Practical Cloud Security Handbook

Secure cloud deployments with AWS, Azure, GCP, and IBM Cloud

Shiv Kumar

bpb

www.bpbonline.com

First Edition 2025

Copyright © BPB Publications, India

ISBN: 978-93-65891-478

To View Complete
BPB Publications Catalogue
Scan the QR Code:

Dedicated to

My wife Shahana
for your endless support, love, and belief in me.
This journey would not have been possible without you

About the Author

Shiv Kumar is a seasoned cloud infrastructure and data engineering expert, currently leading the infrastructure and data engineering division at *VidvanConnect Software Solutions Private Limited*. With over a decade of experience in designing and managing secure, scalable cloud architectures, Shiv works with clients across 33 countries, helping them implement resilient infrastructure and data platforms tailored to global business needs.

He holds a master of science in general studies (mass media communication) and a master of technology in software systems, both from the prestigious *Birla Institute of Technology and Science (BITS), Pilani*. His unique combination of communication and technical expertise allows him to bridge complex technical concepts with practical, business-aligned solutions.

Shiv is deeply passionate about cloud security, DevSecOps, and compliance-driven development. Through this book, Practical Cloud Security Handbook, he brings his vast hands-on experience and global insights to guide professionals in building secure, compliant, and efficient cloud systems.

About the Reviewer

Sahil Dhir is an accomplished professional with more than 14 years of experience in the cyber security realm. As a recognized authority in **governance, risk, and compliance (GRC)**, he leads product vision and strategy for information security solutions, specializing in cloud security architecture and emerging technologies.

For multiple Fortune 500 companies, Sahil has spearheaded the development of enterprise-wide GRC tools and frameworks, demonstrating particular expertise in Identity and Access Management, cloud security, and data protection. His innovative work includes creating comprehensive risk frameworks for generative AI systems, addressing critical aspects such as algorithmic bias, privacy, transparency, and responsible deployment. His deep understanding of regulatory frameworks, including SOX, PCI, and GDPR, has helped organizations strengthen their compliance posture while enabling business growth.

A thought leader in the cybersecurity space, Sahil regularly engages with senior stakeholders to communicate risk strategies and provides technical guidance on new finance technology systems. His expertise in building and scaling GRC programs has benefited multiple Fortune 500 companies, establishing him as a trusted voice in the industry.

Sahil holds extensive experience in security assessments and operations management, with a particular focus on data-driven decision-making to address emerging security challenges. His commitment to staying current with offensive security strategies enables him to develop proactive risk management programs that serve as effective business enablers.

Acknowledgement

Writing this book has been a transformative journey, and I am grateful to all those who made it possible.

First and foremost, I extend my heartfelt thanks to my family for their unwavering support, patience, and encouragement throughout the writing process. Your belief in me has been my greatest strength.

I am deeply appreciative of my colleagues, mentors, and peers in the cloud and cybersecurity space. Your guidance, feedback, and shared experiences have been instrumental in shaping the practical content of this book.

A special thanks to BPB Publications for believing in the vision of this book and providing me the platform to share my insights with a broader audience. Your professionalism, editorial support, and commitment to quality have been invaluable throughout the publishing process.

Finally, to the readers and professionals dedicated to building secure cloud systems—this book is for you.

Last but not least, I want to express my gratitude to the readers who have shown interest in the book. Your support and encouragement have been deeply appreciated.

Thank you to everyone who has played a part in making this book a reality.

Preface

In today's digital landscape, cloud computing has become the backbone of modern infrastructure, powering businesses of every scale with unmatched agility, scalability, and cost-efficiency. With this massive shift towards the cloud, the importance of robust and scalable cloud security has become paramount. Practical Cloud Security Handbook is a step-by-step guide designed for IT professionals, architects, developers, and security engineers who aim to understand and implement secure cloud environments across leading cloud service providers like **Amazon Web Services (AWS)**, **Microsoft Azure**, **IBM Cloud**, and **Google Cloud Platform (GCP)**.

This book was born out of real-world challenges encountered while designing and securing cloud-native and hybrid systems in production environments. It aims to bridge the gap between theoretical security concepts and their practical implementations using **infrastructure as code (IaC)**, DevSecOps pipelines, and native and third-party tools. The book covers a wide spectrum of essential topics, from shared responsibility models and identity access management to monitoring, encryption, compliance, and best practices for cloud-native and non-cloud-native deployments.

Each chapter is structured to walk you through foundational concepts, platform-specific configurations, tools and libraries like Terraform, Jenkins, Ansible, and practical use cases. Whether you are securing data at rest, implementing Zero Trust architecture, automating security testing, or aligning with industry compliance standards like ISO, HIPAA, or CMMI, this book has been crafted to give you actionable insights and hands-on experience.

My goal with this book is to help readers not just understand security principles but to implement them confidently and consistently in real-world cloud environments.

Chapter 1: Introduction to Cloud Security- This chapter sets the foundation for understanding cloud security by introducing the shared responsibility model. It explores the delineation between cloud provider and application owner responsibilities and emphasizes why cloud security is vital in today's digital age. It provides clarity on ownership boundaries to help readers better plan their security posture.

Chapter 2: Cloud-native Architectures- Focusing on modern system design, this chapter examines cloud-native architectures used in diverse industries such as BFSI, AI/ML, big data, and streaming applications. It contrasts traditional and distributed system designs while emphasizing the operational and security benefits of cloud-native solutions.

Chapter 3: Understanding Top Workloads in the Cloud- This chapter walks readers through the most critical cloud workloads including IAM, VPC, Kubernetes, Docker, storage, and compute resources. It explains how these components interact in real deployments and highlights common security considerations for each.

Chapter 4: Concepts of Security- Here, we delve into fundamental security principles like encryption, secure protocols, IAM, and **single sign-on** (**SSO**). It provides the theoretical grounding needed to understand how security mechanisms operate across the cloud ecosystem.

Chapter 5: Securing Storage Services- Security configurations for storage services in AWS, Azure, IBM Cloud, and GCP are the focus of this chapter. It walks through native storage security features, encryption settings, and best practices for secure data storage across different platforms.

Chapter 6: Securing Network Services- This chapter dives into network-level security using **virtual private clouds** (**VPCs**), route tables, and firewall configurations. Platform-specific details are covered, helping readers design secure, segmented, and scalable network architectures across major cloud providers.

Chapter 7: Identity and Access Management- IAM and SSO are at the heart of this chapter, focusing on role-based access, multi-factor authentication, and secure user provisioning. Security configuration details for each cloud provider offer a comprehensive view of access control mechanisms.

Chapter 8: Monitoring, Applying Encryption and Preparation/Testing- Readers are introduced to native and third-party tools used for monitoring cloud infrastructure security. It also covers encryption in transit and at rest, and testing methodologies to validate security configurations for production readiness.

Chapter 9: Security as Code- Exploring the IaC approach, this chapter introduces tools like Terraform and Ansible. It focuses on integrating security configurations into code, enabling version control, automation, and repeatability in cloud deployments.

Chapter 10: Best Practices for Cloud-native Implementations- This chapter shares proven practices for securing cloud-native applications, including implementing Zero Trust models, managing attack surfaces, and enforcing data protection policies. It emphasizes security embedded into every layer of architecture.

Chapter 11: Best Practices for Non-cloud-native Implementations- Addressing legacy and hybrid environments, this chapter outlines strategies for securing non-cloud-native applications. Topics include patch management, **vulnerability assessment and penetration testing (VAPT)**, and adapting Zero Trust to non-cloud setups.

Chapter 12: DevSecOps- DevSecOps brings security into the development pipeline. This chapter explains how to integrate security checks into CI/CD pipelines using tools like Jenkins. It discusses components, planning, and implementation strategies for secure and agile delivery.

Chapter 13: Compliance and Regulatory Considerations- The final chapter provides a comprehensive overview of key regulatory frameworks including ISO, HIPAA, and CMMI. It guides readers on aligning cloud practices with these standards and embedding compliance into their development and deployment lifecycles.

Let us begin our journey into building resilient, secure, and compliant cloud systems.

Code Bundle and Coloured Images

Please follow the link to download the
Code Bundle and the *Coloured Images* of the book:

https://rebrand.ly/69fcbaf

The code bundle for the book is also hosted on GitHub at
https://github.com/bpbpublications/Practical-Cloud-Security-Handbook.
In case there's an update to the code, it will be updated on the existing GitHub repository.

We have code bundles from our rich catalogue of books and videos available at
https://github.com/bpbpublications. Check them out!

Errata

We take immense pride in our work at BPB Publications and follow best practices to ensure the accuracy of our content to provide with an indulging reading experience to our subscribers. Our readers are our mirrors, and we use their inputs to reflect and improve upon human errors, if any, that may have occurred during the publishing processes involved. To let us maintain the quality and help us reach out to any readers who might be having difficulties due to any unforeseen errors, please write to us at :

errata@bpbonline.com

Your support, suggestions and feedbacks are highly appreciated by the BPB Publications' Family.

Did you know that BPB offers eBook versions of every book published, with PDF and ePub files available? You can upgrade to the eBook version at www.bpbonline. com and as a print book customer, you are entitled to a discount on the eBook copy. Get in touch with us at :

business@bpbonline.com for more details.

At www.bpbonline.com, you can also read a collection of free technical articles, sign up for a range of free newsletters, and receive exclusive discounts and offers on BPB books and eBooks.

Piracy

If you come across any illegal copies of our works in any form on the internet, we would be grateful if you would provide us with the location address or website name. Please contact us at business@bpbonline.com with a link to the material.

If you are interested in becoming an author

If there is a topic that you have expertise in, and you are interested in either writing or contributing to a book, please visit www.bpbonline.com. We have worked with thousands of developers and tech professionals, just like you, to help them share their insights with the global tech community. You can make a general application, apply for a specific hot topic that we are recruiting an author for, or submit your own idea.

Reviews

Please leave a review. Once you have read and used this book, why not leave a review on the site that you purchased it from? Potential readers can then see and use your unbiased opinion to make purchase decisions. We at BPB can understand what you think about our products, and our authors can see your feedback on their book. Thank you!

For more information about BPB, please visit www.bpbonline.com.

Join our Discord space

Join our Discord workspace for latest updates, offers, tech happenings around the world, new releases, and sessions with the authors:

https://discord.bpbonline.com

Table of Contents

CHAPTER 1
Introduction to Cloud Security

Introduction

In the digital era, where data is as valuable as gold and cyber threats are a constant concern, this chapter is essential for anyone involved in cloud computing. This chapter provides a foundational understanding of the complex dynamics of cloud security. It highlights the shared responsibility model, a crucial framework that outlines how security tasks are divided between cloud providers and application owners. We will dissect the essentials of cloud security and focus on the why, the how, and the who of protecting cloud environments.

Structure

The chapter covers the following topics:

- Importance of cloud security
- Cloud provider responsibilities
- Application provider responsibilities
- Case study

Objectives

After reading this chapter, you will grasp the critical importance of cloud security in safeguarding data and maintaining operational integrity in cloud environments. You will understand the shared responsibility model, which clearly defines the roles of cloud providers and application owners in upholding security. You will also gain insights into the specific responsibilities of cloud providers, including infrastructure and compliance aspects. By the end of this chapter, you will learn about the essential security duties of application providers, particularly in areas such as application-level security and data encryption. Acquire foundational knowledge to make informed decisions for safeguarding cloud-based resources and applications.

Importance of cloud security

Cloud computing has revolutionized business operations, offering unmatched flexibility, scalability, and cost-efficiency. However, this transformation has also brought forth a new set of challenges, with security paramount among them. Understanding why cloud security is crucial is the first step toward ensuring the safety of your digital assets in the cloud.

> **Note:** **You do not need to be a cloud security expert to benefit from this chapter. However, having a basic understanding of cloud computing and familiarity with cloud security concepts will be beneficial. If you have prior experience with any of the four major cloud platforms, Amazon Web Services (AWS), Azure, IBM Cloud, or Google Cloud Platform (GCP), it is a plus, but it is not mandatory.**

As businesses increasingly migrate to the cloud, ensuring security is no longer optional—it is a necessity. While cloud computing offers numerous advantages, it also introduces unique security challenges that organizations must address. A strong cloud security strategy helps mitigate risks, protect sensitive data, and maintain operational resilience. The following are the key reasons why cloud security is critical:

- **Data protection**: In the cloud, your data is stored on remote servers maintained by cloud providers. Ensuring the **confidentiality, integrity, and availability (CIA)** of this data is imperative. Breaches can lead to data theft, loss, or manipulation, damaging your reputation and potentially causing legal repercussions.

- **Compliance requirements**: Various industries and regions have stringent data protection and privacy regulations. Non-compliance can result in severe fines and penalties. Cloud security helps you meet these requirements and maintain regulatory compliance.

- **Shared responsibility model**: The shared responsibility model underpins cloud security, assigning distinct security responsibilities to both the cloud provider and the user. Understanding these roles is vital to prevent security gaps.

- **Cyber threats**: The digital landscape is fraught with cyber threats, from malware and phishing attacks to **distributed denial-of-service** (**DDoS**) assaults. Cloud security tools and practices are essential defenses against these threats.

- **Business continuity**: Downtime can be costly. Cloud security measures, such as redundancy and disaster recovery planning, ensure business continuity despite unexpected disruptions.

- **Cost-efficiency**: Security breaches can be costly to remediate. Investing in robust cloud security upfront can save you significant IAM expenses down the line.

- **Trust and reputation**: It is crucial to maintain the trust of your customers and partners. Demonstrating strong cloud security practices builds trust and safeguards your reputation.

- **Innovation and growth**: Cloud security enables you to use the cloud's full potential for innovation and growth without compromising your organization's security.

Cloud security transcends technical considerations; it is a fundamental business imperative. It safeguards your data, ensures compliance, protects against cyber threats, and supports users' growth and success in the digital age.

Cloud provider responsibilities

In cloud computing, the responsibilities for ensuring the security and integrity of the infrastructure and services are shared between the cloud provider (such as AWS, Microsoft Azure, IBM Cloud, or GCP) and the cloud user. Understanding what your cloud provider is responsible for is vital in establishing a secure cloud environment. The key responsibilities of a cloud provider are listed as follows:

- **Physical security**: Cloud providers secure physical data centers and facilities where cloud infrastructure is housed. This involves access controls, surveillance, and environmental protection against physical threats.

- **Network security**: Cloud providers establish and maintain the underlying network infrastructure, ensuring the security of data in transit. They implement measures like firewalls, **intrusion detection systems** (**IDSs**), and DDoS mitigation.

- **Data center operations**: Providers manage and maintain the data center operations, including hardware provisioning, maintenance, and updates. This ensures that the underlying infrastructure is reliable and up to date.

- **Virtualization security**: Cloud providers are responsible for securing the virtualization layer, which includes hypervisors and **virtual machine** (**VM**) isolation. They must prevent unauthorized access between VMs.

- **Identity and Access Management (IAM)**: IAM services enable users, groups, and roles to access resources securely. Providers offer tools for user authentication, authorization, and access control.

- **Security of managed services**: Managed services, such as databases and **machine learning (ML)**, are secured by the cloud provider. Users must configure these services securely.

- **Security compliance**: Cloud providers adhere to various security compliance standards and certifications, such as *International Organization for Standardization (ISO) 27001, Systems and Organization Controls 2 (SOC 2)*, and *Health Insurance Portability and Accountability Act (HIPAA)*, to ensure that their infrastructure meets industry-specific security requirements.

- **Backup and disaster recovery**: Cloud providers offer backup and disaster recovery services to protect data and ensure business continuity.

- **Patch management**: Providers are responsible for patching and updating the underlying infrastructure to address security vulnerabilities.

- **Incident response**: Cloud providers have incident response teams and procedures to address security incidents and breaches that affect their infrastructure.

- **Physical-to-logical separation**: Providers ensure that data and workloads of different customers are logically separated in a multi-tenant environment.

- **Global network security**: Cloud providers operate a global network and ensure secure data transfers across regions and continents.

- **Shared responsibility communication**: They communicate the shared responsibility model to customers, clarifying which security aspects are their responsibility and which are the customer's responsibility.

It is important to note that the specific responsibilities of a cloud provider may vary based on the type of cloud service **infrastructure as a service (IaaS)**, **platform as a service (PaaS)**, or **software as a service (SaaS)** and the **service level agreement (SLA)** between the provider and the customer. Cloud users must fully understand the shared responsibility model and configure their cloud resources accordingly to ensure comprehensive security.

Application provider responsibilities

In a cloud computing environment, the responsibilities for security are shared between the cloud provider (e.g., AWS, Azure, GCP, or IBM Cloud), the cloud user, and, in some cases, the application provider. While the cloud provider manages the underlying infrastructure, and the cloud user configures and secures their cloud resources, the application provider plays a crucial role in ensuring the security of the software and services they deliver via the cloud. Here are the key responsibilities of an application provider:

- **Software security**: Application providers are responsible for developing, maintaining, and updating their software securely. This includes identifying and patching vulnerabilities, ensuring secure coding practices, and staying informed about emerging threats.

- **Access controls**: Ensure robust access controls within the application. This involves user authentication, authorization, and **role-based access control (RBAC)** to restrict access to sensitive data and functionalities.

- **Data encryption**: Encrypt data both in transit and at rest. Ensure that sensitive data, such as user credentials and personal information, is encrypted to protect it from unauthorized access.

- **Authentication**: Implement strong authentication mechanisms, such as **multi-factor authentication (MFA)**, to verify the identity of users and prevent unauthorized access.

- **Authorization**: Define and enforce access permissions and authorization rules within the application to control what users can do and see based on their roles and responsibilities.

- **Secure configuration**: Configure the application securely by following the best practices and security guidelines provided by the cloud provider. This includes securing database configurations, API endpoints, and other components.

- **Logging and monitoring**: Implement logging and monitoring within the application to detect and respond to security incidents. Monitor for unusual or suspicious activities and setup alerts for security events.

- **Data backup and recovery**: Establish data backup and recovery mechanisms to ensure data availability and resilience in case of data loss or system failures.

- **Incident response**: Develop an incident response plan outlining how the application provider will respond to security incidents. This includes procedures for identifying, containing, and mitigating security breaches.

- **Compliance and regulations**: Depending on the type of data the application handles, comply with relevant industry regulations and data protection laws, such as the *General Data Protection Regulation (GDPR)* or HIPAA. Implement necessary controls to meet compliance requirements.

- **Third-party integrations**: Secure all third-party integrations, including data transfer and access controls.

- **User education**: Provide user education and guidance on security best practices. Encourage users to use strong passwords, enable security features like MFA, and be cautious of phishing and social engineering attacks.

- **Regular updates**: Continuously update the application to patch security vulnerabilities and improve security features. Stay informed about security advisories and apply security patches promptly.

- **Data privacy**: Protect user data and privacy. Clearly communicate data handling practices, obtain necessary consent, and anonymize or pseudonymize data when appropriate.

- **Secure development lifecycle**: Implement a secure **software development lifecycle (SDLC)** to ensure that security is integrated into every phase of application development.

- **Documentation**: Maintain documentation related to security practices, configurations, and incident response plans for reference and auditing purposes.

- **Security testing**: Conduct regular security testing, including vulnerability assessments and penetration testing, to identify and remediate security weaknesses.

- **Redundancy and high availability**: Ensure the application is designed for redundancy and high availability to minimize downtime and maintain service continuity.

- **Security training**: Train the application development and operations teams on security best practices and response procedures.

- **Collaboration with cloud users**: Collaborate with cloud users (organizations deploying the application) to ensure a cohesive security strategy, especially when configuring access controls, security groups, and networking.

It is important to note that the specific responsibilities of an application provider may vary depending on the type of application, its complexity, and the nature of the cloud services it relies on. Application providers should work closely with cloud users to define and implement security measures that align with the shared responsibility model of the cloud provider.

Illustration

Application providers assume a critical role in ensuring the security of the software and services they deliver via the cloud infrastructure. These responsibilities primarily revolve around safeguarding the software application itself, the data it processes, and access to it. Firstly, application providers are accountable for implementing robust data encryption mechanisms, both in transit and at rest, to protect sensitive information from unauthorized access. They must establish stringent access controls and authentication measures to regulate who can access the application and its associated data.

Moreover, application providers are tasked with setting up comprehensive monitoring and logging systems to promptly detect any security anomalies or breaches. This includes monitoring user activity, application performance, and security events. In the event of a security incident, application providers should have well-defined incident response plans to mitigate the impact and swiftly recover from security breaches. Compliance with relevant industry standards and regulatory requirements is another crucial aspect of their responsibilities, ensuring that the application adheres to the best security practices and legal obligations.

Application providers are often responsible for implementing data backup and recovery mechanisms to safeguard against data loss and service disruptions. They need to establish robust backup strategies and recovery procedures to ensure business continuity. In short, application providers play a pivotal role in the shared responsibility model of cloud security, focusing on securing the software application, managing access controls, encrypting data, monitoring for threats, responding to incidents, ensuring compliance, and maintaining data resilience.

Case study

TechNova, a forward-thinking technology company, migrated its services to AWS. This strategic move promised scalability, efficiency, and innovation, but it also raised concerns about cloud security.

TechNova faced several challenges during this transition. They had diverse teams with varying levels of access requirements, which made managing permissions a complex task. Additionally, safeguarding sensitive data was a top priority, necessitating robust encryption practices. Lastly, with a sprawling AWS environment, they needed a monitoring solution to comprehensively track resource usage, detect anomalies, and facilitate proactive responses.

To address these challenges, TechNova implemented a multi-faceted security strategy. They meticulously designed IAM policies, aligning them with their teams' roles and responsibilities. This not only ensured secure access but also streamlined operational efficiency. TechNova used AWS's encryption capabilities for data protection, implementing encryption for data at rest and in transit using AWS **Key Management Service** (**KMS**). To maintain the integrity of their AWS resources, they employed AWS CloudWatch, a robust monitoring solution that provided real-time insights.

The results of TechNova's migration to AWS, fortified with sound cloud security practices, were transformative. Their enhanced security measures mitigated risks associated with unauthorized access or data breaches. Well-defined IAM policies streamlined access management, reducing administrative overhead. AWS CloudWatch's monitoring capabilities allowed TechNova to proactively manage its resources, ensuring optimal performance and cost-efficiency.

This case study serves as a real-world example, highlighting the pivotal role of cloud security in TechNova's migration journey. It underscores the importance of IAM, encryption, and monitoring solutions in fortifying cloud environments, making it a valuable reference for organizations venturing into cloud adoption.

Conclusion

This chapter is a foundational exploration of cloud security, emphasizing its critical role in safeguarding data, applications, and infrastructure. It introduced the shared responsibilities model, elucidating the distinct roles of cloud providers and application owners. Readers gain insights into why cloud security is paramount and understand the pivotal responsibilities undertaken by both cloud providers and application owners. This chapter sets the stage for a deeper exploration into cloud security, equipping readers with essential knowledge to navigate the complexities of this vital domain.

In the next chapter, we will be focusing on various aspects of cloud-native systems, comparing them with traditional architectures and focusing on specific use cases such as **Banking, Financial Services, and Insurance (BFSI)**, streaming, big data, and **artificial intelligence (AI)**/ML architectures.

Key takeaways

- **Cloud Security is a business imperative**: With the growing reliance on cloud infrastructure, securing data, applications, and services is critical to ensuring operational continuity and customer trust.

- **Understand the shared responsibility model**: Security in the cloud is a joint effort. Cloud providers secure the infrastructure, while application owners must safeguard their applications, data, and configurations.

- **Know your roles**: Cloud providers handle physical security, network protection, managed services, and compliance frameworks. Application providers are responsible for secure development, encryption, monitoring, and incident response.

- **Cyber threats are constant**: Threats like data breaches, DDoS attacks, and insider risks make cloud security an ongoing priority requiring proactive tools and monitoring.

- **IAM, encryption, and monitoring are pillars of defense**: IAM, strong encryption, and continuous monitoring form the backbone of an effective cloud security strategy.

- **Compliance and resilience must be built-in**: Adherence to legal and industry regulations like GDPR, HIPAA, and ISO 27001 ensures credibility and avoids penalties. Redundancy and recovery planning support business continuity.

- **Security enables innovation**: A strong security posture enables organizations to leverage the full benefits of the cloud—scalability, agility, and innovation—without compromising on safety.

Key terms

- **Cloud security**: The practice of protecting cloud-based data, applications, and services from security threats and breaches.

- **Shared responsibilities model**: A framework defining the security responsibilities of both the cloud provider and the application owner in a cloud environment.

- **Identity and Access Management**: A security discipline that focuses on managing user identities and their access to resources in the cloud.

- **Encryption**: The process of converting data into a code to prevent unauthorized access, often used for data at rest and in transit.

- **Data at rest**: Data that is stored on non-volatile storage media, such as databases or file systems.

- **Data in transit**: Data that is actively moving from one location to another, typically over a network.

- **Continuous monitoring**: The practice of continuously monitoring cloud resources and systems to detect and respond to security threats and vulnerabilities.

- **Principle of least privilege**: Granting users and applications the minimum level of access necessary to perform their tasks, reducing the potential for security breaches.

- **Security configuration**: The settings and parameters that define the security posture of cloud resources, including access controls and firewall rules.

- **Penetration testing**: The process of actively assessing the security of a system by simulating attacks to identify vulnerabilities.

- **Vulnerability scanning**: Automated scanning of systems and applications to identify potential security weaknesses.

- **Compliance**: Adherence to regulatory and industry standards and requirements related to data security and privacy.

- **Multi-factor authentication**: A security process in which users are required to provide two or more authentication factors to access a system or application.

- **Serverless computing**: A cloud computing model where cloud providers automatically manage the infrastructure, allowing developers to focus solely on writing code.

- **Key Management Service**: A cloud service that provides secure and centralized management of encryption keys.

- **Incident response**: The process of identifying, managing, and mitigating security incidents and breaches.

- **Data privacy**: The protection of sensitive and personal data to ensure compliance with privacy regulations.

- **Compliance as code**: The practice of defining and managing compliance rules and policies using code and automation.

- **Monitoring and logging**: The collection and analysis of logs and telemetry data to gain insights into the security and performance of cloud resources.

Solved exercises

1. **Why is cloud security important?**

    Answer: Cloud security is vital because it safeguards sensitive data, prevents unauthorized access, ensures compliance, and protects against cyber threats. In a cloud environment, security is a shared responsibility between the cloud provider and the application owner.

2. **What is the shared responsibilities model in cloud security?**

    Answer: The shared responsibilities model defines the division of security responsibilities between the cloud provider (e.g., AWS, Azure, GCP) and the application owner. The provider is responsible for the security of the cloud infrastructure, while the owner is responsible for securing their applications and data.

3. **Can you explain the concept of IAM in cloud security?**

    Answer: IAM is a fundamental component of cloud security that focuses on managing user identities and their access to resources. It involves creating roles, setting permissions, and ensuring the principle of least privilege to control access effectively.

4. **What are some of the common encryption methods used in cloud security?**

    Answer: Common encryption methods in cloud security include AES-256 for data at rest, TLS/SSL for data in transit, and the use of encryption keys managed by services like AWS KMS.

5. **What is the significance of continuous monitoring in cloud security?**

    Answer: Continuous monitoring helps detect security threats, vulnerabilities, and suspicious activities in real-time. It is essential for maintaining the security of cloud resources and responding promptly to potential threats.

6. **Explain how the responsibilities of a cloud provider and application provider differ in the context of encryption.**

    Answer: Cloud providers typically offer encryption services for data at rest and in transit. However, the application provider is responsible for implementing encryption within their applications and managing encryption keys for data security.

7. **Give an example of a cloud monitoring tool and its importance.**

    Answer: One example is AWS CloudWatch. It provides real-time monitoring and alerting for AWS resources, helping organizations maintain the health, performance, and security of their cloud infrastructure.

8. **What is the principle of least privilege, and why is it crucial in cloud security?**

   Answer: The principle of least privilege means granting users and applications the minimum access required to perform their tasks. It is essential in cloud security to limit potential damage from insider threats or compromised accounts.

9. **How can organizations ensure that their cloud security configurations are robust?**

   Answer: Organizations can ensure robust security configurations by conducting regular testing, including penetration testing and vulnerability scanning. They should also keep configurations up-to-date and follow best practices.

10. **What are the key takeaways from this chapter?**

    Answer: The key takeaways include understanding the importance of cloud security, the shared responsibilities model, the role of IAM, encryption methods, continuous monitoring, and the need for robust security configurations.

Unsolved exercises

1. Provide an example of a real-world security breach in a cloud environment and discuss the lessons learned.

2. How can organizations balance security and usability in their cloud environments?

3. What are the potential risks of not following the principle of least privilege in cloud security?

4. Explain the concept of encryption key rotation and why it is essential.

5. What are the compliance considerations for organizations using cloud services?

6. How can organizations ensure data privacy and compliance with regulations like GDPR in the cloud?

7. Discuss the role of MFA in enhancing cloud security.

8. What are the best practices for securing serverless computing in the cloud?

9. Can you provide a case study of an organization that successfully implemented cloud security measures and the benefits they achieved?

10. Describe the process of disaster recovery planning in a cloud environment and its significance in cloud security.

Join our Discord space

Join our Discord workspace for latest updates, offers, tech happenings around the world, new releases, and sessions with the authors:

https://discord.bpbonline.com

CHAPTER 2
Cloud-native Architectures

Introduction

This chapter will explore a vital field in today's technology-driven world. Cloud-native architecture represents a paradigm shift in how applications are designed, built, and managed. They use the flexibility, scalability, and resilience of cloud computing. This chapter will explore various aspects of cloud-native systems, comparing them with traditional architectures and focusing on specific use cases such as **Banking, Financial Services, and Insurance (BFSI)**, streaming, big data, and **artificial intelligence (AI)/ machine learning (ML)** architectures.

Structure

The chapter covers the following topics:

- Traditional architectures
- Typical BFSI architectures
- Streaming architectures
- Big data architectures
- AI/ML architectures
- Case study

Objectives

By the end of this chapter, you will understand the fundamental principles of cloud-native architectures. You will be able to differentiate between traditional and cloud-native architectures. In addition, you will gain insights into BFSI, streaming, big data, and AI/ML architectures in the cloud-native context and develop the ability to analyze and design cloud-native solutions for various use cases critically. Foster a mindset for innovation and problem-solving in cloud-native environments.

Traditional architectures

Before we begin, it is crucial to understand traditional architectures, which have been the foundation of software development and deployment for decades. This section will explore these architectures by highlighting their characteristics, strengths, and limitations.

Characteristics of traditional architectures

Traditional IT architectures have long been the foundation of enterprise systems, offering stability and control. However, they come with inherent limitations in scalability, flexibility, and maintenance. The following are the defining characteristics of traditional architectures:

- **Monolithic design**: Traditional architectures often feature monolithic designs, where applications are built as single, indivisible units. All components, from input handling to data processing and **user interface** (**UI**) rendering, are tightly integrated.

- **On-premises deployment**: These systems are typically deployed on-premises. This means the entire infrastructure, including servers, networking, and storage, is managed within the physical premises of the organization.

- **Manual scaling**: Scaling in traditional architectures is often manual and involves physical hardware upgrades or adding more servers, leading to potential downtime and higher costs.

- **Centralized data management**: Data management is centralized, with a single database often serving as the hub for all data transactions.

- **Predictable load handling**: These systems are designed to handle predictable loads, with resources provisioned to manage peak usage, which might lead to underutilization during off-peak periods.

Advantages of traditional architectures

Despite the rise of modern cloud-based and distributed architectures, traditional architectures continue to offer certain advantages. These benefits make them a viable choice for specific use cases and organizations:

- **Simplicity**: The monolithic nature of these systems can make them simpler to develop, test, and deploy initially, especially for small-scale applications.

- **Control**: On-premises deployment offers complete control over the infrastructure, which some organizations might prefer for regulatory or security reasons.

Limitations of traditional architectures

While traditional architectures offer control and simplicity, they also come with several limitations that can hinder scalability, flexibility, and efficiency. Understanding these challenges is crucial when evaluating modern alternatives. The limitations of traditional architectures are as follows:

- **Scalability challenges**: Scaling requires significant effort and investment, often leading to over-provisioning of resources.

- **Flexibility issues**: Adapting to new technologies or scaling on demand is challenging due to the monolithic and on-premises nature of these systems.

- **Downtime and maintenance**: Updating or maintaining these systems can lead to downtime, impacting business continuity.

- **Resource inefficiency**: Resources might be underutilized, leading to inefficiencies and increased costs.

Transition to cloud-native

The evolution from traditional to cloud-native architectures is driven by the need to address these limitations. Cloud-native systems offer more flexibility, scalability, and efficiency using modern technologies like microservices, containerization, and cloud computing.

Case study: Traditional banking system

Consider a traditional banking system, which often uses a monolithic architecture. Such systems may struggle with scalability during peak transaction periods and might experience downtime during maintenance. The move to a cloud-native architecture can address these challenges, offering better scalability, reduced downtime, and improved customer experience.

Typical BFSI architectures

In the BFSI sector, architectures are designed to handle sensitive data, ensure high security, and maintain uninterrupted services. This section will explore the typical architectures used in the BFSI industry, discussing their key components and how they address the unique challenges of this sector.

Key components of BFSI architectures

The BFSI sector relies on a robust and secure architectural framework to ensure seamless operations, regulatory compliance, and customer satisfaction. The following are the essential components of BFSI architectures:

- **Core banking systems**: These are centralized systems handling day-to-day banking transactions, customer information, and account management. They are often robust and designed for high reliability.

- **Data warehousing and analytics**: BFSI architectures include comprehensive data warehousing solutions for storing and analyzing large volumes of financial data.

- **Customer relationship management (CRM) systems**: CRM systems are essential for managing customer interactions, providing personalized services, and maintaining customer data.

- **Security and compliance layers**: Given the sensitive nature of financial data, BFSI architectures incorporate advanced security measures, including encryption, firewalls, and **intrusion detection systems** (**IDSs**). Compliance with regulations like the *General Data Protection Regulation* (*GDPR*), *Payment Card Industry Data Security Standard* (*PCI DSS*), and the *Sarbanes–Oxley* (*SOX*) *Act* is also a key component.

- **Payment processing systems**: These systems manage various financial transactions, including electronic payments, wire transfers, and credit/debit card processing.

- **Risk management and fraud detection systems**: BFSI architectures include sophisticated algorithms and systems for risk assessment, fraud detection, and mitigation.

Characteristics of BFSI architectures

BFSI architectures are designed to meet the demanding requirements of the financial sector, ensuring security, reliability, and compliance. Key characteristics include:

- **Highly secure**: Security is paramount, with multiple layers of protection against internal and external threats.

- **Scalable and reliable**: These systems must handle high volumes of transactions reliably, scaling as needed without compromising performance.

- **Regulatory compliance**: BFSI architectures are designed to comply with various regional and international regulations.

- **Integration capabilities**: They often require integration with various external and internal systems, such as stock exchanges, credit bureaus, and government regulatory bodies.

- **Disaster recovery and business continuity**: These architectures have robust backup and disaster recovery mechanisms to ensure continuous operation and data integrity.

Traditional BFSI architectures

Traditional BFSI architectures were designed for stability and control but often lacked the flexibility of modern systems. Key features include:

- **Monolithic structure**: Earlier BFSI architectures were often monolithic, with tightly coupled components making them rigid and complex to update or scale.

- **On-premises data centers**: Traditionally, BFSI institutions relied on on-premises data centers with physical security measures.

- **Batch processing systems**: Earlier systems often used batch processing for transactions, which could lead to delays in data availability and transaction processing.

Evolving trends in BFSI architectures

As financial institutions adapt to technological advancements and regulatory demands, BFSI architectures are evolving to enhance efficiency, security, and customer experience. Key trends include:

- **Shift to microservices**: To overcome the rigidity of monolithic structures, BFSI is increasingly adopting microservices architecture, allowing for faster deployment and better scalability.

- **Cloud adoption**: There is a growing trend towards using cloud services for better scalability, flexibility, and cost-effectiveness, while still ensuring data security and regulatory compliance.

- **Real-time processing**: With advancements in technology, BFSI architectures are moving towards real-time processing for transactions and data analytics.

- **Enhanced security measures**: Continuous evolution in security practices, including the use of AI/ML for fraud detection and blockchain for secure transactions.

- **Regulatory technology**: Implementation of new technologies to manage regulatory compliance more efficiently.

Case study: Digital banking transformation

Consider a case where a traditional bank transforms its architecture to support digital banking. This involves integrating mobile banking, online services, real-time analytics, and personalized customer services into their existing system. The case study will explore the challenges faced and the solutions implemented during this transformation.

Streaming architectures

Streaming architectures are designed to handle real-time data processing, enabling businesses to analyze and act upon data as it is generated. This section explores the key components, characteristics, and trends in streaming architectures, focusing on their application in various industries such as media, finance, and **Internet of Things (IoT)**.

Key components of streaming architectures

Streaming architectures are designed to handle continuous data flows efficiently. They consist of several essential components, including:

- **Data sources**: The starting point of any streaming architecture, including IoT devices, social media feeds, financial transactions, etc.

- **Message brokers**: Systems like Apache Kafka or RabbitMQ that facilitate the efficient transfer of data streams between producers and consumers.

- **Stream processing engines**: Technologies like Apache Storm, Flink, or Spark Streaming that process and analyze data in real-time.

- **Data storage**: Real-time data lakes or databases like Apache Cassandra or Amazon DynamoDB are used to store processed data.

- **Analytics and visualization tools**: Tools for real-time analytics and visualization of streaming data, like Elasticsearch, Kibana, or Grafana.

Characteristics of streaming architectures

Streaming architectures are designed to handle real-time data efficiently, offering the following key characteristics:

- **Low latency**: Essential for processing and reacting to real-time data streams quickly.

- **Scalability**: Ability to scale up or down based on the volume of incoming data streams.

- **Fault tolerance**: Mechanisms to ensure continuous operation even in the case of component failures.

- **Data durability**: Ensuring no data loss during transfer and processing.

- **Real-time analytics**: Capabilities to analyze data on the fly and derive insights instantly.

Traditional vs. streaming architectures

Traditional and streaming architectures differ significantly in how they handle data processing and scalability:

- **Batch processing vs. real-time**: Traditional architectures rely on batch processing, whereas streaming architectures process data in real-time.

- **Scalability**: Traditional systems might struggle to scale rapidly, while streaming architectures are designed with scalability in mind.

- **Latency**: High latency in traditional systems versus low latency in streaming architectures.

Evolving trends in streaming architectures

Streaming architectures are continuously evolving to meet the growing demand for real-time data processing and analytics. The following are a few trends in streaming architectures:

- **Cloud-based streaming services**: Services like AWS Kinesis, Google Cloud Pub/Sub, and Azure Event Hubs are becoming popular for their scalability and ease of use.

- **Microservices integration**: Streaming architectures are increasingly integrated with microservices for more dynamic and flexible systems.

- **Advanced analytics**: Integration of ML and AI for predictive analytics in streaming data.

- **Edge computing**: Processing data closer to the source to reduce latency and bandwidth use.

Case study: Real-time financial market analysis

Consider a financial firm that utilizes a streaming architecture to analyze market trends in real-time. The case study will explore how they process vast streams of financial data, including trades, news, and social media, to make rapid investment decisions.

Big data architectures

Big data architectures are specifically designed to handle the immense scale, velocity, and variety of data that modern businesses and technologies generate. This section will cover the essential components, characteristics, and trends of big data architectures, highlighting their role in extracting insights from large datasets.

Key components of big data architectures

To effectively manage and extract insights from vast and complex datasets, big data architectures are composed of several critical layers and technologies. These components work together to handle data ingestion, storage, processing, analysis, and visualization at scale. The following are the key components that form the backbone of a modern big data architecture:

- **Data ingestion layer**: Tools like Apache Flume and Kafka are used to ingest data from various sources at high speeds.

- **Data storage layer**: Distributed storage solutions like **Hadoop Distributed File System** (**HDFS**) or cloud-based storage like Amazon **Simple Storage Service** (**S3**) to store vast amounts of data.

- **Data processing layer**: Technologies such as Apache Hadoop for batch processing and Apache Spark for batch and real-time processing.

- **Data analysis and querying layer**: Tools like Apache Hive and Presto are used to query and analyze large datasets.

- **Data orchestration and workflow management**: Solutions like Apache Airflow and Oozie for orchestrating data pipelines and managing workflows.

- **ML and advanced analytics**: Integration of ML frameworks and tools like TensorFlow or PySpark for advanced analytics.

- **Data visualization and reporting tools**: Tools like Tableau, Power BI, or Apache Superset for visualizing and interpreting the results.

Characteristics of big data architectures

Big data architectures are built to manage the scale, complexity, and diversity of modern data ecosystems. The following characteristics define the robustness and effectiveness of these systems:

- **Scalability**: Ability to handle growing data volumes efficiently.

- **Fault tolerance and reliability**: Systems are designed to be resilient against data loss and system failures.

- **Flexibility**: Capable of handling different types of data (structured, semi-structured, unstructured).

- **High availability**: Ensuring continuous access to data and services.

- **Distributed processing**: Utilizing distributed computing techniques for efficient data processing.

Traditional vs. big data architectures

Big data architectures differ significantly from traditional systems in how they handle data volume, processing, and storage. The following are the key points of comparison:

- **Data volume and variety**: Traditional architectures struggle with the scale and diversity of big data.

- **Processing power**: Big data architectures use distributed computing, unlike centralized processing in traditional systems.

- **Storage mechanisms**: Big data uses distributed storage systems, which are more scalable and cost-effective than traditional RDBMS.

Evolving trends in big data architectures

As data continues to grow in complexity and volume, big data architectures are rapidly evolving to meet modern business and analytical demands. Key trends shaping their development include:

- **Cloud integration**: Increasing adoption of cloud platforms for big data processing due to their scalability and reduced infrastructure costs.

- **Real-time processing**: Shift from batch to real-time data processing for timely insights.

- **Data lakes**: The adoption of data lakes for storing raw data in its native format provides more flexibility than traditional data warehouses.

- **AI/ML integration**: Using AI/ML for smarter data analytics and decision-making processes.

- **Edge computing**: Processing data closer to its source to reduce latency and bandwidth requirements.

Case study: Retail industry analytics

Consider a retail chain implementing a big data architecture to analyze customer behavior, sales trends, and supply chain logistics. The case study will detail how they process and analyze terabytes of data from various sources to optimize their operations and improve customer experiences.

AI/ML architectures

AI/ML architectures are designed to enable complex computational processes that simulate human intelligence and learning capabilities. This section explores the structure, components, and trends in AI/ML architectures, highlighting their role in various applications, from predictive analytics to natural language processing.

Key components of AI/ML architectures

AI/ML architectures are composed of multiple interconnected components that work together to support the complete ML lifecycle—from data acquisition to deployment and maintenance. Understanding the following components is essential for building scalable, efficient, and secure AI/ML systems in the cloud:

- **Data collection and ingestion**: Gathering and ingesting data from diverse sources form the basis for training ML models.

- **Data preprocessing and transformation**: Tools and processes for cleaning, normalizing, and transforming data into a suitable format for analysis.

- **Model training and evaluation environment**: Computing resources and environments for training ML models. This includes using GPUs to train deep learning models and techniques for model validation and evaluation.

- **Model deployment and inference**: Systems for deploying trained models into production and for real-time or batch inference.

- **Data storage and management**: Storing large datasets and model artifacts. It involves databases and data lakes capable of handling structured and unstructured data.

- **Orchestration and workflow management**: Tools like Kubernetes and Apache Airflow are used to manage and orchestrate the ML pipeline.

- **Monitoring and maintenance**: Continuous monitoring of model performance, data drift, and operational metrics, with provisions for model retraining and updating.

Characteristics of AI/ML architectures

AI/ML architectures are specifically designed to support the demands of modern intelligent systems. These architectures are characterized by their ability to handle large-scale data, support diverse models, and enable rapid, automated decision-making. The following are the key characteristics that define effective AI/ML systems in cloud environments:

- **Scalability**: The ability to scale computational resources as per the training and inference needs.

- **Flexibility**: Support for various algorithms, models, and data types.

- **High-performance**: Leveraging high-performance computing resources for intensive model training processes.

- **Automation**: Automated pipelines for training, deployment, and monitoring of models.

- **Real-time processing**: Capabilities for real-time data processing and inference.

Traditional vs. AI/ML architectures

AI/ML architectures introduce a significant shift from traditional system designs by prioritizing intelligence, adaptability, and data-driven automation. The following points highlight the key differences between traditional and AI/ML architectural approaches:

- **Computational intensity**: AI/ML architectures require more computational power than traditional systems, often necessitating specialized hardware like GPUs.

- **Data handling**: AI/ML systems handle a broader variety of data (including unstructured data) and require more sophisticated data processing techniques.

- **Model management**: Unlike traditional architectures, AI/ML architectures include components for ongoing model training, evaluation, and retraining.

Evolving trends in AI/ML architectures

As AI/ML technologies continue to mature, their architectural patterns are evolving to support greater scalability, agility, and security. The following emerging trends are shaping the future of AI/ML system design in cloud and hybrid environments:

- **Cloud-based AI services**: Utilization of cloud platforms offering AI/ML services for scalability and efficiency, such as AWS SageMaker, Google AI Platform, and Azure ML.

- **AutoML**: Automated ML platforms for automating the process of applying ML to real-world problems.

- **Edge AI**: Running AI algorithms on edge devices for faster processing and reduced latency.

- **MLOps**: Practices that integrate ML with **continuous integration/continuous deployment (CI/CD)** and DevOps methodologies.

- **Federated learning**: A distributed approach to training ML models across multiple devices or servers.

Case study: Healthcare diagnostics

A case study involving the deployment of an AI model in healthcare for diagnostics, analyzing medical images to detect anomalies. This case study will explore the architecture's ability to process large datasets, ensure data privacy, and provide accurate, real-time diagnostics.

Illustration

To visually convey the key architectural concepts discussed in this chapter, the following illustration has been designed to encapsulate the core themes and their interrelationships in a cloud-native environment:

- **Central theme**: A large, stylized cloud at the center symbolizes cloud computing as the core theme.

- **Around the cloud**: Five distinct, smaller sections or icons, each representing a specific topic of the chapter.

- **Sections**:
  - **Traditional architectures**:
    - **Icon**: A solid, single-block structure, signifying the monolithic nature of traditional systems.
    - **Colors**: More muted tones to represent older technology.
  - **Typical BFSI architectures**:
    - **Icon**: A bank-like building with a shield, highlighting the focus on security and financial systems.
    - **Colors**: Strong, reliable colors like blue or green.
  - **Streaming architectures**:
    - **Icon**: Dynamic waves or flowing lines illustrating the movement and real-time processing of data streams.
    - **Colors**: Bright, energetic colors like orange or yellow to depict speed and activity.
  - **Big data architectures**:
    - **Icon**: Interconnected nodes and data points, showing the complexity and scale of big data systems.
    - **Colors**: Deep purples or blues, suggesting depth and vastness.
  - **AI/ML architectures**:
    - **Icon**: A stylized brain or circuit pattern representing AI/ML.
    - **Colors**: Futuristic tones like metallic silver or electric blue.

- **Interconnectivity**: Each section icon is connected to the central cloud with dashed lines, indicating its integration with cloud-native architectures.

- **Simplified labels**: Brief, clear labels for each section are placed neatly next to the respective icons.

- **Overall design**: The illustration maintains a clean, modern aesthetic focusing on clarity and ease of understanding. The design uses minimalistic details to keep the focus on the overarching concepts of each architecture type within the cloud-native context.

Case study

A major retail chain, *XYZ Retailers*, faced challenges with its traditional IT infrastructure. The legacy systems were not scalable, leading to difficulties during peak shopping seasons. Moreover, their data analytics capabilities were limited, affecting their ability to understand customer behavior and preferences in real-time.

Objective

XYZ Retailers aimed to transition to a cloud-native architecture to enhance scalability, improve real-time data analytics capabilities, and provide a more personalized shopping experience to its customers.

Implementation

This implementation strategy enabled XYZ Retailers to modernize their infrastructure, improve operational efficiency, and enhance customer experiences. By leveraging cloud-native technologies, they ensured scalability, flexibility, and real-time decision-making, positioning themselves for sustained growth in a competitive retail landscape, as follows:

- **Microservices architecture**: XYZ Retailers decomposed their monolithic application into a set of microservices, each handling a specific function like inventory management, customer service, and payment processing. This enabled independent scaling and updating of different services.

- **Containerization and orchestration**: They containerized these microservices using Docker and used Kubernetes for orchestration. This approach streamlined deployment processes and improved resource utilization.

- **Real-time data processing**: They implemented Apache Kafka for real-time data streaming, allowing them to process customer data as it was generated. This setup was critical for understanding customer behavior in real-time.

- **Cloud-based data storage**: They moved their data storage to a cloud-based solution, using a combination of Amazon S3 for object storage and Amazon Redshift for data warehousing. This provided scalability and flexibility in data management.

- **AI/ML integration**: They integrated AI/ML models for predictive analytics, using AWS SageMaker for training and deploying models. These models helped forecast demand, optimize inventory, and personalize marketing efforts.

- **DevOps practices**: Adopted DevOps practices for CI/CD, enhancing the agility of their SDLC.

The results will be as follows:

- **Enhanced scalability**: The microservices architecture allowed XYZ Retailers to scale services independently based on demand, especially during peak shopping periods.

- **Improved customer insights**: Real-time analytics enabled a deeper understanding of customer preferences, leading to more targeted marketing and improved customer satisfaction.

- **Operational efficiency**: Containerization and orchestration led to better resource utilization and reduced operational costs.

- **Increased sales**: Personalized marketing strategies, driven by AI/ML insights, resulted in higher customer engagement and increased sales.

Case study conclusion

The transition to a cloud-native architecture empowered XYZ Retailers to overcome the limitations of their legacy systems. It enhanced their operational efficiency and provided them with the tools to better understand and serve their customers, ultimately leading to increased revenue and market competitiveness. This case study demonstrates the transformative potential of the cloud.

Conclusion

This chapter explains cloud-native architectures, setting the stage by contrasting them with traditional architectures. It highlights how traditional systems, characterized by their monolithic and on-premises nature, face challenges in scalability and flexibility. This comparison underscores the advantages of cloud-native architectures, which are modular, scalable, and agile. The discussion then zooms into the BFSI sector, illustrating how cloud-native principles are revolutionizing these traditionally rigid structures. The chapter emphasizes the critical importance of security, regulatory compliance, and robust transaction handling in BFSI systems and how they are being transformed by the advent of cloud technologies.

The focus then shifts to exploring streaming architectures, focusing on their requirements for real-time data processing, low latency, and high scalability. It delves into the role of technologies such as message brokers and stream processing engines in facilitating these architectures. Further, the chapter addresses the intricacies of big data and AI/ML architectures, pivotal in handling large data volumes and complex computational tasks. It showcases how big data architectures manage vast, diverse datasets effectively, pointing to the shift towards cloud-based solutions for better scalability and flexibility. In the AI/ML context, the architectural needs for advanced ML workloads are dissected, including aspects like high-performance computing, data preprocessing, and model management. The chapter emphasizes how cloud-native principles like microservices, containerization, and automated orchestration are integral to driving innovation and efficiency in various sectors. It provides a comprehensive overview of the transformative impact of cloud-native architectures, highlighting their significance in modern technological and business landscapes.

In the next chapter, we will be exploring the top workloads in the cloud, those that represent the most common and impactful use cases in modern cloud environments. From **Identity and Access Management (IAM)** for secure operations, to the versatile power of Kubernetes and Docker for containerization, and from advanced AI/ML workloads to storage and analytics, this chapter serves as a foundational guide.

Key takeaways

- **Cloud-native architectures enable agility and scalability**: They break away from monolithic systems by using microservices, containerization, and cloud platforms to deliver scalable, resilient, and agile application infrastructures.

- **Traditional vs. cloud-native**: A shift in mindset: Traditional systems offer control but struggle with flexibility, scalability, and modernization. Cloud-native systems are modular, easier to update, and suited for dynamic business needs.

- **BFSI sector leverages cloud-native for security and compliance**: Financial institutions adopt microservices, real-time processing, and cloud platforms to meet regulatory demands and improve customer service.

- **Streaming architectures process data in real-time**: By using tools like Kafka and Flink, organizations can respond instantly to data from IoT, finance, or media applications, enhancing agility and competitiveness.

- **Big data architectures handle scale, speed, and diversity**: They manage massive datasets using distributed storage, scalable compute layers, and real-time analytics, enabling smarter, faster decisions.

- **AI/ML architectures power intelligent systems**: Built for high computation, data diversity, and automation, cloud-native AI/ML systems support real-time inference, scalable model training, and MLOps for continuous learning.

- **Case studies highlight real-world transformation**: From banks to retailers, cloud-native adoption has led to better scalability, customer insights, and operational efficiency, demonstrating the model's business impact.

- **Innovation relies on cloud-native principles**: The use of microservices, container orchestration (Kubernetes), CI/CD pipelines, and real-time analytics defines modern digital transformation across industries.

Key terms

- **Cloud-native architecture**: A design approach for applications built-in the cloud, focusing on scalability, flexibility, and resilience.

- **Microservices**: An architectural style that structures an application as a collection of loosely coupled services, improving modularity and scalability.

- **Containerization**: A lightweight form of virtualization that packages an application and its dependencies in a container, ensuring consistency across environments.

- **Kubernetes**: An open-source platform for automating the deployment, scaling, and management of containerized applications.

- **DevOps**: A set of practices that combines software **development** (**Dev**) and IT **operations** (**Ops**) to shorten the SDLC and provide continuous delivery.

- **Banking, Financial Services, and Insurance**: It refers to companies that provide a range of financial products/services, such as banking, insurance, and asset management.

- **Streaming architecture**: A design approach for processing data in real-time as it is generated, typically used in applications that require immediate data analysis and response.

- **Big data**: It refers to complex and large data sets that traditional data processing software cannot handle efficiently. Big data architectures are designed to store, process, and analyze this data.

- **Artificial intelligence/machine learning architectures**: Systems designed to enable and support advanced AI/ML algorithms for tasks such as predictive modeling and data analysis.

- **Scalability**: The capability of a system to handle a growing amount of work or its potential to be enlarged to accommodate that growth.

- **Fault tolerance**: The ability of a system to continue operating correctly in the event of the failure of some of its components.

- **Real-time processing**: The processing of data immediately as it is generated, with minimal latency.

- **Data lake**: A storage repository that holds a vast amount of raw data in its native format until it is needed.

- **Edge computing**: A distributed computing paradigm that brings computation and data storage closer to the location where it is needed, to improve response times and save bandwidth.

- **Federated learning**: An ML approach where the algorithm is trained across multiple decentralized devices or servers holding local data samples.

Solved exercises

1. **What is the main difference between traditional and cloud-native architectures?**

   Answer: Traditional architectures feature monolithic designs and on-premises deployments, leading to scalability and flexibility issues. In contrast, cloud-native architectures are modular, scalable, and agile, leveraging microservices, containerization, and cloud computing.

2. **How do cloud-native architectures benefit BFSI institutions?**

   Answer: Cloud-native architectures offer BFSI institutions enhanced scalability, improved security, better regulatory compliance, and the ability to rapidly adapt to changing market conditions.

3. **What role do message brokers play in streaming architectures?**

   Answer: Message brokers in streaming architectures facilitate the efficient transfer and management of data streams between data producers and consumers, crucial for real-time data processing.

4. **Why is scalability a critical feature in big data architectures?**

   Answer: Scalability is essential in big data architectures to handle the ever-increasing volume, velocity, and variety of data efficiently.

5. **How does containerization benefit cloud-native architectures?**

   Answer: Containerization packages applications and their dependencies together, ensuring consistency across different environments, improving deployment processes, and aiding in efficient scalability.

6. **What is the significance of microservices in cloud-native architectures?**

   Answer: Microservices allow for the development, deployment, and scaling of application components independently, enhancing the agility and resilience of cloud-native architectures.

7. **How do AI/ML architectures integrate with cloud-native systems?**

   Answer: AI/ML architectures in cloud-native systems benefit from scalable and flexible cloud resources, which are essential for handling large datasets and complex computational tasks required for AI/ML workloads.

8. **Why is real-time data processing important in cloud-native streaming architectures?**

   Answer: Real-time data processing allows businesses to analyze and act upon data instantaneously, essential for applications like financial trading, live media streaming, and IoT monitoring.

9. **What are the advantages of using cloud-based data storage in big data architectures?**

   Answer: Cloud-based data storage offers scalable, flexible, and cost-effective solutions for storing and managing large volumes of data in big data architectures.

10. **How does Kubernetes support cloud-native architectures?**

    Answer: Kubernetes provides orchestration and management of containerized applications, automating deployment, scaling, and operational aspects of cloud-native applications.

Unsolved exercises

1. Explain how monolithic architecture differs from a microservices architecture.

2. Why is real-time analytics important in streaming architectures, and how is it achieved?

3. Discuss the challenges faced when integrating AI/ML models into cloud-native architectures.

4. How does containerization support the deployment of microservices in cloud-native architectures?

5. What are the key considerations when migrating from a traditional to a cloud-native architecture?

6. Explain how cloud-native architectures address the issue of fault tolerance.

7. Describe the benefits of adopting DevOps practices in cloud-native application development.

8. How do data lakes in big data architectures differ from traditional data warehouses?

9. Discuss the impact of cloud-native architectures on operational efficiency in a business.

10. What is the significance of adopting a federated learning approach in AI/ML architectures?

Join our Discord space

Join our Discord workspace for latest updates, offers, tech happenings around the world, new releases, and sessions with the authors:

https://discord.bpbonline.com

CHAPTER 3

Understanding Top Workloads in the Cloud

Introduction

In the ever-evolving landscape of information technology, cloud computing has emerged as a transformative force, reshaping the way organizations approach IT infrastructure and operations. As we know, cloud computing offers organizations the flexibility, scalability, and efficiency needed to meet their technological demands. This chapter provides an in-depth exploration of key cloud workloads and their associated security considerations.

We will see that within this vast ecosystem of cloud computing, the concept of workloads plays a pivotal role in encompassing the diverse range of tasks, processes, and operations that are executed within a cloud environment. Hence, it is essential to understand the intricacies of workloads for effectively harnessing the power of cloud computing to drive innovation and business growth.

This chapter also delves into the intricacies of cloud technology, from **Identity and Access Management (IAM)** to advanced technologies like **artificial intelligence/ machine learning (AI/ML)**, including **virtual private clouds (VPCs)**, databases, Docker and Kubernetes, and data analytics. Each workload is examined within the context of real-world implementation, highlighting the practical applications and benefits of cloud technology.

Structure

In this chapter, we will discuss the following topics:

- Types of workloads
- Real-world implementation examples
- Advantages and challenges
- Cloud workloads and security

Objectives

By the end of this chapter, through an exploration of compute, storage, and network workloads, you will gain insights into how cloud computing can be leveraged to handle diverse tasks and operations. This chapter will equip you with the knowledge needed to navigate the complex world of workloads in cloud computing and security.

Types of workloads

Workloads in cloud computing represent the diverse set of tasks and operations that are executed within a cloud environment. Understanding the different types of workloads is essential for effectively utilizing cloud resources and optimizing performance. Let us take a detailed look at the various types of workloads.

Compute workloads

Compute workloads are centered around processing tasks and computations. These workloads can be further categorized based on their characteristics and requirements as follows:

- **Batch processing workloads**: Batch processing involves executing a series of tasks or jobs in a specific order without user interaction. It is commonly used for data processing, analysis, and transformation tasks. For instance, a company might perform batch processing to generate monthly financial reports from large datasets.

- **High-performance computing (HPC) workloads**: HPC workloads involve complex calculations and simulations that require significant computational power. These workloads are prevalent in scientific research, weather forecasting, and engineering simulations. For example, simulating airflow over an aircraft's wings to optimize aerodynamics is an HPC workload.

- **Web server workloads**: Web server workloads involve managing incoming web requests, serving web applications, and handling user interactions. These workloads are common for hosting websites, e-commerce platforms, and online services. A web server workload dynamically responds to user requests by generating and delivering web pages.

Storage workloads

Storage workloads revolve around managing data, files, and databases. These workloads are critical for various applications that require reliable and scalable data storage as follows:

- **Database workloads**: Database workloads involve managing structured data using **database management systems** (**DBMS**). These include both relational databases, **structured query language** (**SQL**), and NoSQL databases. Examples of database workloads include storing customer information, order details, and inventory data for an e-commerce platform.

- **File storage workloads**: File storage workloads encompass managing unstructured data like documents, images, and multimedia files. Collaborative tools, content management systems, and backup solutions rely on file storage workloads to organize and store data efficiently.

Network workloads

Network workloads deal with communication between resources and optimizing data delivery. Understanding these workload types is essential for selecting appropriate cloud resources, designing architectures, and optimizing performance. Different workloads have varying resource requirements, scalability needs, and performance expectations, all of which should be carefully considered during cloud deployment and management. They are crucial for ensuring data access and efficient content distribution:

- **Content delivery network (CDN) workloads**: CDNs are used to distribute content, such as images, videos, and web pages, to edge servers located closer to end users. This minimizes latency and reduces the load on origin servers. CDNs are essential for improving user experience and ensuring fast content delivery.

- **Virtual private network (VPN) workloads**: VPN workloads involve securely connecting remote users or offices to a private network over a public network (usually the internet). This is common for ensuring secure communication and data transfer between distributed teams or remote workers.

Real-world implementation examples

In this section, we will examine real-world implementation examples of various types of workloads in cloud computing. These real-world examples illustrate how organizations can leverage cloud computing to implement various workloads to address specific business needs. By choosing the right cloud services, resource configurations, and automation techniques, businesses can achieve efficiency, scalability, and enhanced performance in their operations.

Compute workload example of video rendering

Description: Imagine a creative agency working on a project that involves rendering high-definition videos for a client's marketing campaign.

Implementation:

- **Selecting graphics processing unit-enabled instance**: The agency can choose a cloud provider like **Amazon Web Services** (**AWS**) and use **graphics processing unit** (**GPU**) enabled instances like AWS EC2's G4 instances. GPUs are well-suited for video rendering due to their parallel processing capabilities.

- **Launching instances**: Using the AWS Management Console or API, the agency can launch an EC2 instance, specifying the GPU instance type, security groups, key pair, and network settings.

- **Video rendering software**: The agency installs video rendering software and relevant libraries on the instance. They can use tools like *FFmpeg* or *Adobe Premiere* for rendering tasks.

- **Scaling**: Depending on the workload, the agency can scale up by launching multiple instances to handle rendering jobs concurrently.

- **Automating**: Using scripts or orchestration tools, the agency can automate instance provisioning, rendering job distribution, and termination.

Advantages:

- **Speed**: GPU acceleration results in faster rendering times.

- **Cost-efficiency**: Pay only for the compute resources used during rendering.

- **Flexibility**: Scale resources based on workload demands.

Storage workload example of e-commerce database

Description: An e-commerce platform needs a reliable and scalable database to manage product inventory, customer data, and transactions.

Implementation:

- **Managed database service**: The platform can use a managed database service like Amazon **Relational Database Service** (**RDS**) to setup a MySQL or PostgreSQL database.

- **Database creation**: Using the AWS Management Console or API, they can create an RDS instance, specifying the database engine, instance class, storage, and other settings.

- **Database configuration**: The platform can configure backup schedules, automated snapshots, and replication for high availability.

- **Application integration**: The e-commerce platform integrates the application code with the RDS instance for seamless data access.

- **Scalability**: As the platform grows, they can vertically scale the RDS instance or use read replicas to distribute read traffic.

Advantages:

- **Managed services**: Automated backups, scaling, and security patches provided by the cloud provider.

- **Scalability**: Easily scale database resources as the business grows.

- **Focus on development**: Developers can focus on application features instead of database management.

Network workload example of content delivery

Description: A media streaming service aims to deliver content efficiently to users worldwide.

Implementation:

- **CDN integration**: The service can integrate with a CDN like *Cloudflare* or *Akamai*.

- **Zone creation**: They create a new zone in Cloudflare, providing domain information and configuring DNS settings.

- **Cache configuration**: The service configures caching rules for different types of content, setting expiration times and cache control headers.

- **Global distribution**: The CDN automatically distributes content to edge servers located closer to users across the globe.

- **Purge cache**: In case of content updates, the service can programmatically purge the cache for specific resources using the CDN API.

Advantages:

- **Latency reduction**: Content is delivered from edge servers, reducing latency for users.

- **Scalability**: CDN automatically scales to handle varying traffic loads.

- **Improved user experience**: Faster content delivery improves user experience.

Advantages and challenges

In this section, we will delve into the advantages and challenges associated with different types of workloads in cloud computing. Understanding both the advantages and challenges associated with different types of workloads helps organizations make informed decisions about their cloud deployment and management strategy. By mitigating challenges and leveraging the benefits, businesses can create resilient and efficient cloud environments that support their unique workload requirements.

Advantages

The following are the advantages of cloud computing:

- **Scalability**: Cloud environments offer on-demand resource scalability, allowing you to scale up or down based on workload demands. This elasticity ensures optimal performance without overprovisioning or underutilization.

    o **Example**: During a holiday sale, an e-commerce website can quickly scale its compute and storage resources to handle increased traffic.

- **Cost-efficiency**: Cloud services operate on a pay-as-you-go model, allowing you to pay only for the resources you consume. This eliminates upfront capital expenditures and reduces operational costs.

    o **Example**: A startup can avoid purchasing expensive hardware by using cloud services to launch and scale its application.

- **Flexibility**: Cloud platforms provide a wide range of services to accommodate diverse workloads. This flexibility allows you to choose the most suitable services for your application needs.

    o **Example**: An organization can deploy a combination of compute, storage, and networking services to build a complex application architecture.

- **Global accessibility**: Cloud services are accessible from anywhere with an internet connection. This global accessibility enables remote teams and users to collaborate and access resources easily.

    o **Example**: A multinational corporation can centrally manage its resources and applications while allowing its employees across the world to access them.

- **Managed services**: Cloud providers offer managed services that handle routine tasks such as security patches, backups, and scaling. This allows you to focus on application development rather than infrastructure management.

    o **Example**: Using a managed database service, an application developer can focus on optimizing queries and application logic instead of managing database servers.

Challenges

The following are the challenges of cloud computing:

- **Latency**: Network latency can impact the performance of real-time applications and services, especially if data needs to travel long distances between the user and the cloud server.

    o **Mitigation**: Use CDNs to cache and deliver content from edge locations, reducing latency for users in different regions.

- **Data security**: Storing sensitive data in the cloud raises concerns about data security and compliance with regulations.

    o **Mitigation**: Implement encryption mechanisms, strict access controls, and regular security audits. Use encryption at rest and in transit to protect data from unauthorized access.

- **Vendor lock-in**: Depending heavily on a single cloud provider can limit flexibility and portability, making it challenging to switch providers in the future.

    o **Mitigation**: Design applications using industry-standard APIs and avoid using provider-specific features. Consider multi-cloud or hybrid cloud strategies for better flexibility.

- **Resource management**: Inadequate resource management can lead to overspending, inefficient resource allocation, and performance issues.

    o **Mitigation**: Implement monitoring and auto-scaling to ensure resources are allocated optimally. Regularly analyze resource usage patterns and adjust as needed.

- **Data transfer costs**: Moving large volumes of data in and out of the cloud can incur data transfer costs, impacting the budget.

    o **Mitigation**: Optimize data transfer by compressing files, using data transfer acceleration services, and planning data migrations strategically.

Cloud workloads and security

In the ever-evolving landscape of cloud technology, understanding various workloads and their associated security considerations is paramount. This chapter delves into key cloud workloads such as IAM, VPC, AI/ML, storage, databases, compute instances, Docker and Kubernetes, and data analytics. Real-world implementation examples, including considerations for IAM, will be explored.

Identity and Access Management

IAM is a fundamental aspect of cloud security that ensures proper control and authorization of user access to resources and services within a cloud environment, minimizing security risks. IAM allows organizations to define and manage who can access what resources, under what circumstances, and with what level of permissions creating policies, roles, and permissions to grant access.

IAM is crucial for securing cloud environments, enabling organizations to enforce the principle of least privilege, implement strong authentication, and manage access with granularity. By understanding IAM components and concepts, businesses can ensure that only authorized personnel access resources and services, enhancing overall security posture.

This section provides an in-depth understanding of IAM, its components, and its real-world implementation.

IAM components

IAM consists of several key components that help manage identity and access control in cloud environments:

- **Users**: These are the individuals who interact with the cloud services. Each user is assigned a unique identity.

- **Groups**: Groups are collections of users who share similar job roles or responsibilities. Permissions are assigned to groups rather than individual users for easier management.

- **Roles**: Roles define a set of permissions that can be assumed by users or AWS services. Roles are attached to users or resources, granting specific access privileges.

- **Policies**: Policies are JSON documents that specify the permissions granted to users, groups, or roles. They define what actions are allowed or denied on particular resources.

IAM concepts and implementation

Understanding the core principles and best practices of IAM ensures a secure and well-managed access control system:

- **Principle of least privilege**: This concept dictates that users should only have the minimum permissions necessary to perform their tasks. This reduces the risk of accidental or intentional misuse of resources.

- **Authentication vs. authorization**: Authentication is the process of verifying the identity of a user. Authorization determines what actions a user is allowed to perform after authentication.

- **Multi-factor authentication (MFA)**: Adding an extra layer of security, MFA requires users to provide multiple forms of verification (for example, password and a time-based code) before accessing resources.

- **IAM roles for cross-account access**: Organizations can grant permissions to users or resources across different AWS accounts using IAM roles. This simplifies access management for shared resources.

Real-world implementation example

To better understand IAM in action, consider how organizations apply these concepts in practical scenarios:

- Imagine a software development company called *TechSolutions* using a cloud environment for their projects. Here is how they implement IAM:

  o **User setup**: They create individual IAM users for each team member, like developers and project managers.

  o **Group assignment**: Users are grouped based on roles such as developers, managers, and administrators.

  o **Role creation**: A role named DeploymentRole is created for deploying applications to production environments.

  o **Policy definition**: They create policies like EC2FullAccess and S3ReadOnly to define permissions for users and roles.

  o **MFA implementation**: TechSolutions enforces MFA for all users accessing critical resources.

  o **Cross-account access**: They establish cross-account roles to grant their development team temporary access to resources in the testing account.

- Consider a multinational corporation adopting a cloud infrastructure. They setup IAM policies to allow department heads access to resources relevant to their teams. The DevOps team gets access to the **continuous integration/continuous deployment (CI/CD)** pipelines, while the finance team can access cost-related metrics.

Virtual private cloud

A VPC is a pivotal component of cloud computing that empowers organizations to establish isolated and customizable network environments within a public cloud infrastructure, allowing organizations to segment their resources and secure communication. It offers control over IP addressing, routing tables, and network gateways.

VPCs offer organizations the ability to create isolated network environments within the cloud, promoting security, flexibility, and efficient resource management. By understanding

VPC components and concepts, businesses can design network architectures that align with their specific needs while maintaining robust security measures.

This section provides an in-depth exploration of VPC, its key concepts, components, and a real-world implementation example.

VPC key concepts

A VPC provides a logically isolated network environment within the cloud. The following are some key concepts that define its structure and functionality:

- **Isolation and segmentation**: VPCs allow users to create distinct, isolated network environments. This isolation enhances security and enables multiple projects or departments to coexist without interference.

- **IP addressing**: Users can define IP address ranges for their VPC using CIDR notation. This allows precise control over the address space within the VPC.

- **Subnets**: Subnets divide the VPC's IP address range into smaller segments, aiding in resource grouping and enhanced security through network **access control lists (ACLs)**.

- **Route tables**: Route tables dictate the flow of traffic between subnets, ensuring efficient routing and facilitating communication between resources.

VPC components

To build a functional and secure VPC, various components work together to manage network access and traffic flow:

- **Internet gateway (IGW)**: An IGW serves as the gateway for communication between the VPC and the internet, enabling resources within the VPC to access external services and vice versa.

- **Elastic IP addresses**: Elastic IP addresses are static public IP addresses that can be associated with resources in the VPC, providing a consistent endpoint for internet-facing services.

- **Network ACLs**: ACLs operate at the subnet level and control inbound and outbound traffic, serving as an additional layer of security.

- **Security groups**: Security groups are stateful firewalls that regulate traffic at the instance level, allowing or denying inbound and outbound communication.

VPC real-world implementation example

Consider a cloud deployment scenario for *TechCorp*, a technology enterprise. Here is how they implement VPC:

- **VPC design**: TechCorp creates a VPC with a CIDR block of 10.0.0.0/16, which provides a substantial address space for their resources.

- **Subnet creation**: They setup subnets for different purposes: Web subnet (10.0.1.0/24) for internet-facing applications and database subnet (10.0.2.0/24) for database servers.

- **IGW**: An IGW is attached to the VPC, enabling instances in the web subnet to communicate with the internet.

- **Security groups and ACLs**: TechCorp configures security groups to control access at the instance level and uses ACLs to regulate traffic flow between subnets.

- **Elastic IP assignment**: They assign an Elastic IP to a load balancer in the web subnet to provide a static endpoint for their web application.

A **software as a service (SaaS)** provider uses VPC to isolate customer data. Each customer's data resides in a separate subnet, and network ACLs are configured to control traffic between them, ensuring data privacy and security.

Artificial intelligence and machine learning

AI/ML has transformed the cloud landscape by providing scalable platforms and tools for complex computations, data analysis, and predictive modeling. AI/ML leverages the cloud's scalability for complex computations. Cloud platforms provide AI/ML services and frameworks, making it easier to build, train, and deploy models.

AI/ML integration with the cloud empowers businesses to harness the potential of data-driven decision-making, predictive analysis, and automation. By understanding AI/ML concepts and applications, organizations can create innovative solutions that leverage AI/ML to transform industries, drive efficiency, and deliver enhanced user experiences.

This section delves into the intricate world of AI/ML, exploring its underlying concepts, applications, and a real-world implementation scenario.

AI/ML key concepts

AI/ML forms the foundation of modern intelligent systems. The following are some key concepts that define how AI/ML works:

- **AI**: AI involves creating systems that can simulate human-like intelligence, enabling them to learn from experience, adapt to new information, and perform tasks that typically require human intelligence.

- **ML**: ML is a subset of AI that focuses on creating algorithms and models that enable computers to learn from data. It encompasses supervised learning, unsupervised learning, and reinforcement learning.

- **Deep learning**: A subset of ML, deep learning uses neural networks with multiple layers to extract intricate patterns and features from data, enabling it to perform tasks like image and speech recognition.

- **Data training and inference**: AI/ML models are trained using large datasets to learn patterns and relationships. Once trained, they can make predictions or classifications on new, unseen data (inference).

AI/ML applications and cloud services

AI/ML has revolutionized various industries by enabling intelligent automation and data-driven decision-making. The following are some of its key applications:

- **Predictive analytics**: AI/ML can analyze historical data to predict future trends and outcomes, helping businesses make informed decisions.

- **Natural language processing (NLP)**: NLP enables machines to understand and interpret human language, powering chatbots, sentiment analysis, and language translation.

- **Computer vision**: AI/ML algorithms can interpret and analyze visual data, enabling applications like facial recognition, object detection, and autonomous vehicles.

- **Recommendation systems**: ML algorithms can suggest products, services, or content to users based on their preferences and behavior, enhancing user experience.

AI/ML real-world implementation example

Consider *HealthCareAI*, a healthcare institution leveraging cloud-based AI/ML to enhance patient care:

- **Data collection and storage**: HealthCareAI collects medical data from various sources, such as patient records, medical images, and lab results. They store this data in a cloud-based data lake.

- **Model development**: They build an AI model using deep learning to analyze medical images and detect anomalies in X-rays.

- **Training and validation**: The model is trained using a diverse dataset of X-ray images. It learns to differentiate between normal and abnormal images by identifying patterns.

- **Deployment and inference**: Once trained, the model is deployed to the cloud, allowing healthcare professionals to upload X-ray images for analysis. The model provides insights into potential anomalies.

- **Continual learning**: HealthCareAI periodically re-trains the model with new data to improve accuracy and adapt to evolving medical knowledge.

A healthcare startup uses cloud-based AI/ML to process medical images. They employ a convolutional neural network to detect anomalies in X-rays, benefiting from the cloud's processing power and AI capabilities.

Storage in the cloud

Storage is a fundamental component of cloud computing that provides scalable, reliable, and flexible data management solutions. This section delves into the intricacies of cloud storage, its key characteristics, various types, and a real-world implementation example.

Cloud storage solutions offer organizations the ability to manage and scale their data seamlessly, ensuring data durability, accessibility, and flexibility. By comprehending the nuances of different storage types and how they align with specific business needs, enterprises can optimize their data management strategies and enhance overall operational efficiency.

Cloud storage key characteristics

Cloud storage provides a flexible and efficient way to manage data. The following are some of its essential characteristics:

- **Scalability**: Cloud storage offers the ability to scale storage resources up or down based on demand. This eliminates the need for upfront provisioning and allows organizations to pay for only what they use.

- **Durability and redundancy**: Cloud storage systems ensure data durability through redundancy and replication. Data is stored across multiple physical locations, minimizing the risk of data loss.

- **Accessibility**: Cloud storage enables access to data from anywhere with an internet connection. This flexibility is essential for remote collaboration and data-driven decision-making.

Types of cloud storage

Different types of cloud storage cater to various use cases, ensuring optimal performance and data management:

- **Object storage**: Object storage is ideal for unstructured data like images, videos, and documents. Objects are stored in a flat structure with unique identifiers and metadata.

- **Block storage**: Block storage is used for structured data and provides raw storage volumes that can be attached to **virtual machines (VMs)**. It is suitable for databases and applications requiring direct control over storage.

- **File storage**: File storage provides a hierarchical structure similar to traditional file systems. It is suitable for sharing files among multiple instances or users.

Real-world implementation example

Imagine an e-commerce company called *ShopWiz* using cloud storage to manage its data as follows:

- **Object storage for product images**: ShopWiz employs object storage to store product images and videos. Each item has a unique object identifier and associated metadata, making it easy to retrieve and display on the website.

- **Block storage for databases**: The company uses block storage to manage its relational database. This ensures consistent and reliable data storage for transactions and customer information.

- **File storage for inventory management**: ShopWiz utilizes file storage for its inventory management system. This allows multiple departments to access and update inventory files collaboratively.

- **Scalability for seasonal traffic**: During peak shopping seasons, ShopWiz can easily scale up its storage resources to accommodate increased traffic and data processing demands.

- **Data redundancy for data safety**: ShopWiz's data is replicated across multiple availability zones to ensure data safety and minimize the risk of data loss.

Databases in the cloud

Databases are foundational to modern applications, enabling efficient data storage, retrieval, and management. Cloud platforms offer a range of database services to cater to diverse requirements. This section delves into the nuances of cloud databases, covering relational databases, NoSQL databases, and their real-world implications.

Cloud databases offer a spectrum of choices to accommodate different data management needs. Relational databases suit structured, consistent data, while NoSQL databases cater to flexible, scalable requirements. By aligning database choices with specific application demands, businesses can effectively manage data, ensure performance, and drive value from their cloud investments.

Relational databases

Relational databases provide a structured approach to data management, ensuring consistency and integrity. Key characteristics include:

- **Data structure**: Relational databases use tables with predefined schemas to store structured data. Each table contains rows (records) with columns (attributes).

- **SQL queries**: Relational databases utilize SQL for data manipulation and querying. SQL ensures standardized interactions with the database.

- **Atomicity, consistency, isolation, and durability (ACID) transactions**: Relational databases support ACID transactions, ensuring data integrity and consistency.

NoSQL databases

NoSQL databases offer an alternative to traditional relational databases, providing flexibility and scalability for modern applications. Key features include:

- **Flexible schema**: NoSQL databases offer flexibility in data modeling, accommodating semi-structured and unstructured data. They are suitable for applications with evolving requirements.

- **Scalability**: NoSQL databases are designed for horizontal scalability, making them ideal for high-velocity data and distributed architectures.

- **Consistency, availability, and partition tolerance (CAP) theorem**: NoSQL databases follow the CAP theorem, which emphasizes the trade-off between CAP.

Real-world implementation example

Consider *FashionMall*, an e-commerce platform using cloud databases for its operations:

- **Relational database for transactional data**: FashionMall employs a relational database to manage transactional data like customer orders, payments, and inventory. ACID transactions ensure data consistency.

- **NoSQL database for user profiles**: User profiles, which may have varying attributes, are stored in a NoSQL database. This accommodates evolving user data without altering the schema.

- **Scalability for flash sales**: During flash sales, FashionMall scales its databases horizontally to handle the surge in user activity and order processing.

- **Data warehousing for analytics**: The company utilizes cloud-based data warehousing to consolidate and analyze sales data, helping them make informed decisions about inventory and marketing strategies.

An e-commerce platform uses cloud storage to manage product images and videos. They leverage a NoSQL database to handle high-velocity customer reviews and implement auto-scaling compute instances during peak shopping seasons.

Compute instances in the cloud

Compute instances, often referred to as VMs, form the computational foundation of cloud environments, providing the processing power necessary to run applications and services.

Compute instances are the building blocks of cloud computing, offering flexibility, scalability, and customization. By understanding instance types, provisioning methods, and optimization techniques, organizations can deploy applications that seamlessly adapt to changing demands while optimizing resource utilization and cost-effectiveness.

This section delves into the intricacies of compute instances, their attributes, benefits, and a real-world implementation example.

Key attributes of compute instances

Compute instances provide the backbone for running applications in the cloud, offering flexibility and scalability. The following are their key attributes:

- **Virtualization**: Compute instances are virtualized representations of physical hardware. They allow multiple instances to run on the same physical server, optimizing resource utilization.

- **Flexibility**: Cloud platforms offer a wide range of instance types optimized for different workloads. Users can select configurations based on CPU, memory, storage, and networking requirements.

- **Elasticity**: Compute instances can be easily scaled up or down based on demand. This elasticity ensures that resources match workload fluctuations.

- **Pay-as-you-go**: Cloud providers offer a pay-as-you-go model for compute instances, allowing users to pay only for the resources they consume.

Compute instances benefits

By leveraging cloud-based compute instances, businesses can optimize performance and efficiency. Some of the major benefits include:

- **Resource isolation**: Virtualization ensures resource isolation between instances, preventing performance interference.

- **Rapid provisioning**: Compute instances can be provisioned quickly, enabling faster application deployment and development.

- **Customization**: Users can customize instance configurations to meet specific application requirements, tailoring CPU, memory, and storage.

- **High availability**: Cloud platforms offer features like auto-scaling and load balancing to enhance application availability.

Real-world implementation example

Imagine *TechWeb*, a web hosting company utilizing cloud compute instances for its services:

- **Instance selection**: TechWeb chooses instance types with a balance of CPU and memory for hosting websites. Different instance types cater to varying traffic levels and resource demands.

- **Auto-scaling**: During traffic spikes, TechWeb's application load balancer triggers auto-scaling, creating additional compute instances to handle increased requests.

- **Customization**: TechWeb customizes instances with necessary software stacks and configurations, ensuring compatibility with their clients' web applications.

- **Managed services**: For customers seeking fully managed solutions, TechWeb offers managed compute instances, handling maintenance, backups, and updates.

- **Resource optimization**: Using monitoring tools, TechWeb continuously monitors instance performance to optimize resource allocation and cost-efficiency.

Docker and Kubernetes

Docker containers and Kubernetes orchestration offer a powerful framework for developing, deploying, and managing applications in cloud environments. By embracing containerization and orchestration, organizations can achieve efficient resource utilization, rapid application deployment, and automation of critical tasks, leading to enhanced agility and scalability in their operations.

Containerization with Docker and orchestration with Kubernetes revolutionize application deployment and management. Docker packages applications with dependencies, ensuring consistency across environments. Kubernetes automates the deployment, scaling, and management of containerized applications.

This section explores the concepts of Docker containers, Kubernetes orchestration, their advantages, and a real-world implementation example.

Docker containers

Docker containers revolutionize application deployment by enabling lightweight and consistent environments. Key features include:

- **Containerization**: Docker containers encapsulate applications and their dependencies, ensuring consistent behavior across different environments.

- **Isolation**: Containers provide process-level isolation, allowing multiple applications to run on the same host without conflicts.

- **Portability**: Docker containers can be easily moved between environments, from development to production, and even across cloud providers.

- **Resource efficiency**: Containers share the host operating system kernel, making them lightweight and efficient compared to traditional VMs.

Kubernetes orchestration

Kubernetes provides a powerful orchestration system for managing containerized applications at scale. Its key functionalities include:

- **Deployment**: Kubernetes automates application deployment, ensuring consistent setup and scaling across clusters of machines.

- **Scaling**: Kubernetes scales applications up or down based on demand, maintaining optimal performance and resource utilization.

- **Load balancing**: Kubernetes distributes incoming traffic across containers to ensure even resource utilization and availability.

- **Self-healing**: Kubernetes monitors the health of containers and restarts or replaces failed ones automatically.

Real-world implementation example

Imagine *MicroTech*, a software company adopting microservices architecture using Docker and Kubernetes as follows:

- **Containerization with Docker**: MicroTech divides its monolithic application into smaller microservices, each running in a separate Docker container. This enhances modularity and deployment flexibility.

- **Container registry**: MicroTech uses a Docker registry to store and manage Docker images of its microservices. This centralized repository simplifies version control.

- **Kubernetes deployment**: Using Kubernetes, MicroTech deploys microservices across a cluster of machines. Kubernetes automatically manages load balancing and scaling.

- **CI/CD**: MicroTech implements CI/CD pipelines that automatically build Docker images, run tests, and deploy new versions to Kubernetes clusters.

- **Scaling with Kubernetes**: During peak usage, Kubernetes scales up instances of high-traffic microservices, ensuring performance without manual intervention.

A fintech company adopts a microservices architecture. They use Docker to containerize each microservice, ensuring seamless deployment. Kubernetes manages these containers, automatically scaling services based on demand.

Data, ETL and analytics

Cloud platforms offer powerful tools for data processing, **extract, transform, load (ETL)**, and analytics. Services like data lakes, warehouses, and analytics engines allow organizations to derive insights from their data.

Data analytics in the cloud

Data analytics in the cloud empowers organizations to extract valuable insights from vast volumes of data, driving informed decision-making and business growth. Cloud data analytics empowers organizations to harness the value of data through scalable processing, efficient ETL operations, and insightful analytics. By implementing cloud-based analytics workflows, businesses can gain deeper insights into their operations, customer behaviors, and market trends, driving smarter decisions and competitive advantage.

This section delves into the realm of cloud-based data analytics, covering data processing, ETL operations, and a real-world implementation example.

Data analytics key components

Cloud-based data analytics involves multiple components that streamline the processing, storage, and analysis of vast datasets. These key components include:

- **Data processing**: Cloud platforms offer tools for processing large datasets quickly and efficiently. Parallel processing and distributed computing accelerate data analysis.

- **ETL operations**: ETL pipelines extract data from various sources, transform it into a usable format, and load it into data warehouses or lakes for analysis.

- **Data warehousing**: Cloud data warehousing provides storage and querying capabilities optimized for analytical workloads, enabling fast and complex queries.

- **Big data technologies**: Cloud platforms offer managed services for popular big data frameworks like Hadoop and Spark, facilitating complex analytics.

Data analytics benefits

Cloud-based data analytics brings numerous advantages, making data-driven decision-making more efficient and accessible. The benefits include:

- **Scalability**: Cloud data analytics services can scale resources up or down based on data processing demands, enabling cost-effective handling of fluctuating workloads.

- **Cost-efficiency**: Pay-as-you-go models allow organizations to pay only for the resources used during data processing and analysis.

- **Speed and agility**: Cloud analytics platforms enable quick deployment of data processing and analysis workflows, reducing time-to-insight.

Real-world implementation example

Consider *Retail Insights*, a retail company utilizing cloud data analytics to improve operations:

- **Data collection**: Retail Insights collects sales data, customer interactions, and inventory information from various sources, storing it in a cloud data lake.

- **ETL pipeline**: Using cloud-based ETL tools, they transform raw sales data into a structured format, enriching it with customer demographics and product details.

- **Data warehousing**: The transformed data is loaded into a cloud data warehouse. Retail Insights uses this warehouse to run complex queries for sales trends and inventory optimization.

- **Analytics dashboards**: Cloud analytics services help Retail Insights create interactive dashboards that provide real-time insights to managers and executives.

- **Predictive analytics**: By leveraging machine learning models, Retail Insights predicts customer preferences, enabling targeted marketing campaigns.

A media streaming service analyzes viewer behavior using cloud-based analytics tools. They perform ETL operations on user interaction data stored in a data lake, transforming it into meaningful insights for content optimization.

Conclusion

In the dynamic world of cloud computing, workloads serve as the heartbeat of innovation and efficiency. This chapter has provided a comprehensive exploration of workloads in the context of cloud computing, unraveling the intricacies and significance of these fundamental components. As we conclude this journey, let us recap the essential insights that can empower you to harness the full potential of workloads in the cloud.

Workloads in cloud computing are not merely technical components but the engines driving digital transformation. They empower organizations to innovate, scale, and respond to dynamic market forces. As you embark on your cloud computing journey, the insights gained in this chapter will serve as your compass, guiding you through the ever-evolving cloud landscape and ensuring your ability to harness the full potential of cloud workloads for a brighter digital future.

Incorporating IAM, VPC, AI/ML, storage, databases, Docker, and Kubernetes, and data analytics into cloud workloads optimizes efficiency and security. Real-world implementation examples underscore the practicality of these technologies. By staying abreast of cloud advancements and aligning workloads with business objectives, organizations can harness the full potential of cloud technology while safeguarding their digital assets.

In this chapter, we have journeyed through the expansive realm of cloud technology. From IAM to AI/ML, explored how the cloud empowers organizations. We have delved into storage, databases, and containerization with Docker and Kubernetes, highlighting their pivotal roles in modern IT. Data analytics in the cloud offers scalability and agility, while MFA strengthens security.

The cloud is not just a destination; it is an ecosystem of innovation where technology transcends boundaries. As cloud technology continues to evolve, those who grasp its intricacies will unlock limitless possibilities in this digital expanse.

In the next chapter, we will explore the core concepts of security in cloud computing. We will explore foundational pillars such as encryption, secure protocols, IAM, compliance, incident response, and the importance of security awareness. These concepts are vital for building a strong security posture in modern cloud environments and protecting data in an increasingly connected world.

Key takeaways

The following are the important takeaways from this chapter:

- Workloads in cloud computing encompass a wide range of tasks and operations executed within a cloud environment.

- They are categorized into three main types: Compute workloads, storage workloads, and network workloads.

- Compute workloads involve processing tasks and can be further categorized into batch processing, HPC, and web server tasks.

- GPU-enabled instances are beneficial for compute-intensive tasks like simulations and video rendering.

- Storage workloads revolve around data storage and management.

- Relational database workloads manage structured data, while file storage workloads handle unstructured data like documents and multimedia.

- Network workloads deal with communication between resources and optimizing data delivery.

- CDNs enhance content delivery by reducing latency through edge server distribution.

- Real-world examples illustrate how organizations can leverage cloud computing to address specific business needs.

- AWS EC2 for compute, Amazon RDS for storage, and Cloudflare CDN for network workloads are examples.

- Advantages of cloud workloads include scalability, cost-efficiency, flexibility, global accessibility, and managed services.

- Challenges include latency, data security, vendor lock-in, resource management, and data transfer costs.

- Understanding the types of workloads helps in selecting appropriate cloud resources, designing architectures, and optimizing performance.

- Different types of workloads have varying resource requirements and scalability needs.

- Organizations can optimize workloads by monitoring and adjusting resource allocation, implementing security measures, and following best practices.

- Automation and orchestration tools can streamline workload management.

- Workloads are integral components of the larger cloud ecosystem, interacting with various cloud services and resources.

- Multi-cloud and hybrid cloud strategies can enhance flexibility and reduce vendor lock-in risks.

- IAM is crucial for securing access to cloud resources by controlling user identities, permissions, and authentication mechanisms.

- It enforces the principle of least privilege and prevents unauthorized access.

- VPCs provide isolated network environments within cloud infrastructure, enhancing security and network segmentation.

- Components include subnets, route tables, security groups, and network ACLs.

- Cloud technology enhances AI/ML capabilities by providing scalability, processing power, and access to AI services.

- Real-world applications include image recognition, NLP, and predictive analytics.

- Cloud storage offers scalability, durability, and accessibility for data management.

- Object, block, and file storage cater to different data types and use cases.

- Cloud databases include relational and NoSQL options, each with unique characteristics.

- Relational databases use structured schemas, while NoSQL databases offer flexibility for unstructured data.

- Compute instances, or VMs, provide processing power for cloud applications.

- They offer flexibility, scalability, and resource isolation.

- Docker containers package applications and dependencies, ensuring consistency across environments.

- Kubernetes orchestrates containerized applications, automating deployment, scaling, and management.

- Cloud-based data analytics provides scalability, cost-efficiency, and rapid deployment.

- ETL operations are essential for data extraction, transformation, and loading for analysis.

- MFA enhances cloud security by requiring multiple forms of verification before granting access.

- It mitigates the risk of unauthorized access, even if credentials are compromised.

Key terms

- **Workloads**: The diverse set of tasks, operations, and processes executed within a cloud computing environment.

- **Compute workloads**: Tasks involving computational processing, including batch processing, HPC, and web server tasks.

- **Batch processing workloads**: Workloads that execute a series of tasks or jobs in a specific order without user interaction, commonly used for data processing.

- **HPC workloads**: Complex calculations and simulations that require significant computational power, often used in scientific research and engineering.

- **Web server workloads**: Workloads that manage incoming web requests, serve web applications, and handle user interactions.

- **Storage workloads**: Operations related to data storage and management, including database workloads and file storage workloads.

- **Database workloads**: Workloads that involve managing structured data using DBMS, including relational and NoSQL databases.

- **File storage workloads**: Workloads that manage unstructured data such as documents, images, and multimedia files.

- **Network workloads**: Tasks related to communication between resources, including CDN workloads and VPN workloads.

- **CDN**: A network of distributed servers that deliver web content, such as images and videos, to users from edge locations, reducing latency.

- **GPU-enabled instances**: Cloud computing instances equipped with GPUs, often used for tasks requiring parallel processing, like video rendering.

- **Managed services**: Cloud services provided and managed by the cloud provider, handling routine tasks such as backups, security patches, and scaling.

- **Data security**: Concerns and measures related to protecting data from unauthorized access and breaches, including encryption and access controls.

- **Vendor lock-in**: The dependency on a specific cloud provider's services and technologies, limiting the ability to switch providers easily.

- **Scalability**: The ability to adjust resources (vertical and horizontal scaling) to meet workload demands efficiently.

- **Multi-cloud**: A strategy that involves using multiple cloud providers to reduce reliance on a single vendor and enhance flexibility.

- **Hybrid cloud**: A combination of private and public cloud infrastructure, allowing data and applications to be shared between them.

- **Cost-efficiency**: Achieving optimal resource usage and cost savings in cloud computing by paying only for the resources used.

- **Latency**: The delay in data transmission over a network, which can affect the responsiveness of applications.

- **Optimization strategies**: Techniques and practices to improve the performance, cost-effectiveness, and security of cloud workloads.

- **IAM**: The practice of controlling access to cloud resources by managing user identities, permissions, and authentication mechanisms.

- **VPC**: An isolated network environment within a public cloud infrastructure, providing control over network settings and security.

- **AI**: The simulation of human intelligence in machines to perform tasks like problem-solving, learning, and decision-making.

- **ML**: A subset of AI that uses algorithms to enable machines to learn from and make predictions or decisions based on data.

- **Virtualization**: The process of creating a virtual version of a resource, such as a server, storage device, or network, to optimize resource utilization.

- **Docker**: A containerization platform that packages applications and their dependencies into isolated containers for consistent deployment.

- **Kubernetes**: An open-source container orchestration platform for automating the deployment, scaling, and management of containerized applications.

- **NoSQL database**: A type of database that provides flexibility in data modeling and is suitable for unstructured or semi-structured data.

- **Relational database**: A database system that uses structured schemas and SQL for data storage and retrieval.

- **ETL**: A data integration process that involves extracting data from various sources, transforming it into a usable format, and loading it into a data repository for analysis.

- **MFA**: A security mechanism that requires users to provide multiple forms of verification before granting access to a system or resource.

- **Cloud scalability**: The ability to dynamically adjust computing resources, such as CPU, memory, and storage, to accommodate changing workloads.

- **Containerization**: The practice of packaging applications and their dependencies into containers, providing consistency across different environments.

- **Data analytics**: The process of examining data to discover meaningful patterns, insights, and trends, often facilitated by tools and algorithms.

- **Pay-as-you-go model**: A pricing model in which users are charged based on the resources and services they consume, promoting cost-efficiency.

- **Object storage**: A type of cloud storage designed for storing unstructured data, such as images, videos, and documents.

- **Block storage**: A type of cloud storage that provides raw storage volumes that can be attached to VMs.

- **File storage**: A type of cloud storage that offers hierarchical file system structures for shared access to files.

- **Elasticity**: The ability to automatically scale computing resources up or down based on demand.

- **Load balancing**: The practice of distributing incoming network traffic across multiple servers or instances to optimize performance and ensure high availability.

Solved exercises

1. **What are the three main categories of cloud workloads?**

   Answer: Compute workloads, storage workloads, and network workloads.

2. **What is the primary benefit of using GPU-enabled instances for compute workloads like video rendering?**

   Answer: GPU instances offer parallel processing capabilities, which significantly speed up tasks like rendering and simulation.

3. **Name a managed cloud database service suitable for structured transactional data.**

   Answer: Amazon RDS is ideal for structured transactional data.

4. **How do CDNs enhance network workload performance?**

   Answer: CDNs cache content at edge servers closer to users, reducing latency and improving load times.

5. **What are two key benefits of using Kubernetes in cloud-native environments?**

   Answer: Automated scaling and self-healing (automatic replacement of failed containers).

6. **What is the principle of least privilege in IAM?**

   Answer: It means giving users only the permissions they need to perform their specific tasks, minimizing security risks.

7. **What is the difference between object storage and block storage in cloud environments?**

   Answer: Object storage manages unstructured data with metadata and unique identifiers, while block storage provides raw volumes for structured data and low latency access.

8. **Why is vendor lock-in considered a challenge in cloud computing?**

   Answer: Relying on proprietary services from a single cloud provider can make it difficult and expensive to switch providers later.

9. **How does MFA enhance IAM security?**

   Answer: By requiring multiple verification methods (e.g., password and OTP), MFA adds an extra layer of security beyond passwords.

Unsolved exercises

1. Can you explain the significance of IAM in the context of cloud security?

2. What are the key components of a VPC? How does VPC enhance network security?

3. How does Docker differ from traditional virtualization methods like hypervisor-based VMs?

4. Explain the role of Kubernetes in managing containerized applications. How does it handle automatic scaling?

5. What are the primary advantages of NoSQL databases over traditional relational databases?

6. Describe the ETL process in data analytics. How does it contribute to data analysis?

7. How does cloud-based data analytics offer advantages over on-premises solutions?

8. Explain the role of Docker in application deployment. How does it facilitate consistent environments across different stages of development?

9. How does MFA enhance cloud security? Can you provide an example of MFA in action?

10. Can you give an example of a real-world scenario where cloud-based AI/ML is used? How does the cloud's scalability benefit this scenario?

CHAPTER 4
Concepts of Security

Introduction

Security is an overarching concern that casts a long shadow over the rapidly advancing realm of cloud technology. As organizations embrace the cloud for its scalability, flexibility, and cost-efficiency, they must simultaneously grapple with the ever-evolving landscape of security threats. In this chapter, we embark on a journey through the fundamental concepts of security in the context of cloud technology, shedding light on critical aspects such as encryption, protocols, **Identity and Access Management (IAM)**, **single sign-on (SSO)**, and other residual security topics.

Cloud computing has revolutionized how businesses operate, allowing them to harness the power of remote servers and services for data storage, processing, and application delivery. However, the very nature of cloud computing introduces a new set of security challenges, from protecting data during transmission and storage to managing access permissions and responding to evolving threats.

Encryption stands as the sentinel guarding data, ensuring it remains unintelligible to prying eyes. Protocols create secure pathways through which data flows. IAM and SSO serve as the gatekeepers, controlling who has access to resources and applications. Meanwhile, residual security topics such as compliance, logging, and incident response round out the arsenal of defenses against the ever-persistent and evolving threat landscape.

In this chapter, we will explore these concepts, exploring their significance, implementation strategies, and critical role in fortifying the security posture of cloud-based infrastructures.

As we navigate these vital security waters, we will equip you with the knowledge and insights needed to navigate the cloud securely in an ever-connected world.

Structure

In this chapter, we will discuss the following topics:

- Encryption
- Protocols
- Identity and Access Management
- Security compliance in cloud technology
- Logging and monitoring
- Incident response
- Security training and awareness

Objectives

By the end of this chapter, readers will gain a solid foundation in cloud security concepts, equipping them to navigate the dynamic landscape of secure cloud technology. They will understand the significance of encryption for data security in cloud environments, learn about essential security protocols like **Hypertext Transfer Protocol Secure** (**HTTPS**), **Secure Shell** (**SSH**), and **Message Queuing Telemetry Transport** (**MQTT**) for secure communication, and explore IAM concepts and how they control resource access.

Readers will be able to grasp the importance of compliance with industry regulations and standards in cloud security, discover the role of logging and monitoring in detecting and responding to security incidents, learn the phases of effective incident response, and how to apply them in cloud incidents.

The chapter will help you to understand the necessity of educating users and fostering security awareness in cloud environments.

Encryption

Encryption is a cornerstone of cloud security, essential for protecting data from unauthorized access, whether it is in transit or at rest. In this section, we will explore the principles of encryption, implementation examples, and related code snippets to illustrate how encryption can be applied in various cloud scenarios.

Encryption is a fundamental building block of cloud security, ensuring the confidentiality of data both in transit and at rest. By implementing encryption protocols and leveraging cloud provider services for data encryption and key management, organizations can enhance their security posture and protect sensitive information from unauthorized access or exposure.

Encryption fundamentals

Encryption is the process of converting plaintext data into ciphertext using algorithms and encryption keys. The ciphertext is unreadable without the decryption key, ensuring data confidentiality. In cloud security, two primary forms of encryption are used: data in transit encryption and data at rest encryption.

Data in transit encryption

Data in transit encryption ensures that data remains confidential while being transmitted over networks. A common implementation is using the TLS/SSL protocol. Here is a Python example demonstrating how to establish an encrypted connection with the popular **requests** library:

```python
import requests

# Define the URL to the cloud service
url = "https://api.example.com/data"

# Send a GET request with SSL/TLS encryption
response = requests.get(url)

# Process the response
if response.status_code == 200:
    encrypted_data = response.content
    # Decrypt the data if necessary
    # ...
else:
    print("Error:", response.status_code)
```

Data at rest encryption

Data at rest encryption safeguards data stored on disks or in databases within cloud environments. Cloud providers often offer **server-side encryption** (**SSE**), where data is automatically encrypted before storage. Here is an example using AWS S3 bucket encryption in Python:

```python
import boto3

# Initialize the S3 client
s3 = boto3.client('s3')
```

```python
# Specify the S3 bucket and object
bucket_name = 'my-bucket'
object_key = 'my-data.txt'

# Enable encryption for the object
s3.put_object(
    Bucket=bucket_name,
    Key=object_key,
    ServerSideEncryption='AES256'
)
```

Key management

Proper encryption also involves secure key management. In the cloud, **Key Management Services** (**KMS**) are used to generate, store, and manage encryption keys. Below is an example of AWS KMS key creation and data encryption in Python:

```python
import boto3

# Initialize the KMS client
kms = boto3.client('kms')

# Create a new KMS key
response = kms.create_key()
key_id = response['KeyMetadata']['KeyId']

# Encrypt data using the KMS key
plaintext_data = "Sensitive information"
response = kms.encrypt(
    KeyId=key_id,
    Plaintext=bytes(plaintext_data, 'utf-8')
)

# Store or transmit the ciphertext securely
ciphertext = response['CiphertextBlob']
```

Protocols

Protocols are critical in establishing secure communication channels and maintaining data integrity within cloud environments. In this section, we will explore the essential protocols used in cloud security, provide implementation examples, and share related code snippets to demonstrate their usage.

Protocols like HTTPS, SSH, and MQTT are instrumental in securing communication and data transfer within cloud environments. By using these protocols with appropriate libraries and tools, organizations can establish secure connections, access remote resources, and exchange data with confidence, ensuring the confidentiality and integrity of their information.

Hypertext Transfer Protocol Secure

HTTPS is the standard for secure communication on the web, combining HTTP with SSL/TLS encryption to protect data in transit. Here is a Python example illustrating how to make an HTTPS request using the **requests** library:

```
import requests


# Define the URL with HTTPS
url = "https://api.example.com/data"


# Send an HTTPS GET request
response = requests.get(url)


# Process the HTTPS response
if response.status_code == 200:
    encrypted_data = response.content
    # Decrypt the data if necessary
    # ...
else:
    print("Error:", response.status_code)
```

Secure Shell

SSH is a cryptographic network protocol used for secure remote access to servers and data transfer. The following is an example of using SSH with Python's **paramiko** library to establish an SSH connection and execute a command on a remote server:

```
import paramiko


# Initialize an SSH client
ssh_client = paramiko.SSHClient()
ssh_client.set_missing_host_key_policy(paramiko.AutoAddPolicy())
```

```
# Connect to the remote server
ssh_client.connect('remote-server.example.com', username='your_username',
password='your_password')

# Execute a command on the remote server
stdin, stdout, stderr = ssh_client.exec_command('ls -l')

# Print the output
print(stdout.read().decode())

# Close the SSH connection
ssh_client.close()
```

Message Queuing Telemetry Transport

MQTT is a lightweight, publish-subscribe protocol commonly used in IoT and cloud applications for efficient message exchange. The following is a Python example using the paho-mqtt library to publish and subscribe to MQTT messages:

```
import paho.mqtt.client as mqtt

# Define MQTT broker and topic
broker_address = "mqtt.example.com"
topic = "my_topic"

# Create an MQTT client
client = mqtt.Client()

# Connect to the MQTT broker
client.connect(broker_address)

# Publish a message
message = "Hello, MQTT!"
client.publish(topic, message)

# Subscribe to a topic
def on_message(client, userdata, message):
    print(f"Received message: {message.payload.decode()}")
```

```
client.on_message = on_message
client.subscribe(topic)

# Start the MQTT loop
client.loop_forever()
```

Identity and Access Management

IAM is a fundamental concept in cloud security that revolves around managing user identities and controlling their access to cloud resources. In this section, we will explore IAM principles, provide implementation examples, and share related code snippets to demonstrate how IAM can be effectively applied in cloud environments.

IAM is a cornerstone of cloud security, ensuring that the right users have the right access to resources. By effectively implementing IAM solutions provided by cloud service providers like **Amazon Web Services (AWS)**, **Google Cloud Platform (GCP)**, and Azure, organizations can maintain strict control over access permissions, enforce security policies, and protect their cloud assets from unauthorized access or misuse.

IAM fundamentals

IAM encompasses user authentication, authorization, and permissions management. Proper IAM implementation ensures that only authorized users can access specific resources or perform defined actions.

Amazon Web Services Identity and Access Management

AWS IAM is a widely used IAM service that allows you to control access to AWS resources. Here is an example using AWS IAM in Python to create a new user and assign permissions:

```
import boto3

# Initialize the IAM client
iam = boto3.client('iam')

# Create a new IAM user
user_name = 'new_user'
iam.create_user(UserName=user_name)
```

```
# Define a policy for the user
policy_document = {
    "Version": "2012-10-17",
    "Statement": [
        {
            "Effect": "Allow",
            "Action": "s3:ListBucket",
            "Resource": "arn:aws:s3:::example-bucket"
        },
        {
            "Effect": "Allow",
            "Action": [
                "s3:GetObject",
                "s3:PutObject"
            ],
            "Resource": "arn:aws:s3:::example-bucket/*"
        }
    ]
}


# Attach the policy to the user
policy_name = 's3-access-policy'
iam.put_user_policy(UserName=user_name, PolicyName=policy_name,
PolicyDocument=json.dumps(policy_document))
```

Google Cloud Identity and Access Management

Google Cloud IAM is used to manage access to GCP resources. Here is an example using GCP IAM in Python to grant a user permission to a GCP project:

```
from google.oauth2 import service_account
from googleapiclient import discovery


# Define the service account key file
key_file_path = 'path/to/service_account_key.json'


# Initialize the IAM API client
credentials = service_account.Credentials.from_service_account_file(key_file_
path, scopes=['https://www.googleapis.com/auth/cloud-platform'])
```

```
iam = discovery.build('iam', 'v1', credentials=credentials)


# Define the user's email
user_email = 'user@example.com'


# Grant the user the roles/editor role on the project
project_id = 'my-project-id'
policy = iam.projects().getIamPolicy(resource=project_id).execute()
policy['bindings'].append({'role': 'roles/editor', 'members': ['user:' +
user_email]})
iam.projects().setIamPolicy(resource=project_id, body={'policy': policy}).
execute()
```

Azure Identity and Access Management

Azure IAM is used to manage access to Azure resources. Here is an example using Azure IAM in Python to create a new user and assign them a role:

```
from azure.identity import DefaultAzureCredential
from azure.management.resources import ResourceManagementClient


# Initialize the Azure Resource Management client
credential = DefaultAzureCredential()
resource_client = ResourceManagementClient(credential, 'your-subscription-id')


# Define the user's details
user_principal_name = 'user@example.com'
role_name = 'Contributor'
scope = '/subscriptions/your-subscription-id'


# Create a new user and assign the role
resource_client.role_assignments.create(scope,role_name, user_principal_
name)
```

Security compliance in cloud technology

Ensuring security compliance is a crucial aspect of cloud technology, especially for organizations subject to regulatory requirements. In this section, we will explore the concept of security compliance, provide implementation examples, and share related code snippets to help organizations meet industry-specific standards and regulations.

Security compliance is essential for organizations to protect sensitive data and maintain trust with customers and partners. By leveraging the compliance tools and resources provided by cloud service providers like AWS, GCP, and Azure, organizations can assess, enforce, and report on compliance with regulatory frameworks, ensuring that their cloud deployments meet industry-specific standards and best practices.

Security compliance fundamentals

Security compliance involves adhering to industry-specific regulations, standards, and best practices to protect data and maintain trust. Common regulatory frameworks include *General Data Protection Regulation (GDPR)*, *Health Insurance Portability and Accountability Act (HIPPA)*, *Payment Card Industry Data Security Standard (PCI DSS)*, and more.

Implementing compliance in AWS

AWS offers various compliance tools and resources to help organizations meet regulatory requirements. Here is an example using AWS Config to monitor and enforce compliance rules:

```
import boto3

# Initialize the AWS Config client
config = boto3.client('config')

# Define a custom AWS Config rule for compliance
rule_name = 'my-custom-compliance-rule'
description = 'Ensure EC2 instances are properly tagged'
scope = {
    'ComplianceResourceTypes': ['AWS::EC2::Instance']
}
input_parameters = {
    'tagKey': 'Environment',
    'tagValue': 'Production'
}

# Create the AWS Config rule
config.put_config_rule(
    ConfigRuleName=rule_name,
    Description=description,
    Scope=scope,
```

```
Source={
    'Owner': 'AWS',
    'SourceIdentifier': 'EC2_INSTANCE_PROPERLY_TAGGED'
},
InputParameters=input_parameters
)
```

Implementing compliance in GCP

GCP provides compliance solutions to assist organizations in adhering to regulations. Here is an example using GCP Security Command Center to assess compliance with *Center for Internet Security (CIS) Benchmarks*:

```python
from google.cloud import securitycenter

# Initialize the Security Command Center client
client = securitycenter.SecurityCenterClient()

# Define the CIS benchmark finding filter
filter_ = 'resource.type="gce_instance" AND source_properties.cis-benchmark-
compliance="FAILED"'

# Query Security Command Center for non-compliant resources
findings = client.list_findings(parent="organizations/your-organization-id",
filter_=filter_)

# Process and remediate non-compliant resources
for finding in findings:
    resource_name = finding.resource_name
    # Remediate the non-compliance as needed
```

Implementing compliance in Azure

Microsoft Azure offers compliance solutions and tools to help organizations meet regulatory requirements. Here is an example using Azure Policy to enforce compliance rules:

```python
from azure.identity import DefaultAzureCredential
from azure.management.policyinsights import PolicyInsightsClient
from azure.management.policyinsights.models import ComplianceStateType
```

```
# Initialize the Azure Policy Insights client
credential = DefaultAzureCredential()
policy_client = PolicyInsightsClient(credential)

# Define the compliance state filter
filter_ = "policyAssignmentId eq '/subscriptions/your-subscription-id/
providers/Microsoft.Authorization/policyAssignments/your-policy-assignment-
id' and complianceState eq 'NonCompliant'"

# Query Azure Policy Insights for non-compliant resources
non_compliant_resources = list(policy_client.query_results.
list(query=filter_))

# Remediate non-compliant resources as needed
for resource in non_compliant_resources:
    resource_id = resource.policy_assignment_id
    # Remediate the non-compliance as needed
```

Logging and monitoring

Logging and monitoring are essential components of cloud security, enabling organizations to detect and respond to security incidents promptly. In this section, we will explore the significance of logging and monitoring, provide implementation examples, and share related code snippets to demonstrate their application in cloud environments.

Logging and monitoring are indispensable for detecting and responding to security incidents in cloud environments. By using cloud-native services like AWS CloudWatch, GCP Cloud Monitoring and Logging, and Azure Monitor, organizations can gain visibility into their resources, setup alerts for suspicious activities, and respond swiftly to security threats, enhancing their overall security posture.

Logging and monitoring fundamentals

Logging involves recording events and activities within a cloud environment, while monitoring is the real-time analysis of these logs for anomalies and security threats. Combined, they provide the visibility needed to identify and respond to security incidents effectively.

AWS CloudWatch for logging and monitoring

Amazon CloudWatch is a comprehensive service for logging and monitoring AWS resources. Here is an example of setting up CloudWatch Logs and alarms using Python's Boto 3 library:

```python
import boto3

# Initialize the CloudWatch client
cloudwatch = boto3.client('cloudwatch')

# Create a CloudWatch Log Group
log_group_name = 'my-log-group'
cloudwatch.create_log_group(logGroupName=log_group_name)

# Create a CloudWatch Log Stream
log_stream_name = 'my-log-stream'
cloudwatch.create_log_stream(logGroupName=log_group_name,
logStreamName=log_stream_name)

# Put a log event into the Log Stream
log_event = 'Error: Unauthorized access attempt'
cloudwatch.put_log_events(
    logGroupName=log_group_name,
    logStreamName=log_stream_name,
    logEvents=[
        {
            'timestamp': 1234567890,
            'message': log_event
        }
    ]
)

# Create a CloudWatch Alarm
alarm_name = 'my-alarm'
cloudwatch.put_metric_alarm(
    AlarmName=alarm_name,
    AlarmDescription='Unauthorized access alarm',
    ActionsEnabled=True,
    AlarmActions=['arn:aws:sns:us-east-1:123456789012:my-topic'],
    MetricName='Errors',
    Namespace='LogMetrics',
    Statistic='Sum',
```

```
    Period=60,
    EvaluationPeriods=1,
    Threshold=1,
    ComparisonOperator='GreaterThanOrEqualToThreshold'
)
```

GCP Cloud Monitoring and Logging

Google Cloud Monitoring and Logging provide comprehensive observability for GCP resources. Here is an example of setting up logs and alerts using the Google Cloud SDK:

```
# Create a new Log Sink
gcloud logging sinks create my-log-sink pubsub.googleapis.com/projects/my-
project-id/topics/my-topic --log-filter='severity>=ERROR'


# Create an alert policy
gcloud monitoring alert-policies create my-alert-policy --notification-
channels='projects/my-project-id/notificationChannels/my-notification-
channel' --conditions=metric.type="logging.googleapis.com/user/my-log-sink"
AND metric.label.severity="ERROR"
```

Azure Monitor and Azure Log Analytics

Azure Monitor and Azure Log Analytics provide robust monitoring and logging capabilities for Azure resources. Here is an example of creating a Log Analytics workspace and configuring alerts using Azure CLI:

```
# Create a Log Analytics workspace
az monitor log-analytics workspace create --resource-group my-resource-
group --workspace-name my-log-analytics-workspace --location eastus


# Configure a diagnostic setting to send logs to Log Analytics
az monitor diagnostic-settings create --name my-diagnostic-settings
--resource my-resource-id --workspace my-log-analytics-workspace --logs
'[{"category": "SecurityEvents", "enabled": true}]'


# Create an action group for alerts
az monitor action-group create --name my-action-group --resource-group my-
resource-group --short-name my-action-group --email-action email@example.
com


# Create an alert rule
az monitor metrics alert create --name my-alert-rule --resource my-
```

```
resource-id --resource-group my-resource-group --condition "count >= 1"
--window-size 5m --action my-action-group --description "Security alert"
--severity 3
```

Incident response

Incident response is a critical aspect of cloud security, ensuring that organizations can effectively detect, contain, and mitigate security incidents. In this section, we will explore the principles of incident response, provide implementation examples, and share related code snippets to demonstrate how to respond to security incidents in cloud environments.

Incident response fundamentals

Incident response is a structured approach to addressing and managing security incidents. It involves several key phases, including detection, analysis, containment, eradication, recovery, and lessons learned.

Incident detection in AWS

AWS offers various tools and services for incident detection, such as AWS CloudTrail for logging and AWS Config for resource tracking. Here is an example of setting up AWS CloudTrail and configuring an S3 bucket to store logs:

```
import boto3

# Initialize the CloudTrail client
cloudtrail = boto3.client('cloudtrail')

# Create a new CloudTrail trail
trail_name = 'my-cloudtrail-trail'
cloudtrail.create_trail(
    Name=trail_name,
    S3BucketName='my-cloudtrail-logs-bucket',
)

# Start the trail
cloudtrail.start_logging(Name=trail_name)
```

Incident analysis in GCP

GCP offers tools like Google **Cloud Security Command Center** (**Cloud SCC**) for incident analysis. Here is an example of using Cloud SCC to analyze security findings:

```
from google.cloud import securitycenter

# Initialize the Security Command Center client
client = securitycenter.SecurityCenterClient()

# List all security findings
findings = list(client.list_findings(parent="organizations/your-organization-
id"))

# Analyze and respond to security findings
for finding in findings:
    # Analyze the finding and take appropriate action
```

Incident containment and mitigation in Azure

Microsoft Azure provides resources like Azure Security Center for incident containment and mitigation. Here is an example of using Azure Security Center to initiate a **virtual machine (VM)** remediation:

```
# Trigger a VM remediation using Azure Security Center
az vm remediate --name my-vm --resource-group my-resource-group
```

Incident recovery and lessons learned

Incident recovery involves restoring affected systems and data to their normal state, while lessons learned involve evaluating the incident response process to improve future responses.

Incident response playbooks

Incident response playbooks are predefined procedures that guide incident responders through the steps to take during an incident. These playbooks can be implemented using various automation tools and scripts tailored to your organization's specific needs.

Security training and awareness

Security training and awareness are critical components of cloud security, helping organizations educate their employees and users to recognize and prevent security threats are vital for organizations to strengthen their security posture and reduce the risk of security breaches. By providing employees and users with the knowledge and tools to recognize and respond to security threats, organizations can create a security-conscious culture and minimize the human factor in security incidents.

In this section, we will explore the importance of security training and awareness, provide implementation examples, and share related resources to help organizations create effective security education programs.

Importance of security training and awareness

Security training and awareness are essential for fostering a security-conscious culture within an organization. They empower employees and users to understand security best practices, recognize threats, and respond appropriately.

Security training programs

Organizations should establish security training programs that cover a range of topics, including:

- **Phishing awareness**: Training employees to identify phishing emails and avoid falling victim to phishing attacks.

- **Password management**: Educating users on creating strong passwords and using password managers.

- **Data handling**: Teaching proper data handling procedures, especially when dealing with sensitive or confidential information.

- **Device security**: Promoting secure device usage, including laptops, mobile devices, and IoT devices.

- **Cloud security**: Providing guidance on securely using cloud services, configuring security settings, and recognizing cloud-related threats.

Security training implementation example

Here is an example of implementing a simple security training module in Python, covering the topic of password management:

```python
def password_training():
    print("Welcome to Password Management Training!")
    print("You will learn how to create strong passwords.")

    while True:
        password = input("Enter a new password: ")

        if len(password) < 8:
            print("Password is too short. It should be at least 8
characters.")
        elif not any(char.isupper() for char in password):
```

```
            print("Password should contain at least one uppercase letter.")
        elif not any(char.islower() for char in password):
            print("Password should contain at least one lowercase letter.")
        elif not any(char.isdigit() for char in password):
            print("Password should contain at least one digit.")
        else:
            print("Congratulations! Your password is strong.")
            break

if __name__ == "__main__":
    password_training()
```

Security awareness programs

In addition to formal training, organizations should create ongoing security awareness programs. These programs can include:

- **Regular security newsletters**: Providing employees with security updates, best practices, and tips through newsletters.

- **Simulated phishing campaigns**: Running simulated phishing campaigns to test employees' awareness and training effectiveness.

- **Security awareness events**: Hosting events or webinars to raise awareness about emerging threats and best practices.

- **Reporting mechanisms**: Establishing a clear process for reporting security incidents or suspicious activities.

Security awareness implementation example

Here is an example of implementing a simulated phishing campaign using Python and the **smtplib** library to send simulated phishing emails to employees:

```
import smtplib


# Simulated phishing email content
subject = "Urgent: Verify Your Account"
body = "Click the link below to verify your account:\nhttps://phishingsite.
com/verify"
sender_email = "phishing@example.com"
recipient_email = "employee@example.com"


# Send the simulated phishing email
with smtplib.SMTP("smtp.example.com") as server:
```

```
    server.login(sender_email, "password")
    server.sendmail(sender_email, recipient_email, f"Subject: {subject}\n\
n{body}")
```

Conclusion

In this chapter, we have explored the essential concepts of security in cloud technology. To summarize, we learnt that encryption is the bedrock of data security, both in transit and at rest. Security protocols like HTTPS and SSH establish secure communication channels. IAM is pivotal in controlling who accesses what in the cloud. Compliance is adhering to industry standards and regulations, which is crucial for data protection. Logging and monitoring are fundamental for detecting and responding to security incidents. Incident response is a structured approach vital for addressing security incidents effectively. Educating and raising awareness among users is essential for a robust security posture, which is achieved through security training and awareness. These concepts form the foundation of cloud security. Mastering them is imperative in today's digital landscape to protect data, maintain trust, and foster innovation securely.

In the next chapter, we will explore the security and configuration of cloud storage services across AWS, Azure, IBM Cloud, and GCP. We will learn how to secure object and block storage using encryption, access controls, and monitoring tools. Step-by-step guidance and best practices will help us confidently manage and protect cloud data in real-world scenarios.

Key takeaways

The following are the important takeaways from this chapter:

- **Encryption is essential**: Encryption is crucial for protecting data in transit and at rest. Implement encryption protocols and leverage cloud provider services to ensure data confidentiality.

- **Security protocols matter**: Security protocols like HTTPS, SSH, and MQTT are fundamental in establishing secure communication channels for your cloud applications.

- **IAM is the gatekeeper**: IAM plays a pivotal role in controlling user access to cloud resources. Leverage IAM services offered by cloud providers to manage permissions effectively.

- **Compliance is a must**: Adhering to industry-specific standards and regulations is essential for protecting sensitive data. Utilize compliance tools and practices provided by cloud providers to ensure adherence.

- **Logging and monitoring are crucial**: Effective logging and monitoring are indispensable for timely detection and response to security incidents in the cloud. Implement cloud-native solutions to gain visibility into your resources.

- **Structured incident response**: Implement a structured incident response process that includes detection, analysis, containment, eradication, recovery, and lessons learned phases to effectively address security incidents.

- **Security training and awareness**: Educate and raise awareness among your workforce about security best practices. Regular training programs and awareness initiatives are vital to creating a security-conscious culture.

- **Cultivate a security-first culture**: Foster a security-first mindset within your organization. Security is a collective responsibility, and an informed workforce is your first line of defense against cyber threats.

- **Continuous learning is key**: Security is an ongoing journey, not a destination. Stay up-to-date with evolving threats and best practices to adapt and strengthen your cloud security measures.

Key terms

- **Encryption**: The process of converting data into a code to prevent unauthorized access, protecting data confidentiality.

- **HTTPS**: A secure version of HTTP, used for secure communication over the internet, employing encryption.

- **SSH**: A cryptographic network protocol for secure remote access to servers and secure data communication.

- **IAM**: A framework for managing and controlling user access to resources, ensuring proper authentication and authorization.

- **SSO**: A mechanism that allows users to access multiple applications with a single set of credentials, enhancing convenience and security.

- **Compliance**: Adherence to industry-specific standards, regulations, and best practices to ensure data security and privacy.

- **Logging**: The process of recording events and activities in a system or application, critical for security incident detection and analysis.

- **Monitoring**: Real-time observation and analysis of system activities and events to identify security threats and anomalies.

- **Incident response**: A structured approach to handling and mitigating security incidents, including detection, analysis, containment, eradication, and recovery phases.

- **Security training**: Educational programs and initiatives aimed at teaching user's and employee's security best practices and awareness.

- **Phishing**: A cyberattack technique that involves tricking individuals into revealing sensitive information, often by posing as a trusted entity.

- **Cloud compliance**: Ensuring that cloud services and deployments adhere to regulatory requirements and industry standards.

- **Security protocol**: A set of rules and conventions used to secure communication and data exchange between systems.

- **Vulnerability assessment**: The process of identifying weaknesses in a system's security that could be exploited by attackers.

- **Penetration testing**: Ethical hacking to identify vulnerabilities and assess the security of a system or network.

- **Zero Trust security**: A security model based on the principle of never trust, always verify, where trust is not assumed even for users inside the network.

- **Security awareness**: Promoting knowledge and awareness of security risks and best practices among users and employees.

Solved exercises

1. **What is the primary purpose of encryption in cloud security?**

   Answer: Encryption protects data confidentiality by converting it into unreadable code, ensuring that only authorized users can access it.

2. **What does IAM stand for, and why is it important in cloud security?**

   Answer: IAM stands for Identity and Access Management. It controls and restricts user access to cloud resources, ensuring only authorized users can perform specific actions.

3. **Why is compliance important in cloud security?**

   Answer: Compliance ensures organizations adhere to regulations and standards, protecting sensitive data and maintaining legal and industry requirements.

4. **What is logging, and how does it help in cloud security?**

   Answer: Logging records system events and activities, helping with auditing, incident detection, and forensic investigations in case of security breaches.

5. **What is the purpose of a security awareness program?**

   Answer: A security awareness program educates users about best practices, potential threats, and safe behaviors to reduce the risk of security breaches.

6. **What is SSO, and how does it benefit users?**

   Answer: SSO allows users to access multiple applications with one login, improving convenience and security while reducing password fatigue.

7. **How does HTTPS enhance security in web communication?**

    Answer: HTTPS encrypts data between a user's browser and a website, ensuring secure communication and preventing data interception.

8. **What is the principle of Zero Trust security?**

    Answer: Zero Trust follows the principle of never trust, always verify, meaning no entity is automatically trusted, and all access requests must be authenticated.

9. **What are two common security protocols used for secure cloud communication?**

    Answer: HTTPS (for secure web browsing) and SSH (for secure remote access to servers).

10. **What is multi-factor authentication (MFA), and why is it useful?**

    Answer: MFA requires multiple forms of verification (e.g., password and a one-time code), adding an extra layer of security to prevent unauthorized access.

Unsolved exercises

1. Explain the concept of encryption in cloud security, and why it is important.

2. What are some common security protocols used for secure communication in cloud environments, and when should they be employed?

3. Describe the role of IAM in cloud security. How does it help control access to resources?

4. Why is compliance critical in cloud security, and can you provide examples of industry-specific compliance standards?

5. Explain the significance of logging and monitoring in cloud security. How do these practices contribute to incident detection and response?

6. What are the key phases in an incident response plan, and how would you handle a security incident in a cloud environment?

7. Discuss the importance of security training and awareness in cloud technology. How can organizations effectively educate their workforce about security best practices?

8. What is SSO, and how does it enhance security in cloud environments? Can you explain its implementation and benefits?

9. Describe the principles and components of Zero Trust security. How can organizations implement a Zero Trust model in their cloud deployments?

10. How would you conduct a simulated phishing campaign as part of a security awareness program? What are the key objectives and outcomes of such campaigns?

CHAPTER 5

Securing Storage Services

Introduction

This chapter will focus on securing storage services in various popular cloud platforms such as **Amazon Web Services (AWS)**, **Microsoft Azure, IBM Cloud**, and **Google Cloud Platform (GCP)**. We will provide detailed guidance on various security measures and configurations for these popular cloud platforms in this chapter. A basic understanding of cloud computing concepts will be beneficial.

Structure

The chapter covers the following topics:

- Storage security in AWS
- Storage security in Azure
- Storage security in IBM
- Storage security in GCP
- Storage configurations in AWS
- Storage configurations in Azure
- Storage configurations in IBM

- Storage configurations in GCP
- Illustration
- Case study

Objectives

By the end of this chapter, you will have a clear understanding of the basic principles of storage security in various cloud environments. You will be able to implement various security measures and configure storage services in AWS, Azure, IBM, and GCP for enhanced security.

Storage security in AWS

As our digital world continues to evolve, businesses are increasingly migrating to cloud storage systems to manage, process, and store vast amounts of data. With this migration, securing these storage systems has become paramount to ensure data integrity, confidentiality, and availability.

The following diagram illustrates the pivotal elements of cloud security, each represented as interconnected circles within a larger encompassing sphere, symbolizing their collective role in fortifying an organization's cloud environment:

Figure 5.1: Cloud security

AWS is a well-known cloud service provider offering various storage services such as Amazon **Simple Storage Service (S3)**, **Elastic Block Store (EBS)**, **Elastic File System (EFS)**, and **Glacier**. Each of these services is designed for different use cases, but they all share the common goal of securely storing data. Let us discuss how you can enhance the security of your AWS storage services.

Encryption

AWS provides two types of encryption: At rest and in transit. They are discussed as follows:

- **Encryption at rest**: This is when your data is encrypted when it is not actively being used or moved. AWS provides options to encrypt at rest using keys managed through AWS **Key Management Service** (**KMS**). You can also use a customer-provided key or even choose to let AWS manage the keys for you.

- **Encryption in transit**: This is when your data is encrypted when it is being moved from one place to another. AWS provides the option to encrypt data in transit using **Secure Sockets Layer** (**SSL**)/**Transport Layer Security** (**TLS**).

AWS S3, for instance, allows you to set default encryption on a bucket, which means any new object uploaded to the bucket will be encrypted automatically.

Access control

AWS offers robust mechanisms to control who can access your data. They are as follows:

- **IAM policies**: With AWS **Identity and Access Management** (**IAM**), you can create policies that define who (which users or services) can do what (which actions they can perform) with your resources.

- **Bucket policies**: In Amazon S3, you can attach policies directly to your buckets, specifying which IP addresses or IAM users can access them.

- **Access control lists** (**ACLs**): ACLs are more granular access controls that can be attached to individual objects within an S3 bucket.

- **Pre-signed URLs**: These URLs provide temporary access to a private object in S3. They are valid for a limited period that you define.

Security monitoring and alerts

AWS provides monitoring and alerting services to help you monitor your storage. These services are:

- **CloudTrail**: This service records all AWS API calls, including calls to the S3 API, and delivers log files to you for audit.

- **CloudWatch**: This is a monitoring service for AWS resources and the applications you run on AWS. You can create alarms that watch for certain thresholds and send notifications or automatically change the resources you monitor when those thresholds are crossed.

Versioning and backup

AWS provides built-in tools for data backup and recovery. These tools are as follows:

- **Versioning**: In Amazon S3, you can use versioning to keep multiple versions of an object in one bucket. If you accidentally delete an object, you can restore it.

- **Snapshots**: For EBS volumes, you can create snapshots that can be used as the starting point for new EBS volumes or to protect data for long-term durability.

Securing your storage in AWS is not just about setting up the right permissions and encryption; it also involves constant monitoring and having a backup and recovery plan. The more proactive you are in protecting your data, the better off you will be.

Storage security in Azure

Microsoft Azure offers a suite of cloud storage services, such as Blob Storage, Disk Storage, File Storage, and Queue Storage. These services are designed to handle a wide range of data storage needs. This section will outline the key methods to enhance the security of your data in Azure's storage services.

Encryption

Like AWS, Azure also provides encryption at rest and in transit. They are described as follows:

- **Encryption at rest**: Azure automatically encrypts data before storing it and decrypts it before retrieval. This is managed by Azure **Storage Service Encryption** (**SSE**) for data at rest. It uses Azure Key Vault to hold and manage encryption keys securely.

- **Encryption in transit**: Azure supports TLS for data in transit. It ensures that data traveling between your application and the Azure Storage services remains private and unaltered.

Access control

Azure provides robust mechanisms to manage who can access your data and what they can do with it. These mechanisms are:

- **Azure Active Directory (Azure AD)**: It provides secure IAM. You can define access rights at the level of the storage account.

- **Shared access signature (SAS)**: A SAS is a string containing a security token that can be attached to a URL, which delegates access to resources in your storage account. You can provide a client with an SAS that allows specific access to a private resource for a specific amount of time.

- **Role-based access control (RBAC)**: RBAC provides fine-grained access management for Azure resources, allowing you to grant access for specific tasks like reading, writing, or listing.

- **Access keys**: Azure provides two keys that are used for authentication when the storage account is accessed.

Security monitoring and alerts

Azure provides a couple of monitoring and alerting services to help maintain your storage's security. These services are as follows:

- **Azure Monitor**: It collects, analyzes, and acts on telemetry from your cloud and on-premises environments. It helps you understand how your applications are performing and proactively identifies issues affecting them.

- **Azure Security Center**: It provides unified security management and advanced threat protection for workloads running in Azure. It can be configured to send alerts about suspicious activities.

Data backup and replication

Azure offers several options for backing up and replicating your data. They are:

- **Azure Backup**: It is a straightforward service that allows you to back up Azure **virtual machines** (**VMs**) and other data to a backup vault in Azure. This ensures you can restore data if there is a failure or loss.

- **Data Replication:** Azure offers various replication options to ensure your data is available when needed. These include **locally redundant storage** (**LRS**), **zone-redundant storage** (**ZRS**), **geo-redundant storage** (**GRS**), and **read-access geo-redundant storage** (**RAGRS**).

By combining encryption, secure access control, vigilant monitoring, and data backup, you can create a robust security infrastructure for your Azure Storage services. It is about understanding the available security measures and implementing them as per your data storage requirements.

Storage security in IBM

IBM Cloud offers a range of cloud storage options, including IBM Cloud Object Storage, Block Storage, and File Storage. These services cater to different data storage needs, and ensuring their security is crucial. Here, we will look at some of the key techniques to enhance the security of your IBM Cloud storage services.

Encryption

IBM also provides encryption for data at rest and in transit:

- **Encryption at rest**: IBM Cloud storage services encrypt your data at rest using **Advanced Encryption Standard** (**AES**) 256-bit encryption. You do not need to do anything to enable this; it is automatically applied.

- **Encryption in transit**: Data transmitted to and from IBM Cloud storage services can be encrypted using SSL/TLS, preventing unauthorized interception of your data during transmission.

Access control

Controlling who can access your data in IBM Cloud is achieved through IAM:

- **IBM Cloud IAM**: You can create policies that define who (which users or services) can perform what actions on your resources. For example, you can grant read-only access to certain users and full access to others.

- **ACLs**: You can use ACLs to manage access to buckets and objects within IBM Cloud Object Storage. ACLs allow you to grant specific permissions to specific users or groups.

Security monitoring and alerts

IBM Cloud offers tools to monitor your storage and alert you about the potential security threats. These tools are:

- **IBM Cloud activity tracker**: This service records user-initiated activities that change the state of a service in your account. This helps you audit how your cloud resources are being used and can help detect unusual or unauthorized activities.

- **IBM Cloud security advisor**: This service aggregates security information from multiple sources, providing a centralized view of your security status. It can send notifications when it identifies potential vulnerabilities or threats.

Data backup and replication

IBM Cloud provides options for backing up and replicating your data, ensuring it is safe and available when you need it. These options are as follows:

- **Snapshots**: For IBM Block Storage, you can create snapshots that serve as a point-in-time copy of your data. You can use these snapshots to restore your data in the event of a loss.

- **Cross-region replication**: For IBM Object Storage, you can enable cross-region replication, where your data is automatically replicated to buckets in different regions. This enhances data durability and availability.

By understanding and implementing these security measures, you can ensure that your data stored in IBM Cloud is well protected. Remember, good security is not a set-it-and-forget-it affair; it requires continuous monitoring and regular updates to meet evolving threats.

Storage security in GCP

GCP provides several storage services, including Google Cloud Storage, Persistent Disk, and Filestore. These services accommodate different data storage needs, ensuring their security is paramount. In this section, we will examine key takeaways to enhance your GCP storage services' security.

Encryption

Like other providers, GCP provides encryption for data at rest and in transit:

- **Encryption at rest**: GCP automatically encrypts all data before it is written to disk. It uses several layers of encryption, and keys are managed through Google KMS. You also have the option of supplying your encryption keys if you prefer.

- **Encryption in transit**: GCP uses SSL/TLS to secure data when it is moving between your application and Google storage services, or when it is moving within the Google Network.

Access control

GCP provides multiple mechanisms to control who can access your data. These mechanisms are:

- **Cloud IAM**: With IAM, you can create policies specifying who (which users or services) can do what (which actions they can perform) with your resources.

- **ACLs**: For more granular access controls, ACLs can be applied to individual objects in a Google Cloud Storage bucket.

- **Signed URLs and signed policy documents**: These provide time-limited resource access. When a signed URL is created, the resource is accessible irrespective of the resource's ACLs.

Security monitoring and alerts

GCP offers services to help you monitor your storage and receive alerts about potential security threats. These services are as follows:

- **Cloud audit logs**: This service records operations performed in your GCP account. It generates logs for each API operation on your storage buckets, helping you track changes and spot any unusual activity.

- **Google Cloud's Operations suite (formerly Stackdriver)**: This is a hybrid monitoring, logging, and diagnostics tool that can help you gain insight into how your applications are running. It provides capabilities such as uptime checks, alerts, and incident tracking to help keep your services healthy.

Data backup and replication

GCP provides several options for backing up and replicating your data. These are:

- **Snapshots**: For Persistent Disk, you can create snapshots, which are a point-in-time copy of your data. These snapshots can be used to back up data and create new disks that contain the same data.

- **Multi-region storage class**: For Cloud Storage, you can use the multi-region storage class to automatically replicate your data across multiple geographically distant regions. This increases data availability and reliability.

In conclusion, securing your data in GCP involves using the right encryption methods, managing access control, continuously monitoring your environment, and setting up proper data backup and replication. With these practices, you can significantly enhance the security posture of your data stored in GCP.

Storage configurations in AWS

AWS provides several storage services, each designed for specific use cases. This guide will focus on Amazon S3 and Amazon EBS, two of the most widely used AWS storage services.

The following diagram showcases a user interacting with a cloud infrastructure, illustrating bidirectional communication between a computer and the cloud, as well as between a database and the cloud, emphasizing the seamless flow of data and interactions in a cloud environment:

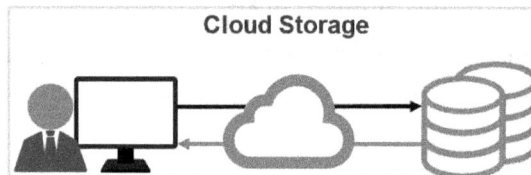

Figure 5.2: Cloud storage configuration

Amazon S3

S3 is an object storage service that offers industry-leading scalability, data availability, security, and performance.

Steps to configure an S3 bucket

The following are the steps to configure S3 in an AWS environment:

1. Create an S3 bucket:

   a. Sign in to the AWS Management Console and open the Amazon S3 console.

   b. Click on **Create bucket**.

   c. Enter a DNS-compliant name for your bucket, select the region where you want the bucket to reside, and click **Next**.

   You can optionally configure bucket properties and permissions as per your requirements.

2. Add objects to your bucket:

   a. Click on the name of your newly created bucket, then click on **Upload**.

   b. Click **Add files**, select the file to upload, and click **Open** to upload the file into your bucket.

3. Setup bucket policies:

   a. Click on the name of your bucket and go to the **Permissions** tab.

   b. Under **Bucket Policy**, click on **Edit**. You can now add IAM policies in JSON format to specify who can access your bucket and what actions they can perform.

4. Enable versioning (optional):

   a. In the bucket settings, go to the **Management** tab and scroll down to **Bucket versioning** and click on **Edit**.

   b. Check **Enable versioning** and click **Save changes**.

Amazon Elastic Block Store

EBS provides block-level storage volumes for use with Amazon EC2 instances. It is designed to deliver high, predictable performance for workloads that require a database, a file system, or access to raw block-level storage.

Steps to configure EBS

The following are the steps to configure EBS in AWS in the environment:

1. Create an EBS volume:

   a. Open the Amazon EC2 console, in the navigation pane, choose **Volumes**, and then choose **Create volume**.

    b.   Specify the volume type, size, IOPS (if necessary), and the **Availability Zone (AZ)**, then click **Create volume**.

2.   Attach the EBS volume to an EC2 instance:

    a.   Select the new volume, choose **Actions**, and then choose **Attach volume**.

    b.   In the **Attach volume** dialog box, start typing the name or ID of the instance you want to attach the volume to, select the instance, and then choose **Attach**.

3.   Make the EBS volume available for use:

    Connect to your EC2 instance and make the volume available using the file system-specific command. This process varies depending on whether the volume has a file system created on it.

Remember, these are the basic steps for configuring storage in AWS. Each use case may require additional configuration, such as setting up lifecycle policies in S3 or configuring IOPS for EBS volumes. Always refer to the official AWS Documentation for the most accurate and detailed instructions.

Storage configurations in Azure

Microsoft Azure provides several storage services for different types of data. This guide will focus on Azure Blob Storage and Azure Disk Storage, which are commonly used for object and block storage, respectively.

Azure Blob Storage

Azure Blob Storage is Microsoft's object storage solution for the cloud. Azure Blob Storage is ideal for serving images or documents directly to a browser, storing files for distributed access, storing data for backup and restore, disaster recovery, and archiving.

Steps to configure Azure Blob Storage

The following are the steps to configure Azure Blob Storage:

1.   Create a storage account:

    a.   Sign in to the Azure portal.

    b.   In the left-hand menu, select **Create a resource**, then select **Storage | Storage account**.

    c.   Fill in the fields for your storage account name, deployment model, account kind, performance, replication, and access tier. Then, create a new resource group or select an existing one. Select a location for your storage account and click on **Review + Create**, then **Create**.

2. Create a Blob container:

   a. Navigate to your new storage account in the Azure portal.

   b. In the left-hand menu for the storage account, scroll to the **Blob service** section, then select **Containers**.

   c. Click + **Container**. Name your container, set the public access level as required, and click **Create**.

3. Upload data to the Blob container:

   a. Select the new container, then click on **Upload**.

   b. In the upload pane, select the files you want to upload and click **Upload**.

Azure Disk Storage

Azure Disk Storage provides persistent, secured disk storage for Azure VMs.

Steps to configure Azure Disk Storage

The following are the steps to configure Azure Disk Storage:

1. Create a disk:

   a. In the Azure portal, select **Create a resource**, then select **Disks**.

   b. Fill in the subscription, resource group, name, region, AZ, and other fields as needed, then click **Create**.

   c. Attach the disk to a VM.

   d. Navigate to the VM to which you want to attach the disk.

   e. In the left-hand menu, select **Disks**, then click + **Add data disk**.

   f. In the dropdown for the new disk, select the disk you just created. Fill in the other fields as required, then click **Save**.

2. Configure the disk on the VM:

   After attaching a disk to a VM, you may need to connect to the VM and configure the disk at the operating system level. This process varies depending on the OS.

As with AWS, these are the basic steps for configuring storage in Azure. Depending on your use case, you may need additional configuration steps, such as setting up blob lifecycle management or configuring disk performance tiers. Always refer to the official Azure documentation for the most accurate and detailed instructions.

Storage configurations in IBM

IBM Cloud offers several storage solutions, among which the most commonly used are IBM Cloud Object Storage and Block Storage.

IBM Cloud Object Storage is a highly scalable cloud storage service, designed for high durability, resiliency, and security. Let us go over the steps to configure these services.

Steps to configure IBM Cloud Object Storage

The following are the steps to configure IBM Cloud Object Storage:

1. Create an object storage instance:

   a. Log in to the IBM Cloud console.

   b. Click on **Catalog**, then select **Storage** under the **Categories** dropdown. Select **Object Storage**.

   c. Provide a name for your service, select a resource group, a location, and a pricing plan, then click on **Create**.

2. Create a bucket:

   a. From your object storage instance dashboard, click on **Buckets**.

   b. Click on **Create bucket**. Choose a unique name for your bucket, select a location, storage class, and optionally enable versioning and encryption. Click **Next** and then **Create bucket**.

   c. Upload objects to your bucket:

   d. Navigate to the bucket you just created, then click on **Upload**.

   e. Choose **Add files**, select the files you want to upload from your machine, and click **Upload**.

IBM Cloud Block Storage

IBM Cloud Block Storage offers durable and high-performing storage for your cloud-based applications.

Steps to configure IBM Cloud Block Storage

Here are the steps to configure cloud block storage in an IBM environment:

1. Create a block storage volume:

   a. In the IBM Cloud console, click on **Catalog**, then select **Storage** under the **Categories** dropdown. Select **Block Storage for VPC**.

    b.   Provide a name for your volume, select a resource group, a location, and a profile (which determines the performance characteristics of the volume). Select the capacity for your volume, then click **Create**.

    c.   Attach the block storage volume to a virtual server instance.

    d.   Navigate to your block storage volume in the IBM Cloud console.

    e.   Click on **Actions**, then select **Attach volume**.

    f.   Select the virtual server instance to which you want to attach the volume, then click **Attach volume**.

Remember that these are basic steps, and your particular use case may need further configurations. For instance, you may need to setup Object Storage lifecycle policies or tune Block Storage performance. Always refer to IBM Cloud's official documentation for the most accurate and comprehensive instructions.

Storage configurations in GCP

GCP provides a multitude of storage services for different data types and use cases. In this guide, we will focus on Google Cloud Storage and Persistent Disk, which are widely used for object and block storage, respectively.

Google Cloud Storage

Google Cloud Storage is a scalable, fully managed, highly reliable, and cost-efficient object/blob store.

Steps to configure Google Cloud Storage

The following are the steps to configure Google Cloud Storage:

1.   Create a Cloud Storage Bucket:

    a.   Sign in to the Google Cloud Console.

    b.   Navigate to the navigation menu, select **Storage | Browser**.

    c.   Click on the **Create bucket** button.

    d.   Give your bucket a unique name, choose a storage class according to your needs, and select the location where you want your data to be stored. Then, click **Create**.

2.   Upload data to your bucket:

    a.   Click on the name of your newly created bucket, then click **Upload files** (or **Upload folder** if you want to upload a directory).

    b.   Select the file(s) or folder from your computer and click **Open** to upload the data.

Google Cloud Persistent Disk

Persistent Disk provides block storage for Google Cloud's VM instances.

Steps to configure Persistent Disk

The following are the steps to configure Persistent Disk storage in the Google Cloud environment:

1. Create a disk:

    a. From the Google Cloud Console, navigate to the navigation menu, select **Compute Engine | Disks**.

    b. Click on the **Create instance** button.

    c. Give your disk a name, choose the disk type and size according to your needs, and select the zone where you want your disk to be located. Then, click on **Create**.

    d. Attach the disk to a VM instance.

    e. Navigate to **Compute engine | VM instances**.

    f. Click on the name of the instance you want to attach the disk to.

    g. Under **Additional disks**, click on the **Add item** button.

    h. In the **Source type** field, select **Existing disk** and select the disk you created earlier. Then, click **Done** and **Save**.

2. Mount and format the disk:

    a. Connect to your instance using SSH.

    b. Identify the disk, format it with a filesystem, and mount it.

Remember, these are the basic steps for configuring storage in GCP. Each use case may require additional configuration, such as setting up lifecycle management in Cloud Storage or configuring performance for Persistent Disks. Always refer to the official GCP documentation for the most accurate and detailed instructions.

Illustration

Suppose a photographer, *Jane*, runs an online store to sell her high-resolution photos. She uses AWS, Azure, IBM Cloud, and GCP to store her photos in S3, Blob Storage, IBM Cloud Object Storage, and Google Cloud Storage, respectively. Jane ensures her photos are protected by enabling versioning and server-side encryption on AWS, Azure, and IBM. She also uses IAM roles and policies, SAS, and Google Cloud IAM to control access. Meanwhile, she uses EBS, Azure Disk Storage, IBM Cloud Block Storage, and Google Cloud Persistent Disk to store the application data of her online store.

Case study

A healthcare startup decided to use cloud storage to store its patient data. They chose AWS for its advanced security features. However, due to misconfiguration of S3 bucket policies, some of their patient data was accidentally exposed to the public. This resulted in a breach of confidential information. After this incident, they conducted a thorough review of their storage security configurations, tightened their IAM policies, and enabled SSE for all their S3 buckets. They also employed a dedicated cloud security team to manage and monitor their storage security.

Conclusion

Choosing the right storage solution and configuring it properly is a critical aspect of cloud computing. Different cloud providers offer diverse storage services tailored to specific use cases, whether it is object storage for large volumes of unstructured data or block storage for databases and applications. Security considerations, including access control and encryption, play a vital role in ensuring the protection of data stored in the cloud. By carefully selecting and configuring cloud storage, businesses can benefit from scalable, flexible, and secure storage solutions that meet their specific needs.

In this chapter, we discussed the security and configuration of storage services in AWS, Azure, IBM Cloud, and GCP. For each platform, we provided an overview of its security features and step-by-step guidance for configuring its storage services. We highlighted the importance of taking precautions, such as using IAM roles, bucket policies, ACLs, and encryption to secure your data.

In the next chapter, we will explore the security capabilities and strengths of major cloud platforms, including AWS, Azure, Google Cloud Platform, and IBM Cloud. AWS offers a vast and mature ecosystem with global scalability, making it ideal for enterprises with diverse and large-scale needs. Microsoft Azure stands out for its seamless integration with Microsoft tools and strong hybrid cloud support, making it a natural fit for organizations already embedded in the Microsoft ecosystem. Google Cloud Platform excels in data analytics, AI, and open-source compatibility, making it a preferred choice for data-driven teams. IBM Cloud, with its focus on hybrid environments, AI through Watson, and strong compliance features, is particularly well-suited for regulated industries such as healthcare, finance, and government. As you read through this chapter, reflect on how each provider's strengths align with your organization's security requirements and long-term cloud strategy.

Key takeaways

The following are the important takeaways from this chapter:

- **Understanding storage types**: Recognize the differences between object storage (ideal for storing large amounts of unstructured data) and block storage (suited for databases, applications, and file systems). Each storage type serves specific use cases and offers unique advantages.

- **Proper configuration**: Follow step-by-step guides for configuring storage services in cloud providers like AWS, Azure, IBM Cloud, and GCP. Ensure proper setup of buckets, containers, volumes, and other storage resources.

- **Prioritizing security**: Implement strong security measures for cloud storage, including IAM roles and policies, ACLs, and encryption (both server-side and client-side). Limit public access and monitor unusual activities.

- **Data lifecycle management**: Enable features like versioning to keep track of changes to objects in storage. Setup lifecycle policies to automate actions such as transitioning objects to lower-cost storage classes or deleting objects after a certain time.

- **Consider regional constraints**: When creating storage resources, consider the region where the data will be stored. Ensure compliance with data residency and latency requirements based on your application and regulatory needs.

- **Regularly review configurations**: Periodically review and update storage configurations and security settings to stay aligned with best practices and evolving business needs.

- By keeping these key takeaways in mind, businesses can make informed decisions about their cloud storage needs and effectively manage their data in the cloud. Cloud storage security is essential to protect sensitive data from unauthorized access or loss.

- Each cloud platform AWS, Azure, IBM, and GCP offers unique security features and configuration practices.

- Always adhere to the principle of least privilege when setting up access control.

- Regular audits and updates are integral to maintaining a secure cloud storage system.

- Correct configurations can enhance storage security and efficiency.

- Understanding the similarities and differences between various platforms can help you choose the right storage service for your needs.

Key terms

- **Object storage**: A storage architecture that manages data as objects, as opposed to other storage architectures like file systems or block storage which manage data as a file hierarchy or as blocks within sectors and tracks.

- **Block storage**: A type of data storage typically used in **storage area network** (**SAN**) environments where data is stored in volumes, also known as **blocks**.

- **Amazon S3**: An object storage service offered by AWS that offers scalability, data availability, security, and performance.

- **Azure Blob Storage**: Microsoft Azure's object storage solution for the cloud, optimized for storing massive amounts of unstructured data, such as text or binary data.

- **Bucket**: A logical unit of storage in Amazon S3 where data is stored in the form of objects.

- **Versioning**: A means of keeping multiple variants of an object in the same bucket in Amazon S3, used to preserve, retrieve, and restore every version of every object stored.

- **Bucket policy**: A resource-based AWS IAM policy that you can use to manage permissions on a specific S3 bucket.

- **IBM Cloud Object Storage**: IBM Cloud Object Storage solution for the cloud, designed to handle large amounts of unstructured data.

- **Google Cloud Persistent Disk**: GCP block storage solution, designed for use with VM instances.

- **Amazon EBS**: AWS block storage solution that provides persistent block-level storage volumes for use with EC2 instances.

- **Mounting**: The process of attaching a file system, a partition, or a storage device to a directory in the operating system.

- **IBM Cloud Block Storage**: IBM Cloud Block Storage solution for the cloud, designed for use with virtual servers.

- **Google Cloud Storage**: Google object storage solution for the cloud, designed for storing large amounts of unstructured data.

- **Container in Azure Blob Storage**: A logical unit of storage in Azure Blob Storage that stores a set of blobs (objects) and provides a flat namespace within the account.

- **Azure Disk Storage**: Microsoft Azure's block storage solution, designed for use with VMs.

Solved exercises

1. **What is the difference between object storage and block storage?**

   Answer: Object storage is designed for storing large amounts of unstructured data, while block storage is suited for databases, applications, and file systems.

2. **What is the difference between object storage and block storage?**

   Answer: Object storage is designed for storing large amounts of unstructured data, while block storage is suited for databases, applications, and file systems.

3. **Which AWS service is used for object storage?**

   Answer: Amazon S3 is used for object storage in AWS.

4. **In Azure, what is the equivalent service to AWS S3?**

   Answer: In Azure, the equivalent service to AWS S3 is Azure Blob Storage.

5. **What are the basic steps to configure an S3 bucket in AWS?**

   Answer: Basic steps include creating an S3 bucket, adding objects to the bucket, setting up bucket policies, and optionally enabling versioning.

6. **What is IBM Cloud storage service for object storage called?**

   Answer: IBM Cloud Object Storage.

7. **What is the name of the block storage service in GCP?**

   Answer: Google Cloud Persistent Disk.

8. **Which AWS service provides block-level storage volumes for use with Amazon EC2 instances?**

   Answer: Amazon EBS.

9. **What is the process of attaching an EBS volume to an EC2 instance called?**

   Answer: It is called mounting.

10. **In IBM Cloud, what is the service used for block storage?**

    Answer: IBM Cloud Block Storage.

11. **Which GCP service is equivalent to Amazon S3 for object storage?**

    Answer: Google Cloud Storage.

Unsolved exercises

1. What are the key security features to consider when configuring storage services in the cloud?

2. How do you enable versioning for an S3 bucket in AWS?

3. In the context of Azure Blob Storage, what is a container and how do you create one?

4. What are the steps to configure IBM Cloud Object Storage?

5. How do you attach a Google Cloud Persistent Disk to a VM instance?

6. What are the steps to upload data to a Google Cloud Storage bucket?

7. How do you make an EBS volume available for use after attaching it to an EC2 instance?

8. What is the significance of setting up bucket policies in S3?

9. In the case of Azure Disk Storage, what actions are necessary on the VM after attaching a disk?

10. Why is it important to periodically review and update storage configurations and security settings in the cloud?

CHAPTER 6

Securing Network Services

Introduction

In the increasingly complex and interconnected digital age, the security of network services has become a paramount concern for businesses worldwide. With the adoption of cloud services from leading providers like **Amazon Web Services (AWS)**, **Microsoft Azure**, **IBM Cloud**, and **Google Cloud Platform (GCP)**, securing these services has become a challenge that IT professionals must contend with daily.

This chapter will provide a detailed examination of **virtual private clouds (VPCs)** and inter-VPC communication within these four popular platforms, along with a thorough overview of security configurations to ensure robust and resilient network services.

The content in this chapter will gradually move from beginner to intermediate level concepts and is designed in a step-by-step manner to facilitate self-learning. It is highly recommended to follow the sequence and do hands-on as you progress for an immersive learning experience.

Structure

The chapter covers the following topics:

- Virtual private cloud in AWS
- Virtual private cloud in Azure

- Virtual private cloud in IBM
- Virtual private cloud in GCP
- Inter-VPC communication and route tables in AWS
- Inter-VPC communication and route tables in Azure
- Inter-VPC communication and route tables in IBM
- Inter-VPC communication and route tables in GCP
- Security configurations in AWS
- Security configurations in Azure
- Security configurations in IBM
- Security configurations in GCP
- Illustration and case study

Objectives

By the end of this chapter, you will have a clear understanding of VPC and how it secures network services. You will learn about the configuration and deployment of VPC in AWS, Azure, IBM Cloud, and GCP and inter-VPC communication, and the role of route tables. You will be able to setup and secure network services using VPC's security configurations on the major cloud platforms.

Virtual private cloud in AWS

AWS provides a VPC service that allows users to launch AWS resources in a custom, **virtual network** (**VNet**). Essentially, it is your slice of the AWS Cloud, isolated and distinct from others. This creates a secure environment for your applications and data.

VPC architecture

A VPC in AWS is a region-level construct. It spans all the **Availability Zones** (**AZs**) in that region, enabling you to create a robust and resilient architecture for your applications. Within a VPC, you can segment the network into one or more subnets, which reside in specific AZs. These subnets can either be public, where resources can access and be accessed by the internet, or private, where resources are hidden from the internet.

The following are the key components of an AWS VPC:

- **Subnets**: These are segments of the VPC's IP address range where you can place groups of isolated resources.
- **Internet gateways (IGW)**: This is a horizontally scalable, redundant, and highly available VPC component that allows communication between resources in your VPC and the internet. It is required to enable internet access for your public subnet.

- **Network Address Translation (NAT) gateways**: NAT gateways enable instances in a private subnet to connect to the internet or other AWS services but prevent the internet from initiating a connection with those instances.

- **Route tables**: A route table contains a set of rules, called **routes**, that are used to determine where network traffic is directed. Each subnet in your VPC must be associated with a route table; the table controls the traffic leaving that subnet.

- **Security groups and network access control lists (NACLs)**: Security groups operate at the instance level. They regulate inbound and outbound traffic to instances and operate only in allow rules. NACLs, however, operate at the subnet level, allowing or denying traffic entering and exiting network interfaces in the subnet.

- **VPC peering**: AWS allows the creation of VPC peering connections. This is a networking connection between two VPCs enabling routing using each VPC's private IP addresses as if they were in the same network.

VPC in action

Imagine a scenario where you have a multi-tier application with a web frontend and a database backend. You can create a VPC with two subnets. The first subnet, a public subnet, hosts the web servers that need to connect to the internet to serve web traffic.

The second subnet, a private subnet, hosts the backend databases and is not accessible from the internet, protecting sensitive data from outside intrusion. You can setup security and network access rules to control traffic between your subnets, applications, and the wider internet.

The aim is to offer a detailed understanding of AWS VPCs and their critical components. With this knowledge, you can create private, isolated sections of the AWS Cloud where you can launch AWS resources in a secure and scalable manner.

Virtual private cloud in Azure

In the Microsoft Azure platform, the concept of a VPC is embodied by a service called **Azure VNet**. Azure VNets provide an isolated, secure environment in Azure where you can launch your services.

VNet architecture

A VNet is a region-level construct, similar to a VPC in AWS. However, Azure approaches regions a little differently. Instead of being confined to a single region, an Azure VNet can span regions, known as **peering**. This ability allows you to connect VNets across regions, forming a larger, interconnected network.

The following are the key components of an Azure VNet:

- **Subnets**: Like in AWS, Azure allows the creation of one or more subnets within a VNet. These are smaller, customized networks within your VNet where you can deploy Azure resources.

- **Network security group (NSG)**: NSGs are akin to firewalls. They contain inbound and outbound rules that allow or deny traffic to and from resources within your VNet.

- **Network interfaces**: These are the interconnection points through which an Azure resource (like a **virtual machine (VM)**) connects with a VNet. They can be associated with a subnet and an NSG.

- **VPN gateway**: This is a specific type of VNet gateway that sends encrypted traffic across a public connection to an on-premises location. It can also send traffic between VNets.

- **Route tables**: Route tables in Azure work similarly to AWS, with rules determining where network traffic is directed. They can be associated with subnets to dictate the flow of traffic within a VNet.

VNet in action

Let us consider a use case for better understanding. Assume you have an application that needs to connect to your on-premises data center and also to resources in another region. You can create a VNet in Azure, segment it into appropriate subnets for your application, and establish a secure connection from your VNet to your on-premises data center using a VPN gateway.

To connect your application to resources in another region, you can establish VNet peering between the two regions. Each of these networks would have appropriate NSG rules and routing tables to manage and secure traffic.

To summarize, Azure VNets provide a robust set of features to create isolated networks in Azure, connect with on-premises networks, and communicate securely with other VNets. Understanding these components and how they interact provides the foundation for managing and securing network services in Azure.

Virtual private cloud in IBM

IBM Cloud also offers the VPC concept, providing you with a secure, isolated VNet in the IBM Cloud. With IBM VPC, you get granular control over your cloud networking environment, including selection of your IP address range, creation of subnets, and configuration of route tables and network gateways.

VPC architecture

A VPC in IBM is similar to a region in AWS or Azure. Each VPC is tied to a specific IBM Cloud region and spans all the AZs in that region. Within a VPC, you can create one or more subnets, each tied to a different AZ, enhancing the resilience and high availability of your applications.

The following are the key components of an IBM VPC:

- **Subnets**: Just like AWS and Azure, a subnet in IBM VPC is a range of IP addresses in the VPC. You can create multiple subnets within a VPC and deploy resources across them.

- **Public gateways**: Public gateways in IBM VPC are like IGWs in AWS. They allow resources within your VPC to communicate with the internet.

- **Floating IPs**: These are public IP addresses that can be dynamically assigned to an instance. They can also be moved between instances, providing flexible IP address management.

- **Security groups**: Security groups act as virtual firewalls at the instance level. They regulate inbound and outbound traffic to instances.

- **Network ACLs**: Network ACLs operate at the subnet level. They allow or deny traffic to and from resources within a subnet.

- **VPC peering**: VPC peering allows you to connect two VPCs as if they were part of the same network.

VPC in action

Let us consider a scenario where you have a three-tier web application with a web server, application server, and database server. You can create a VPC and three separate subnets within it. The web servers can be placed in a public subnet (with a public gateway) to communicate with the internet, while the application and database servers can be placed in private subnets for security.

You can use security groups and network ACLs to ensure that only legitimate traffic flows between the web, application, and database servers. Moreover, you can use floating IPs to expose your web server to the internet.

In conclusion, IBM VPC provides you with a comprehensive set of tools and features to build a secure, scalable, and high-performing VNet in the IBM Cloud. Understanding these components and their interactions will help you better manage and secure your network services in the IBM Cloud.

Virtual private cloud in GCP

GCP offers a VPC service, enabling users to define their VNet with private IP addresses, managing their network both within GCP and with other networks via gateways and peering.

VPC architecture

In GCP, a VPC is a global construct spanning across all regions. Unlike other cloud providers, GCP does not restrict VPCs to a single region. Instead, you can have resources in different regions, all part of the same VPC, without needing to establish peering connections between them. Within a VPC, you can create subnets, which are regional constructs, allowing for a robust and resilient networking setup.

The following are the key components of a GCP VPC:

- **Subnets**: Subnets in GCP are analogous to those in other cloud platforms. They are IP address ranges within the VPC where you can deploy your resources. However, these are regional constructs in GCP, unique to its architecture.

- **Firewall rules**: GCP uses firewall rules (similar to security groups and NACLs in AWS) that govern the traffic to and from instances within your VPC. These rules can be defined at an instance level or across the whole VPC.

- **Routes**: Routes dictate the flow of traffic within the VPC. By default, GCP creates certain system routes. However, custom routes can also be defined.

- **Cloud VPN and Cloud Interconnect**: These two services allow your VPC to connect to other networks. Cloud VPN enables a secure connection over the public internet to your on-premise network, while Cloud Interconnect offers a direct, private connection between GCP and your on-premise network.

- **VPC peering**: VPC peering in GCP allows you to establish a networking connection between two VPCs, enabling traffic to route between them using internal IP addresses.

VPC in action

Consider a scenario where you have a distributed application deployed across multiple regions. With GCP's global VPC, you can create one VPC with different subnets in each region. Each instance within the VPC can communicate with each other using internal IP addresses, improving the performance and security of your applications.

Furthermore, you can create firewall rules that allow only specific traffic to flow between your resources, enhancing your network's security. If you need to connect your VPC to an on-premise network, you can use Cloud VPN or Cloud Interconnect based on your requirements.

Overall, understanding the structure and components of GCP VPC enables you to build scalable and secure networks in the GCP, effectively managing and securing your network services.

Inter-VPC communication and route tables in AWS

AWS provides mechanisms for secure communication between different VPCs. One common method is through VPC peering. Additionally, route tables play a crucial role in controlling network traffic within a VPC and with other VPCs.

VPC peering

VPC peering is a networking connection between two VPCs that enables routing using each VPC's private IP addresses as if they were in the same network. VPCs across different AWS accounts or even across different AWS Regions can be peered together.

To create a VPC peering connection, you need to configure a request between two VPCs. Once the peering connection is established, you can route traffic between these VPCs as if they were in the same network.

Inter-VPC communication

VPC peering allows direct communication between instances in peered VPCs as if they are within the same network. It is important to note that VPC peering connections are neither transitive nor a gateway. If VPC A is peered with VPC B, and VPC B is peered with VPC C, VPC A and VPC C do not have a peering relationship by default. Each peering connection is treated individually.

Route tables

Route tables determine where network traffic is directed. Each subnet in your VPC must be associated with a route table, which controls the traffic leaving that subnet. A subnet can only be associated with one route table at a time, but multiple subnets can share the same route table.

When creating a VPC, a default route table is created automatically. This table will have a default local route that allows all subnets within the VPC to communicate. For traffic to flow between VPCs, you need to manually add routes in your route tables pointing to the **Classless Inter-Domain Routing (CIDR)** block of the other VPC.

Inter-VPC communication with route tables

For VPC peering to work, you need to add the necessary routes to your route tables. For instance, if you have VPC A with CIDR 10.0.0.0/16 and VPC B with CIDR 192.168.0.0/16 peered together, your route tables might look like this:

VPC A route table:

Destination: 10.0.0.0/16, Target: local

Destination: 192.168.0.0/16, Target: pcx-aaaabbbb (VPC peering connection)

VPC B route table:

Destination: 192.168.0.0/16, Target: local

Destination: 10.0.0.0/16, Target: pcx-aaaabbbb (VPC peering connection)

With this setup, any instance in VPC A can communicate with any instance in VPC B and vice versa, using their private IP addresses.

In summary, understanding inter-VPC communication and route tables in AWS is fundamental to managing and securing network services efficiently. Through VPC peering and proper route table configuration, you can establish secure, direct communication between different VPCs.

Inter-VPC communication and route tables in Azure

Microsoft Azure, similar to AWS, provides features for secure communication between different VNets (VNet, equivalent to VPC in AWS), commonly via VNet peering. Route tables are also used to control network traffic within and across VNets.

VNet peering

VNet peering in Azure allows for network communication between two VNets using the private IP addresses of VMs as if they were in the same network. VNets can be peered across different Azure subscriptions and even across different Azure regions, enabling a global, interconnected network.

VNet peering involves two VNets:

- A local VNet
- A peer VNet

A peering needs to be setup from the local VNet to the peer VNet, and the peer VNet also needs a peering that points back to the local VNet. Once these are established, resources in either VNet can communicate with each other.

Inter-VNet communication

With VNet peering, resources in either VNet can communicate directly with each other. However, Azure VNet peering connections are non-transitive. This means if VNet A is peered with VNet B, and VNet B is peered with VNet C, there is no direct peering connection between VNet A and VNet C. Each peering connection is treated individually.

Route tables

Route tables in Azure dictate the flow of traffic between subnets within a VNet and between different VNets. When you create a subnet within a VNet, Azure creates a system route table for that subnet, but you can also create custom route tables based on your requirements.

Route tables consist of one or more routes, each route specifying a destination CIDR block and the next hop type, which is where packets are sent if they match the destination CIDR.

Inter-VNet communication with route tables

To enable traffic flow between peered VNets, you need to add the necessary routes to your route tables. For instance, if VNet A with CIDR 10.0.0.0/16 is peered with VNet B with CIDR 192.168.0.0/16, your route tables might include these entries:

VNet A route table:

Address prefix: 192.168.0.0/16, next hop type: VNet peering

VNet B route table:

Address prefix: 10.0.0.0/16, next hop type: VNet peering

With these entries, any resource in VNet A can communicate with any resource in VNet B and vice versa using their private IP addresses.

In conclusion, understanding how inter-VNet communication and route tables work in Azure is key to managing and securing your network services efficiently. By correctly setting up VNet peering and route table configurations, you can establish secure and direct communication between different VNets.

Inter-VPC communication and route tables in IBM

IBM Cloud allows secure communication between different VPCs using VPC peering. Route tables, as in other cloud platforms, control network traffic within a VPC and across peered VPCs.

VPC peering

VPC peering in IBM Cloud enables two VPCs in the same region to communicate with each other via their private IP addresses, as if they are part of the same network. The peer

VPCs can be part of the same IBM Cloud account or different accounts, as long as they belong to the same region.

A VPC peering connection in IBM Cloud is a bidirectional relationship. A request is initiated from one VPC, which then needs to be accepted by the other VPC. Once the peering connection is established, resources within these VPCs can communicate with each other directly.

Inter-VPC communication

Inter-VPC communication in IBM Cloud, once a peering connection is established, allows instances in the peered VPCs to communicate directly with each other, using their private IP addresses. Note that VPC peering connections in IBM Cloud are non-transitive, similar to AWS and Azure. If VPC A is peered with VPC B, and VPC B is peered with VPC C, VPC A and VPC C do not have a direct peering relationship.

Route tables

In IBM Cloud, a route table is a set of rules, called **routes**, that are used to determine where network traffic is directed. Each subnet in a VPC is associated with a route table, and all traffic leaving the subnet is governed by the route table. By default, a main route table is created with every VPC, and all subnets in the VPC that do not have an explicitly associated route table are associated with the main route table.

Inter-VPC communication with route tables

To enable network traffic between peered VPCs, you need to add routes in your route tables for each VPC, specifying the CIDR block of the other VPC. For example, if VPC A with CIDR 10.0.0.0/16 is peered with VPC B with CIDR 192.168.0.0/16, you would add the following routes:

VPC A route table:

Destination: 192.168.0.0/16, target: VPC peering connection

VPC B route table:

Destination: 10.0.0.0/16, target: VPC peering connection

With these routes, any instance in VPC A can communicate with any instance in VPC B and vice versa, using their private IP addresses.

To sum up, understanding inter-VPC communication and route tables in IBM Cloud is crucial for effectively managing and securing your network services. By correctly configuring VPC peering and route tables, you can establish secure, direct communication between different VPCs.

Inter-VPC communication and route tables in GCP

In GCP, the networking construct comparable to the VPC. GCP allows secure communication between different VPCs, typically through VPC Network Peering. Route tables, similar to other platforms, are used to control network traffic within and across VPCs.

VPC Network Peering

VPC Network Peering in GCP allows two VPC networks to connect and exchange traffic by private IP addresses, as if they were part of the same network. This peering is accomplished without any additional gateways, VPNs, or separate physical hardware, and the traffic between instances in peered VPCs travels across Google's backbone network, not the public internet.

Notably, GCP's VPC Network Peering is a bit different from its counterparts in that it supports transitive peering. This means if VPC A is peered with VPC B, and VPC B is peered with VPC C, VPC A and VPC C can communicate through VPC B, provided that the correct routing configurations are in place.

Inter-VPC communication

With VPC Network Peering established, resources in peered VPCs can communicate directly with each other, using their private IP addresses. GCP automatically creates routes for each VPC in the peering that direct traffic to the IP ranges in the other VPC.

Route tables

In GCP, each VPC network has a system-generated route for each of its subnets. The route's destination is the subnet's IP range, and the next hop is the default IGW. GCP automatically creates and deletes these routes when subnets are added or removed. You can also create custom static routes to direct some packets to specific next hops.

Inter-VPC communication with route tables

For VPC Network Peering to work, you do not usually need to manually add routes in your route tables, as GCP automatically creates the necessary routes. However, you can create custom static routes if needed. Note that with the possibility of transitive peering, you may have to carefully manage your route tables to avoid unintended network paths.

For instance, if VPC A with CIDR 10.0.0.0/16 is peered with VPC B with CIDR 192.168.0.0/16, GCP would automatically add these routes:

VPC A route table:

Destination: 192.168.0.0/16, next hop: VPC peering to VPC B

VPC B route table:

Destination: 10.0.0.0/16, next hop: VPC peering to VPC A

This configuration would allow any instance in VPC A to communicate with any instance in VPC B and vice versa, using their private IP addresses.

In summary, understanding inter-VPC communication and route tables in GCP is essential for effectively managing and securing your network services. Through VPC Network Peering and proper route table configuration, you can establish secure, direct communication between different VPCs.

Security configurations in AWS

In this section, we will look at the steps to configure security measures in the AWS environment.

Create a VPC

The first step is to create a VPC, which gives you an isolated network within AWS:

1. Sign in to the AWS Management Console and open the Amazon VPC console at **https://console.aws.amazon.com/vpc/**

2. In the navigation pane, choose **Your VPCs**.

3. Choose **Create VPC**.

4. In the **Create VPC** dialog box, configure your VPC by entering a name and an IP CIDR block, for example, `10.0.0.0/16`.

5. Choose **Yes, Create**.

Create a subnet

Next, create a subnet within your VPC. Subnets allow you to partition your network within AWS:

1. In the Amazon VPC console, choose **Subnets** in the navigation pane.

2. Click **Create subnet**.

3. Enter a name, choose your VPC from the dropdown, assign a CIDR block, and choose an AZ.

4. Click **Create**.

Create an internet gateway and attach to your VPC

An IGW enables your VPC to connect to the internet:

1. In the VPC dashboard, click on **Internet gateways**.

2. Click **Create internet gateway**, then enter a name for your gateway and click **Create**.

3. After the IGW has been created, select it, click **Actions**, and then **Attach to VPC**.

4. Choose your VPC and click **Attach**.

Create a route table

Route tables control where network traffic is directed:

1. In your VPC dashboard, click **Route tables**.

2. Click **Create route table**, then give it a name, and select your VPC.

3. Click **Create**.

After creating the route table, you need to edit the routes to add the IGW:

1. Select the newly created route table.

2. Under the **Routes** tab, click **Edit routes**.

3. In the **Destination** box, enter `0.0.0.0/0`.

4. For **Target**, select your IGW, then click **Save routes**.

Finally, associate your route table with your subnet:

1. Under the **Subnet associations** tab, click **Edit subnet associations**.

2. Select your subnet and click **Save**.

Create security groups

Security groups act like a firewall for associated Amazon EC2 instances, controlling both inbound and outbound traffic at the instance level:

1. In the AWS Management Console, navigate to the EC2 Dashboard.

2. Under **Network & Security**, click **Security Groups**.

3. Click **Create security group**.

4. Give your security group a name and description. Make sure to select the correct VPC.

5. Under the **Inbound** tab, click **Add Rule**. Choose the type of traffic (SSH, HTTP, etc.) and source (IP ranges).

6. Under the **Outbound** tab, specify the type of outbound traffic allowed.

7. Click **Create**.

Network access control list

NACLs provide a rule-based tool for controlling network traffic ingress and egress at the protocol and subnet level:

1. Go to the VPC dashboard and click **Network ACLs**.

2. Click **Create network ACL**, give it a name, select your VPC, and click **Create**.

3. Select your newly created NACL and click on **Inbound rules**, then **Edit inbound rules**.

4. Add rules to allow inbound traffic from trusted IP addresses and click **Save**.

5. Do the same for **Outbound rules**. Remember to associate your NACL with your subnet.

6. Under the **Subnet associations** tab, click **Edit subnet associations**.

7. Select your subnet and click **Save**.

Each of these components plays a crucial role in securing your AWS network infrastructure. It is important to review and understand each concept and how they interact to ensure a robust security configuration.

Security configurations in Azure

Let us discuss the steps to configure security measures in Azure environment.

Create a VNet

A VNet in Azure provides an isolated and secure environment to run your VMs and applications:

1. Sign in to the Azure portal.

2. In the left-hand menu, select **Create a resource**.

3. In the **Search the Marketplace** box, type **Virtual Network**, and select it from the dropdown.

4. Click **Create**, then enter the required details like name, address space, subscription, resource group, location, etc.

5. Click **Review + create**, then **Create**.

Create a subnet

Next, create a subnet within your VNet. Subnets allow you to segment the network within Azure.

1. Navigate to the VNet you created.

2. Under **Settings**, choose **Subnets**.

3. Click **+ Subnet**.

4. Give your subnet a name and specify the address range (CIDR block).

5. Click **Ok**.

Create a network security group

NSGs act as a virtual firewall for your VMs, controlling inbound and outbound traffic:

1. In the left-hand menu of the Azure portal, select **Create a resource**.

2. In the **Search the Marketplace** box, type **Network Security Group**, and select it from the dropdown.

3. Click **Create**, then enter a name for your NSG, choose your subscription, create a new resource group or use an existing one, and choose a location.

4. Click **Create**.

After creating the NSG, you will need to configure the inbound and outbound security rules:

1. Navigate to your newly created NSG.

2. Under **Settings**, select either **Inbound security rules** or **Outbound security rules**.

3. Click **+ Add** and create your rules, specifying details like source, destination, protocol, port range, and action (Allow/deny).

4. Click **Add**.

Associate your NSG with your subnet

To apply the security rules to your subnet, you will need to associate your NSG with your subnet:

1. Navigate to your NSG.

2. Under **Settings**, select **Subnets**.

3. Click **+ Associate**, then select your VNet and the subnet you wish to associate with the NSG.

4. Click **Ok**.

Create a route table

Route tables allow you to direct network traffic in customized ways:

1. In the left-hand menu of the Azure portal, select **Create a resource**.

2. In the **Search the Marketplace** box, type **Route table**, and select it from the dropdown.

3. Click **Create**, then enter the necessary details like name, subscription, resource group, location, etc.

4. Click **Create**.

After creating the route table, you will need to configure routes:

1. Navigate to your newly created route table.

2. Under **Settings**, select **Routes**.

3. Click + **Add**. Enter the necessary details like a route name, address prefix, next hop type, and next hop address.

4. Click **Ok**.

Then associate your route table with your subnet:

1. Under **Settings** in your route table, select **Subnets**.

2. Click + **Associate**, then select your VNet and subnet.

3. Click **Ok**.

Each of these components plays a critical role in securing your Azure network infrastructure. It is essential to review and understand each concept and how they interact to ensure a robust security configuration.

Security configurations in IBM

This section discusses the steps to configure security measures in the IBM environment.

Create a VPC

To create a VPC on IBM Cloud, follow these steps:

1. Sign in to the IBM Cloud console.

2. In the navigation menu, click on **VPC infrastructure**.

3. From the VPC dashboard, click on **Create VPC**.

4. Fill in the necessary details like name, resource group, and default network ACL.

5. Choose your desired location and click **Create**.

Create a subnet

To create a subnet on IBM Cloud, follow these steps:

1. From the VPC dashboard, go to the **Subnets** section.

2. Click on **Create subnet**.

3. Fill in the necessary details such as name, VPC (choose the one you created earlier), zone, CIDR block, public gateway, etc.

4. Click **Create**.

Create a security group

Security groups act as a virtual firewall for your instances in VPC. To create a VPC on IBM Cloud, follow these steps:

1. In the VPC dashboard, go to the **Security groups** section.

2. Click on **Create security group**.

3. Fill in the necessary details like name, VPC, and resource group.

4. Click **Create**.

After creating a security group, set the inbound and outbound rules:

1. Open the security group you just created.

2. Go to the **Inbound rules** section and click **Add rule**. Set the rule details like protocol, port min, port max, and source.

3. Similarly, add outbound rules under the **Outbound rules** section.

Apply a security group to instances

Once the security group has been created and rules have been defined, it can be applied to instances:

1. In the VPC dashboard, go to the **Instances** section.

2. Select the instance you want to apply the security group to.

3. In the instance details page, go to the **Network interfaces** section.

4. Click on the **network interface card** (**NIC**) attached to your instance.

5. In the network interface details page, go to the **Security groups** section and click **Edit**.

6. Select the security group you created earlier and click **Save**.

Network ACLs

NACLs provide a rule-based tool for controlling network traffic ingress and egress at the subnet level:

1. In the VPC dashboard, go to the **Network ACLs** section.

2. Click **Create ACL**.

3. Fill in the necessary details like name, VPC, and resource group, and then click **Create**.

4. Select your newly created NACL and set inbound and outbound rules similar to how you set them for the security group.

Each of these steps is instrumental in establishing and maintaining robust network security configurations on the IBM Cloud. Ensuring your understanding of each step is critical to securing your network effectively.

Security configurations in GCP

This section discusses the steps to configure the security measures in the GCP environment.

Create a VPC

To create a VPC on GCP, follow these steps:

1. Sign in to the Google Cloud console.

2. Select your project and go to the **VPC network** section.

3. Click **Create VPC network**.

4. Fill in the necessary details like name, description, and subnets (you can add subnets directly here or later as needed).

5. Click **Create**.

Create a subnet

To create a subnet on the GCP cloud, follow these steps:

1. Navigate to the **VPC networks** section.

2. Click on the VPC you created.

3. In the VPC details page, go to the **Subnets** tab and click **Add subnet**.

4. Fill in the necessary details like name, region, and IP address range.

5. Click **Add**.

Create firewall rules

Firewall rules in GCP control traffic to and from your VM instances. To create firewall rules on the GCP cloud, follow these steps:

1. Navigate to the **VPC networks** section.

2. Click on **Firewall**.

3. Click **Create firewall rule**.

4. Fill in the necessary details like name, network (choose the VPC you created), priority, direction of traffic, action on match, targets, source filter, and specified protocols and ports.

5. Click **Create**.

Create and configure a Cloud Router

Cloud Router allows dynamic routing between your VPC and non-Google networks:

1. Navigate to the **Hybrid connectivity** section.

2. Click on **Routers**.

3. Click **Create Router**.

4. Fill in the necessary details like name, region, network, Google **Autonomous System Number (ASN)**, etc.

5. Click **Create**.

Cloud NAT

Cloud NAT allows instances without external IP addresses to access the internet in a controlled and efficient manner:

1. Navigate to the **VPC network** section and select **Cloud NAT**.

2. Click **Create NAT gateway**.

3. Fill in the necessary details like name, region, Cloud Router, NAT IP addresses, etc.

4. Click **Create**.

Each of these steps is vital for establishing and maintaining strong network security configurations in GCP. To effectively secure your network, it is crucial to understand each step and how they interact with each other. The successful setup of these elements will significantly enhance the security of your network in GCP.

Illustration and case study

Consider a fictional company, *Globex Corporation*, that operates across multiple cloud platforms, including AWS, Azure, IBM Cloud, and GCP. In these cloud environments, they have established VNets hosting a range of critical applications and services. To ensure effective network security and traffic management, they utilize VPCs, VPC peering, and route tables across all platforms.

Globex Corporation encountered challenges related to latency and data security while transferring information between its AWS and Azure environments. To address these issues, they implemented VPC peering between their AWS and Azure setups. This solution enabled secure and efficient data transfer using private IP addresses, eliminating the need for data to traverse the public internet. Additionally, they strategically employed route tables to optimize traffic routing, significantly enhancing overall network performance and security.

Conclusion

VPCs provide an isolated, private section of the cloud where you can launch resources within a defined virtual network. Leading cloud providers like AWS, Azure, IBM Cloud, and GCP offer VPCs with customizable IP address ranges, subnets, route tables, and network gateways. VPC peering enables private communication between VPCs, with route tables directing network traffic and adjustable rules controlling flow within and across networks.

This chapter offered a comprehensive guide to configuring secure VPCs, with detailed steps for IBM Cloud and GCP, highlighting the role of subnets and security layers. While AWS and Azure were introduced, a deeper exploration of their VPC setups could further enrich the content. A consistent, in-depth approach across all platforms would position this as a definitive reference for cloud network security.

In the next chapter, we will focus on **Identity Access Management (IAM)** and **single sign-on (SSO)** across major cloud platforms, including AWS, Azure, IBM Cloud, and GCP. You will explore how authentication, authorization, and role-based access controls are implemented, along with best practices to secure user identities in cloud environments.

Key takeaways

- VPCs are essential for creating isolated, secure environments in cloud platforms.

- Both IBM and GCP have systematic methods to setup and secure VPCs, emphasizing subnets, security groups, firewall rules, and other network-related configurations.

- Real-world applications, like the scenario with Globex Corporation, highlight the importance of proper VPC setup and its implications on security and data transfer.

- Consistency in setup and security configurations across different platforms ensures seamless integration and operation.

- VPC peering and route tables play a pivotal role in managing and directing traffic, ensuring efficient and secure communication between different environments.

Key terms

- **VPC**: An isolated cloud-based environment where resources can be launched within a defined VNet.

- **Subnet**: A range of IP addresses in the VPC.

- **Security group**: Acts as a virtual firewall that controls the inbound and outbound traffic to network resources.

- **Firewall rules**: Defined rules to control incoming and outgoing traffic based on protocols, ports, and source/destination IPs.

- **Cloud Router**: Allows dynamic routing between a VPC and non-Google networks.

- **NACLs**: Rule-based tools for controlling network traffic at the subnet level.

- **VPC peering**: A network connection between two VPCs, enabling private communication.

- **Route tables**: Used to direct network traffic, determining where the traffic should be directed based on IP protocol data.

- **Cloud NAT**: Allows instances without external IP addresses to access the internet in a controlled manner.

Solved exercises

1. **What is a VPC?**

   Answer: A VPC is an isolated cloud-based environment where resources can be launched within a defined VNet.

2. **How do security groups function in an IBM VPC?**

   Answer: Security groups act as a virtual firewall that controls the inbound and outbound traffic to network resources within the VPC.

3. **In GCP, what tool is used to control traffic to and from VM instances?**

   Answer: Firewall rules are used to control traffic to and from VM instances in GCP.

4. **What is the purpose of Cloud NAT in GCP?**

   Answer: Cloud NAT allows instances without external IP addresses to access the internet in a controlled and efficient manner.

5. **What are NACLs used for in IBM?**

   Answer: NACLs provide a rule-based tool for controlling network traffic ingress and egress at the subnet level.

6. **Why did Globex Corporation establish VPC peering between their AWS and Azure environments?**

   Answer: They did so to enable secure and efficient data transfer via private IP addresses, avoiding data traversal via the public internet.

7. **In IBM Cloud, where would you go to create a subnet after creating a VPC?**

   Answer: From the VPC dashboard, you would navigate to the **Subnets** section.

8. **Which GCP feature allows dynamic routing between your VPC and non-Google networks?**

   Answer: Cloud Router allows for this dynamic routing.

9. **How do you apply a security group to instances in IBM?**

   Answer: In the VPC dashboard, go to the **Instances** section. Select the desired instance, navigate to the **Network interfaces** section, click on the NIC attached to your instance, and then edit the **Security groups** section to apply the desired security group.

10. **What is the significance of route tables in VPCs?**

    Answer: Route tables are used to direct network traffic. The rules can be adjusted to control the flow of traffic within the VPC and across peered VPCs.

Unsolved exercises

1. How do VPCs in AWS and Azure differ from those in IBM and GCP?
2. Illustrate a scenario where VPC peering can be detrimental if not correctly configured.
3. Describe the step-by-step process to setup firewall rules in AWS.
4. How do Cloud Routers in GCP enhance network security and efficiency?
5. If Globex Corporation wished to expand its operations, what additional security measures might it consider for its VPCs across platforms?
6. What is the difference between inbound and outbound rules in a security group, and why are both important?
7. How can companies ensure data privacy while using VPC peering across different platforms?
8. Explain the significance of CIDR blocks when creating subnets in a VPC.
9. What considerations should be made when deciding the priority for firewall rules in GCP?
10. Discuss the advantages and disadvantages of using Cloud NAT in GCP.

CHAPTER 7
Identity and Access Management

Introduction

In this chapter, we will dive into the core concepts of **Identity and Access Management (IAM)** and **single sign-on (SSO)** across various cloud platforms, namely **Amazon Web Services (AWS)**, **Microsoft Azure**, **IBM Cloud**, and **Google Cloud Platform (GCP)**. As the world becomes more digitally connected, managing user identities, their access, and their credentials becomes increasingly critical. It is vital to understand how these concepts operate within each cloud environment and how to secure these configurations.

Structure

The chapter covers the following topics:

- Identity and Access Management in AWS
- Identity and Access Management in Azure
- Identity and Access Management in IBM
- Identity and Access Management in GCP
- Single sign-on in AWS
- Single sign-on in Azure
- Single sign-on in IBM

- Single sign-on in GCP
- Security configurations for IAM and SSO in AWS
- Security configurations for IAM and SSO in Azure
- Security configurations for IAM and SSO in IBM
- Security configurations for IAM and SSO in GCP
- Illustration
- Case study

Objectives

By the end of this chapter, you will have a clear understanding of the fundamentals of IAM and SSO and their significance. The chapter will help you navigate and implement IAM and SSO in AWS, Azure, IBM Cloud, and GCP. You will be able to apply security configurations for IAM and SSO in these platforms.

Prerequisites

Prior knowledge of basic cloud computing concepts is recommended. Familiarity with the mentioned cloud platforms would be beneficial but not compulsory, as this chapter aims to explain the concepts from the ground up.

Identity and Access Management in AWS

IAM in AWS enables you to securely control access to AWS services and resources for your users. With IAM, you can manage users, security credentials such as access keys, and permissions that control which AWS resources users can access.

Before we dive into the workings of IAM, let us understand a few key concepts:

- **Users**: A user is an identity with specific permissions that can be associated with a person or service. Users interact with AWS by signing into the AWS Management Console, making programmatic requests, or using the AWS CLI.

- **Groups**: A group is a collection of IAM users. You can manage permissions for multiple users by assigning policies to a group to which the users belong.

- **Roles**: A role is an AWS entity with permissions but without any credentials (passwords or access keys) associated. You can assume a role to temporarily take on different permissions for specific tasks.

- **Policies**: A policy is an entity that, when associated with an identity or resource, defines its permissions. AWS evaluates these policies when a principal (user or role) makes a request.

- **Access keys**: These are credentials for APIs and CLI. Each user has access keys (access key ID and secret access key) to interact with AWS services.

Working with IAM

When you first create an AWS account, you begin with a single sign-in identity that has complete access to all AWS services and resources in your account, known as the **root user**. AWS recommends that you use this account to create your first IAM user.

When you create an IAM user, you grant it permissions by associating policies. Policies are JSON documents that allow or deny access to specific AWS services or resources. They provide granular control, allowing you to specify not just the actions a user can perform but also the resources those actions can affect.

AWS IAM roles

IAM roles allow you to delegate access to users or services that need to work with resources in your AWS account. When you create a role, you establish trust between your account and another AWS account, an AWS service, an **identity provider** (**IdP**), or an application. This entity is then known as the **trusted entity**.

An IAM role does not have any credentials associated with it. Instead, when you assume a role, it provides you with temporary security credentials for your role session.

Security best practices for AWS IAM

There are several security best practices to consider while working with AWS IAM:

- **Grant least privilege**: Only allow permissions necessary to perform a task. If a user needs additional permissions, they can be granted on a case-by-case basis.

- **Enable MFA**: **Multi-factor authentication** (**MFA**) adds an extra layer of protection on top of usernames and passwords.

- **Rotate credentials regularly**: Regularly rotating security credentials (like AWS access keys) reduces the risk of them being misused.

- **Audit IAM roles and permissions**: Regularly review and audit IAM roles and permissions to remove any unnecessary permissions.

- **Use IAM roles for EC2 instances**: If you have applications running on EC2 that need to access other AWS services, use IAM roles and assign them to the instances.

IAM is an essential service within AWS, and understanding how it works is crucial for managing security effectively in the AWS environment. With the right implementation of IAM, you can ensure a highly secure and scalable user management infrastructure.

Take a moment to think. If you are the administrator of an organization, what access level would you assign to a new developer joining your team?

Identity and Access Management in Azure

In Microsoft Azure, IAM is managed through **Azure Active Directory (Azure AD)**. Azure AD is Microsoft's cloud-based IAM service, which helps employees sign in and access resources.

Understanding Azure AD

Azure AD is not the same as traditional on-premises AD. It is an **identity as a service (IDaaS)** solution that offers several features such as user and group management, cloud-based apps SSO, self-service password management, and more.

The key concepts of Azure AD IAM include:

- **Users**: Users are the email accounts that are allowed access to the Azure resources. These can be sourced from the Azure AD itself, a Microsoft account, or a guest account from another Azure AD.

- **Groups**: Groups in Azure AD allow you to manage a collection of users. Instead of assigning roles to individual users, you can assign roles to a group, and all users who are members of the group inherit these roles.

- **Roles**: Azure has hundreds of built-in roles that can be assigned at different scopes (management group, subscription, resource group, and resource).

- **Managed identities**: Azure managed identities provide an identity for applications to use when connecting to resources that support Azure AD authentication.

- **Azure AD Connect**: Azure AD Connect is a tool that connects and syncs your AD with Azure AD on-premises.

Working with Azure AD

Once you have created your Azure account and are ready to add users and groups, you can start assigning roles. These roles carry permissions that decide what actions the users or groups can perform and on which resources. Role assignments can be inherited, so if you assign a role to a group at the subscription level, it gets passed down to all resource groups and resources in that subscription.

Azure AD roles

Azure AD roles are used for access management in Azure AD. They allow you to assign permissions to users, groups, and applications at a certain scope to perform specific operations.

Some common Azure AD roles include:

- **User Administrator**: This role can manage all aspects of users and groups, including resetting passwords for limited admins.

- **Billing Administrator**: This role can make purchases, manage subscriptions and support tickets.

- **Global Administrator**: This role has access to all administrative features, and can assign other administrative roles to users.

Security best practices for Azure AD IAM

The following are a few best practices for managing security in Azure AD:

- **Enable MFA**: Like AWS, enabling MFA adds an extra layer of security to your user sign-ins.

- **Regularly review role assignments**: It is a good practice to review and reevaluate role assignments regularly to ensure they align with the principle of least privilege.

- **Monitor sign-in and audit logs**: Azure AD provides sign-in logs and audit logs, which help you monitor and gain insights into user behaviors and potential security risks.

- **Enable conditional access**: With Azure AD Conditional Access, you can enforce controls on access to apps in your environment based on specific conditions from a central location.

- **Use managed identities for Azure resources**: Instead of creating a service principal, consider using a managed identity. Managed identities provide an identity for applications to use when connecting to resources.

Azure's IAM capabilities through Azure AD offer comprehensive access and identity management solutions for the Azure cloud. By effectively managing identities and access, you can ensure a secure and compliant environment.

Before moving on, here is an exercise: Try to imagine a scenario where you would need to use the principle of least privilege. How would you apply it in your Azure environment?

Identity and Access Management in IBM

IBM Cloud IAM is a service that securely authenticates users and controls their access to resources in the IBM Cloud. It allows you to manage users and their access across your account in a centralized, simple, and automated manner.

Understanding IBM IAM

IBM IAM service provides various mechanisms to control access, including users, service IDs, access groups, and API keys. The following are some key concepts:

- **Users**: Users are individuals with unique credentials who are given access to the IBM Cloud.

- **Service IDs**: Service IDs represent applications or services, rather than individuals. These are used to grant resource permissions to services or apps within IBM Cloud.

- **Access groups**: Access groups are collections of users or service IDs to which you can collectively assign access policies.

- **API keys**: API keys are used as a method for a program to make authorized API calls.

- **Policies**: Policies are the rules that determine who has what kind of access to which resources.

Working with IBM IAM

Once you create an IBM Cloud account, you have complete control over your cloud resources. This root user can then create new users, assign them to access groups, and provide them with the necessary API keys to enable programmatic access to IBM Cloud services.

Assigning users to access groups simplifies the process of managing permissions, as changes made to an access group's policies automatically apply to all members of that group.

IBM IAM roles

IAM roles in IBM Cloud allow you to assign specific access rights to users or service IDs. Roles are basically collections of permissions that you can assign to a user or service ID. Examples of predefined roles in IBM Cloud include manager, editor, operator, and viewer.

Security best practices for IBM IAM

The following are some of the best practices for managing security in IBM IAM:

- **Principle of least privilege**: Always assign the least amount of privilege necessary for a user to perform their tasks.

- **Monitor activity**: Regularly monitor user activity and access patterns to identify any suspicious activity.

- **Manage API keys**: Keep track of your API keys, rotate them regularly, and avoid embedding them in your code directly.

- **Use access groups**: To make access management easier, use access groups to assign the same set of permissions to multiple users or services.

- **Implement 2FA**: Implement **two-factor authentication** (**2FA**) for an added layer of security during user authentication.

IBM's IAM services provide the necessary tools to manage access to your cloud resources securely and efficiently. By properly implementing IAM in IBM Cloud, you can create a secure and compliant cloud environment.

In the next section, we will discuss IAM in GCP. Keep going and remember to think critically about how you would apply these principles in real-life scenarios.

Here is a thought exercise: Imagine a scenario where you have multiple teams working on different projects within the same IBM Cloud account. How would you organize users and access groups? How would you ensure security and separation of responsibilities among these groups?

Identity and Access Management in GCP

IAM in GCP provides predefined roles that give granular access to specific Google Cloud resources and prevent unwanted access to other resources. IAM offers a unified view of security policy across your entire organization, with built-in auditing to ease compliance processes.

Understanding GCP IAM

GCP IAM provides the right tools to manage resource permissions with minimum fuss and high automation. The following are some key concepts:

- **Members**: Members can be a Google Account for end users, a service account for apps and **virtual machines** (**VMs**), a Google Group, or a G Suite or Cloud Identity domain that can access a resource.

- **Roles**: A role is a collection of permissions. Permissions determine what operations are allowed on a resource. IAM roles can be primitive (Owner, Editor, and Viewer), predefined, or custom.

- **Policies**: A policy binds a set of members to a role. When you attach a policy to a resource, it determines who (the members) has what type of access (the role) on that resource.

- **Service accounts**: A service account is a special kind of account used by an application or a VM, not a person. Applications use service accounts to make authorized API calls.

Working with GCP IAM

After creating a Google Cloud account, you have complete control over your resources. You can then assign IAM roles to members. Members can be individuals, groups, domains, or even service accounts.

IAM policies, which consist of roles and members, are set on resources. A policy attached to a resource will apply to all the resource's child resources. For example, a policy set on a project will apply to all resources in the project.

GCP IAM roles

There are three types of roles in IAM:

- **Primitive roles**: Which include Owner, Editor, and Viewer, affect all resources in the project.

- **Predefined roles**: Which provide granular access for a specific service and are managed by Google Cloud.

- **Custom roles**: Which provide granular access according to a user-defined list of permissions.

Security best practices for GCP IAM

To manage security effectively in GCP IAM, consider the following best practices:

- **Principle of least privilege**: Only grant the minimum permissions necessary for a role.

- **Regularly audit permissions**: Make use of Cloud Audit Logs to regularly review and monitor access.

- **Use strong authentication**: Implement two-step verification for all users.

- **Rotate service account keys**: Regularly rotate and manage service account keys to minimize the impact of key compromise.

- **Use predefined roles**: Whenever possible, use predefined roles instead of primitive roles to follow the principle of least privilege.

GCP IAM capabilities offer comprehensive access and identity management solutions for the Google Cloud. With the appropriate implementation of IAM, you can ensure a secure and efficient cloud environment.

In the following sections, we will move on to discussing SSO, starting with AWS.

Before moving on, reflect on a scenario where you need to assign access to a new developer joining your team in a Google Cloud project. Which type of role would you assign them and why? Consider both the principle of least privilege and the need to maintain productivity and efficiency.

Single sign-on in AWS

AWS SSO is a cloud-based service that simplifies the management of SSO access to AWS accounts and business applications. AWS SSO helps users manage their user identities and provides users with an easy-to-use portal from which they can access their assigned AWS accounts, roles, and business applications.

Understanding AWS SSO

AWS SSO gives administrators centralized control to manage SSO access to multiple AWS accounts and business applications. The following are some key concepts:

- **AWS SSO user portal**: This is a user interface from which users can access the AWS accounts and roles they are assigned to.

- **SSO applications**: These are third-party business applications that support SAML 2.0 and are integrated with AWS SSO for SSO access.

- **SSO access:** This is the permission given to users to access AWS accounts and business applications using AWS SSO.

- **SSO configuration**: These are the settings for AWS SSO, including the identity source, permission sets, and more.

Working with AWS SSO

To start using AWS SSO, an administrator needs to configure the identity source, which can be AWS Managed Microsoft AD, an existing Microsoft AD, or an external IdP like Okta or Azure AD.

Once the identity source is setup, administrators can define which AWS accounts the users have access to and which roles they can assume within those accounts. Administrators can also integrate business applications with AWS SSO to provide users with a single portal for accessing all their applications.

When a user logs into the AWS SSO user portal, they are presented with a list of AWS accounts, roles, and applications they have access to. They can click on an account or role to get temporary credentials or on an application to be automatically signed in.

AWS SSO security best practices

The following are the best practices:

- **Use MFA**: Enable MFA for AWS SSO users to add an additional layer of security to the sign-in process.

- **Apply the least privilege principle**: Only assign users the minimum set of permissions they need to perform their tasks.

- **Monitor activity**: Use AWS CloudTrail to record and monitor all AWS SSO sign-in events.

- **Regularly review access rights**: Periodically review and update AWS SSO permissions to ensure they are still appropriate for each user.

AWS SSO provides a central location to manage SSO access to multiple AWS accounts and business applications, making it easier for administrators to manage access rights and for users to access their resources.

In the following sections, we will discuss SSO in Azure and IBM. Keep up the good work and remember to reflect on these concepts and think about how you would apply them in real-world scenarios.

Consider this exercise: If you were managing a team working on multiple AWS accounts and using several business applications, how would you setup AWS SSO to ensure a balance between access convenience and security?

Single sign-on in Azure

Azure AD provides secure, enterprise-grade IAM capabilities, including SSO. Azure AD SSO simplifies access to applications by providing users with a single set of credentials to access multiple applications.

Understanding Azure AD SSO

Azure AD SSO provides a seamless way for users to access their enterprise cloud applications. The following are some key concepts:

- **Azure AD users**: Users in Azure AD can be sourced from an on-premises AD or created directly within Azure AD.

- **SSO applications**: Applications that support SSO can be integrated with Azure AD to enable SSO access.

- **Azure AD SSO configuration**: These are the settings in Azure AD for enabling and managing SSO.

Working with Azure AD SSO

To enable SSO for an application, an administrator adds the application to Azure AD and configures SSO. Azure AD supports different types of SSO, including SAML-based, OpenID Connect, and password-based SSO.

Users can access their SSO-enabled applications through the Azure AD access panel or directly from the application's sign-in page. When a user signs in to an application through Azure AD, they are redirected to Azure AD for authentication. After successful authentication, they are redirected back to the application with a token representing their authenticated session.

Azure AD SSO security best practices

The following are the best practices:

- **Use MFA**: Enable MFA for Azure AD users to add an additional layer of security to the sign-in process.

- **Monitor sign-in activity**: Use Azure AD reports to monitor sign-in activity and identify any unusual behavior.

- **Regularly review access**: Periodically review and update Azure AD access rights to ensure they are still appropriate for each user.

- **Least privilege access**: Grant users only the access they need to perform their tasks.

Azure AD SSO provides a straightforward, secure way for users to gain access to multiple applications using a single set of credentials. It not only reduces the burden of password management but also enhances the security posture of an organization.

Next, we will discuss SSO in IBM. Keep up the good work, and remember to think about how you would apply these concepts in real-world scenarios.

Consider the following exercise: If you were managing a team using multiple cloud-based applications, how would you setup Azure AD SSO to provide them with secure and efficient access to their resources? What would you consider when deciding which type of SSO to use for an application?

Single sign-on in IBM

IBM offers SSO capabilities in its cloud platform, IBM Cloud. IBM Cloud SSO service allows users to use one set of credentials to authenticate across multiple applications and services, eliminating the need to manage multiple usernames and passwords.

Understanding IBM SSO

IBM Cloud provides SSO as a standalone service that can be bound to applications running on the platform. The following are a few key concepts related to IBM Cloud SSO:

- **Service instances**: In the context of IBM Cloud SSO, a service instance represents an isolated environment that stores the configuration, users, and applications associated with a specific SSO service.

- **IBM Cloud Identity**: IBM Cloud Identity is a core component of the IBM SSO service. It provides the user repository and authentication services required to implement SSO.

- **Applications**: Applications are the services and tools that users need to access. In IBM Cloud SSO, administrators define and configure the applications that users can access.

Working with IBM Cloud SSO

To implement SSO with IBM Cloud, administrators start by creating an instance of the SSO service in IBM Cloud. This service instance can be configured with a range of identity sources, including IBM Cloud Identity, an on-premises **Lightweight Directory Access Protocol** (**LDAP**) directory, or a third-party IdP.

Once the identity source is configured, administrators define the applications that users can access through SSO. These applications can include both IBM Cloud services and external applications that support SAML 2.0 or OpenID Connect.

With SSO configured, users can log in once to IBM Cloud and then access any of their assigned applications without having to reauthenticate.

IBM Cloud SSO security best practices

The following are the key best practices:

- **Use MFA**: Enable MFA in IBM Cloud Identity for an additional layer of security during the authentication process.

- **Least privilege access**: Assign users only the permissions they need to perform their tasks.

- **Monitor sign-in activity**: Use IBM Cloud Activity Tracker to monitor sign-in activity and identify any unusual behavior.

- **Regularly review access**: Regularly review and update access rights to ensure they are still appropriate for each user.

IBM Cloud SSO provides a straightforward, secure method for users to access their cloud applications. It simplifies identity management and enhances security by reducing the risk of password-related security breaches.

In the next sections, we will discuss SSO in IBM. Keep going and remember to reflect on these concepts and consider how they would apply in real-world scenarios.

Consider this exercise: As an administrator for a company using IBM Cloud, how would you setup SSO to streamline access for your users? What security measures would you put in place to protect your users' identities and access?

Single sign-on in GCP

SSO is a feature that allows users to use one set of login credentials (such as a username and password) to access multiple applications. The service authenticates the end user for all the applications the user has been given rights to and eliminates further prompts when the user switches applications during the same session. In GCP, this capability is provided by Google Workspace (formerly known as **G Suite**) SSO and Cloud Identity.

Understanding Google Workspace SSO

Google Workspace SSO is designed to authenticate users, allowing them to access several services, like GCP Console, Cloud Storage, Compute Engine, and more, without needing to log in separately to each one. This simplifies the login process for end users and can help improve security around user authentication.

The following are the key concepts in Google Workspace SSO:

- **Google Workspace identity**: A Google Workspace identity refers to a user account that exists in a Google Workspace domain. This identity can be used to access Google services, including GCP resources.

- **SSO profile**: A Google Workspace SSO profile specifies the SSO configuration for a user or a group of users, including the IdP's URLs and certificate.

- **Service provider**: A service provider is a URL that hosts the application, which users will be redirected to after authentication.

- **IdP**: An IdP is a trusted provider that lets you use SSO to access other websites.

Working with Google Workspace SSO

To use Google Workspace SSO, an administrator configures the Google Workspace domain to integrate with a third-party IdP. Once configured, users can access GCP resources using their Google Workspace identity.

In the case of a third-party application, users are redirected to an external IdP, where they authenticate using their enterprise credentials. After successful authentication, they are redirected back to the application with an SSO token.

Google Workspace SSO supports both SAML-based and OpenID Connect-based authentication, providing flexibility to businesses in choosing their preferred identity solution.

Security best practices for Google Workspace SSO

The following are the key best practices:

- **Enable MFA**: Enable MFA for additional security.

- **Regular audit**: Regularly review and monitor the list of applications that are enabled for SSO.

- **Session timeout**: Configure the session timeout to automatically log out users after a period of inactivity.

- **Encryption**: Always use encryption for data communication.

SSO in GCP, managed via Google Workspace, provides a straightforward, secure way for users to gain access to GCP resources. It not only reduces the burden of password management but also enhances the security posture of an organization.

In the following section, we will discuss security configurations for IAM and SSO in different platforms, starting with AWS. Keep learning and remember to think about how these concepts would apply in real-world scenarios.

Before moving forward, consider this exercise: If you were a security admin at a company using GCP, how would you setup SSO to ensure secure and efficient access to cloud resources for your team members? How would you balance convenience and security?

Security configurations for IAM and SSO in AWS

Follow the given steps to secure AWS IAM:

1. **Create individual IAM users**: In your AWS Management Console, navigate to the IAM service. Here, go to the **Users** section and select **Add user**. Provide a username and select the access type—programmatic access, AWS Management Console access, or both. For console access, you can auto-generate a password or create a custom one.

2. **Grant least privilege access**: In the **Set permissions** section, attach existing policies directly for users if the policy you want to attach already exists. If not, create a new one by choosing **Create policy**. Use the policy generator to select permissions. Remember, only give the necessary permissions to perform the required job functions.

3. **Use IAM groups**: For managing multiple users, it is easier to create IAM groups. You can create a group in the IAM console under the **User groups** section. Click **Create new group**, name your group, and attach the necessary policies to this group. Then, add users to this group.

4. **Enable MFA**: MFA adds a layer of security to your AWS account. Go to the **Security credentials** tab of the user details in the IAM console. Here, under the **Assigned MFA device**, select **Manage**. You can then add a virtual MFA device or a hardware one. Follow the prompts to activate the MFA.

The following are the steps to secure AWS SSO:

1. **Setup AWS SSO**: First, you need to setup AWS SSO. From the AWS SSO console, you can choose your identity source. The options available are AWS Managed Microsoft AD, an existing Microsoft AD, or an external IdP.

2. **Assign users and groups**: Next, assign your users and groups. You can manage SSO access and permissions across your AWS accounts. To do this, you create permission sets, which are similar to IAM roles. These permission sets will define access for the users.

3. **Use AWS SSO permission sets**: You can create custom policies within permission sets to define access for your users. Alternatively, use AWS managed policies if they suit your requirements.

4. **Enable MFA for SSO**: To increase security, navigate to your AWS SSO settings and enforce MFA for all users. This can often be found in the **Security** section.

5. **Regularly review and update permissions**: AWS recommends regularly reviewing the permissions you have assigned. You can use AWS CloudTrail to monitor activity and keep permissions up to date. Make sure you always follow the principle of least privilege.

Remember, IAM and SSO are vital for securing access to your resources in AWS. Regular review and adherence to AWS security best practices will help ensure the integrity of your infrastructure.

Exercise: Setup a new user and assign it to a group with specific policies. Enable MFA for this user. Reflect on how these steps can help improve your AWS account's security.

Up next, we will be delving into security configurations for IAM and SSO in Azure, IBM, and GCP.

Security configurations for IAM and SSO in Azure

Microsoft Azure provides comprehensive solutions for IAM and SSO through Azure AD. Configuring these services properly is key to maintaining a secure and efficient environment in Azure.

Follow the given steps to secure Azure IAM and SSO:

1. **Create Azure AD users and groups**: In the Azure portal, navigate to the Azure AD section. Here, you can add new users and groups under the **Users and Groups** section, respectively. Provide the necessary details for each user and group.

2. **Assign roles to users/groups**: Azure offers various built-in roles such as Owner, Contributor, Reader, etc. Assign these roles to users or groups based on their responsibilities. This can be done by navigating to the **Access control (IAM)** section of any resource and then adding a role assignment.

3. **Practice least privilege access**: Make sure to follow the principle of least privilege while assigning roles. Users should be given the minimum levels of access they need to perform their functions. This reduces the risk of unauthorized access to resources.

4. **Enable MFA**: You can enable MFA for users to add an additional layer of security. This can be done in the **Security** section of Azure AD.

Follow the given steps for Azure SSO security configuration:

1. **Configure Azure AD for SSO**: To setup SSO, first, you need to configure Azure AD. This involves adding and verifying a custom domain that matches the domain used for your company's user accounts.

2. **Setup SSO for applications**: Azure AD allows you to setup SSO for thousands of pre-integrated applications. In Azure AD, you can go to enterprise applications, select the desired application, and then setup SSO.

3. **Assign users/groups to the application**: After setting up SSO for an application, you need to assign users or groups to the application. This can be done under the **Users and Groups** section of the specific application in Azure AD.

4. **Enable Azure AD Conditional Access**: Azure AD Conditional Access allows you to implement automated access control decisions based on certain conditions for accessing your cloud apps. This can be done in the **Security** section of Azure AD.

Remember, maintaining security in Azure involves continuous monitoring and management of access permissions. Regularly review your IAM and SSO configurations, keep your permissions up to date, and always follow the principle of least privilege.

Exercise: Try setting up a new user and assigning a role to the user. Enable MFA for this user. Then, setup SSO for an application and assign the user to the application. Review how these steps can enhance your Azure account's security.

Next, we will discuss the security configurations for IAM and SSO in IBM and GCP. Keep going, you are doing great!

Security configurations for IAM and SSO in IBM

IBM Cloud uses IBM Cloud IAM for authentication, authorization, and access control. IBM Cloud also provides an SSO service that enables users to log in once and then switch between applications without needing to log in again.

Let us explore how to secure IAM and SSO configurations in IBM Cloud:

1. **Create IBM Cloud IAM users**: To create new users, navigate to the **Manage** menu and then to **Access (IAM)** in the IBM Cloud console. Here, you can add new users and provide the necessary details for each user.

2. **Assign access policies to users**: IBM Cloud IAM allows you to assign users permissions to access resources within the account. You can create access policies for each user by specifying the service, role (like Manager, Viewer, Operator), and resource instance.

3. **Practice the principle of least privilege**: Assign only the permissions needed for a user to perform their tasks, following the principle of least privilege. This approach minimizes potential damage from accidents or misuse of permissions.

4. **Enable MFA**: For extra security, enable MFA in the **Security** section under **Manage**. This adds an extra layer of protection by requiring users to verify their identity using a second factor, such as a phone or hardware token, in addition to their password.

The following are the steps to secure IBM Cloud SSO:

1. **Setup IBM Cloud SSO**: First, you need to create an IBM Cloud SSO instance. This can be done from the IBM Cloud catalog. Once created, you can configure your identity sources, such as LDAP or SAML.

2. **Assign users to applications**: Within the SSO instance, navigate to the **Applications** tab and add applications to the instance. Once an application is added, you can assign users or groups to the application.

3. **Configure access policies**: For each application, you can define access policies based on user or group, IP range, device type, and other factors. These policies can help control who can access what within your applications.

4. **Enable MFA**: You can enforce MFA at the application level in IBM Cloud SSO. This can be done under the application's settings in the SSO instance. By enabling MFA, you add another level of protection for your applications.

Security is a continuous process, so you should regularly review your IAM and SSO settings, keep permissions up to date, and always adhere to the principle of least privilege.

Exercise: Setup a new user with specific access permissions and enable MFA for that user. Create an SSO instance, add an application, and assign the new user to that application. Reflect on how these steps can enhance the security of your IBM Cloud environment.

Next, we will delve into the security configurations for IAM and SSO in GCP.

Security configurations for IAM and SSO in GCP

GCP offers IAM and SSO services to help administrators authorize who can take action on specific resources. Here is a step-by-step guide to secure IAM and SSO in GCP:

1. **Create GCP IAM users**: Create users in Google Workspace or Cloud Identity. Google Workspace is more suitable for businesses that require additional productivity tools like Gmail, Google Docs, etc. Cloud Identity is a standalone service that only provides identity services.

2. **Assign roles to users**: GCP offers predefined roles that give granular access to GCP resources. You can also create custom roles. Roles can be assigned to users, groups, or service accounts at the organization, folder, or project level.

3. **Practice the principle of least privilege**: Assign the minimum level of access necessary for users to perform their tasks.

4. **Use service accounts for applications**: Service accounts provide an identity for services running on your GCP resources. Using service accounts rather than user accounts for applications is a best practice for maintaining security.

The following are the steps for GCP SSO security configuration:

1. **Setup SSO**: SSO is setup by default for Google Workspace and Cloud Identity. Users can use their Google Workspace or Cloud Identity credentials to sign in to SSO-enabled applications.

2. **Configure SSO for third-party applications**: SSO can be configured for third-party applications by creating an SSO app and configuring SAML settings. The third-party application should support SAML 2.0.

3. **Assign users to the application**: After setting up SSO for an application, users or groups can be assigned to the application. This can be done from the admin console under the **Apps** section.

4. **Enable context-aware access**: Context-aware access allows you to enforce granular access controls based on a user's identity and the context of their request. This can be setup from the admin console under **Security** settings.

Remember, maintaining security in GCP involves continuous monitoring and management of access permissions. Regularly review your IAM and SSO configurations, keep your permissions up to date, and always follow the principle of least privilege.

Exercise: Try setting up a new user and assigning a role to the user. Setup SSO for a third-party application and assign the user to the application. Review how these steps can enhance your GCP account's security.

You have now learned about securing IAM and SSO configurations in AWS, Azure, IBM Cloud, and GCP. By understanding these concepts, you are now equipped to manage identity and access across a range of cloud platforms.

Illustration

Consider a company named *Tech Corp.* that has its infrastructure spread across AWS, Azure, GCP, and IBM Cloud. To manage their resources efficiently and securely, they implement IAM and SSO across all these platforms. By following the principle of least privilege, they assign only necessary permissions to users based on their job functions. They also utilize SSO to simplify their user experience, enabling employees to switch between applications without logging in multiple times.

Case study

Foodie Corp., a multinational food delivery company, recently migrated to a multi-cloud infrastructure using AWS, Azure, and GCP. They faced a challenge in managing the access rights of their employees and ensuring a seamless login experience across multiple applications. By implementing IAM and SSO, they were able to manage and monitor their resource access efficiently. They followed the principle of least privilege for role assignment and enabled MFA for additional security. By configuring SSO for their applications, they reduced login fatigue and improved their employees' user experience.

Conclusion

In this chapter, we explored the concepts of IAM and SSO in four major cloud platforms: AWS, Microsoft Azure, IBM Cloud, and GCP. We learned how to configure IAM and SSO securely, the best practices for role assignment, and the importance of practicing the principle of least privilege. We also learned how to enable MFA and how to configure SSO for third-party applications.

In the next chapter, we will be focusing on three essential components of cloud security: Monitoring security, applying encryption, and preparing/testing security configurations across four major cloud platforms: AWS, Microsoft Azure, IBM Cloud, and GCP, with a focus on both native and non-native tools.

Key takeaways

- IAM is central to cloud security, providing the framework for defining who can access what resources and under what conditions across cloud platforms.

- SSO enhances user convenience and reduces credential sprawl by allowing users to access multiple services with a single set of login credentials.

- All four major cloud platforms, AWS, Azure, IBM Cloud, and GCP, offer robust IAM and SSO capabilities, including support for **role-based access control (RBAC)**, **multi-factor authentication (MFA)**, and identity federation.

- AWS IAM enables fine-grained policies using JSON-based permissions, roles, and policies.

- Azure Active Directory provides tight integration with Microsoft services and strong SSO features across enterprise applications.

- IBM Cloud IAM supports federated identity management and integrates with IBM Verify for enhanced authentication.

- Google Cloud IAM uses predefined roles, custom roles, and service accounts to manage access, and supports **Identity-Aware Proxy (IAP)** for Zero Trust.

- Implementing least privilege principles and regularly reviewing IAM roles and policies is essential for minimizing security risks.

- Federation and external identity provider integration allow centralized identity control across multiple cloud services and organizations.

- A well-configured IAM and SSO setup strengthens your cloud security posture and simplifies compliance with enterprise policies and industry regulations.

Key terms

- **AWS**: Amazon's cloud computing platform provides a mix of **infrastructure as a service (IaaS)**, **platform as a service (PaaS)**, and packaged **software as a service (SaaS)** offering.

- **Azure:** Microsoft's public cloud computing platform, offering solutions including IaaS, PaaS, and SaaS.

- **GCP**: Google Cloud service, which provides computing resources for deploying and running applications and services.

- **IAM**: A system for defining and controlling the permissions of individual users and the circumstances under which users are (or are not) allowed to access a network or its resources.

- **Virtual private cloud (VPC)**: A cloud-based network used to partition resources within the public cloud, which can be securely linked to a private network.

- **CMEK**: A mechanism allowing users to manage their encryption keys in cloud environments, particularly in GCP.

- **Encryption**: The process of converting data into a code to prevent unauthorized access.

- **Azure Monitor**: Azure's comprehensive solution for collecting, analyzing, and acting on telemetry data from cloud and on-premises environments.

- **Google Cloud Security Scanner**: A web application security scanner for applications running in Google App Engine, it looks for vulnerabilities like **cross-site scripting (XSS)**, flash injection, mixed content, and outdated/insecure libraries.

- **Security Command Center**: A service in GCP that provides insights into the security posture of the data and applications.

- **Penetration testing**: Authorized simulated cyberattacks on a computer system, meant to evaluate the security of a system.

- **RBAC**: A system where individual access to a system is determined based on roles within an organization. Specific permissions are assigned to specific roles.

- **S3**: An AWS service that offers scalable object storage for data backup, archival, and analytics.

- **API**: A set of tools and protocols that allow different software applications to communicate with each other.

- **VPC Service Controls**: In GCP, they provide perimeter protection for sensitive data in GCP services.

Solved exercises

1. **Which GCP service allows you to control who has access to which resources in your cloud environment?**

   Answer: GCP IAM service.

2. **What is the purpose of VPC in GCP?**

   Answer: It is used to define private IP address ranges, create subnets, configure routing, and control inbound and outbound traffic.

3. **By default, how does GCP handle data encryption for data stored at rest?**

   Answer: GCP encrypts customer data stored at rest by default.

4. **What is CMEK in the context of GCP encryption?**

   Answer: Customer-managed encryption keys.

5. **In AWS, what is the service primarily used for creating and managing access keys?**

   Answer: AWS IAM.

6. **Which Azure service helps users monitor, maintain, and manage resources in the cloud?**

   Answer: Azure Monitor.

7. **For which cloud platform is Google Cloud Security Scanner specifically designed?**

   Answer: GCP.

8. **What does VPC stand for in the context of cloud network security?**

   Answer: Virtual private cloud.

9. **Which cloud platform offers a Security Command Center for gaining visibility into the security posture?**

   Answer: GCP.

10. **If an organization wants to use its encryption keys in GCP, what feature would they utilize?**

    Answer: CMEK.

Unsolved exercises

1. What is the primary difference between the default encryption provided by GCP and CMEK?

2. Which AWS service provides detailed insights into the behavior of your resources to help maintain application health and detect anomalous behavior?

3. In Azure, what is the service that aids in providing a unified security management system?

4. Name a GCP tool used for logging, monitoring, and alerting.

5. Which cloud platform provides VPC Service Controls for securing APIs and services?

6. How can an organization restrict access to a specific AWS S3 bucket so that only certain IAM users can access it?

7. In the context of Azure's IAM, what is the significance of RBAC?

8. What is the purpose of penetration testing in a cloud environment?

9. Which service in GCP would you use if you want to d   efine private IP address ranges and create subnets?

10. If a company wants to monitor API calls in their AWS environment, which AWS service should they utilize?

Join our Discord space

Join our Discord workspace for latest updates, offers, tech happenings around the world, new releases, and sessions with the authors:

https://discord.bpbonline.com

CHAPTER 8

Monitoring, Applying Encryption, and Preparation/Testing

Introduction

In the evolving world of technology, security plays a crucial role in cloud computing environment. This chapter focuses on three essential components of cloud security: Monitoring security, applying encryption, and preparing/testing security configurations across four major cloud platforms: **Amazon Web Services (AWS)**, **Microsoft Azure**, **IBM Cloud**, and **Google Cloud Platform (GCP)** with a focus on both native and non-native tools.

Structure

The chapter covers the following topics:

- Monitoring cloud security in AWS
- Monitoring cloud security in Azure
- Monitoring cloud security in IBM Cloud
- Monitoring cloud security in GCP
- Applying encryption in AWS
- Applying encryption in Azure
- Applying encryption in IBM Cloud

- Applying encryption in GCP
- Preparation/testing the security configurations in AWS
- Preparation/testing the security configurations in Azure
- Preparation/testing the security configurations in IBM Cloud
- Preparation/testing the security configurations in GCP
- Case study

Objectives

By the end of this chapter, you will understand the importance of continuous monitoring and encryption in cloud security. You will be able to differentiate between native and non-native tools for cloud security monitoring and gain practical knowledge of applying and managing encryption in different cloud platforms. Also, you will learn how to prepare and test security configurations to ensure the robustness of your cloud infrastructure.

Prerequisites

Readers should have a basic understanding of cloud computing and cloud security concepts. Familiarity with the four cloud platforms (AWS, Azure, IBM Cloud, and GCP) is beneficial but not necessary, as the chapter will provide a step-by-step guide to implementing the discussed topics on each platform.

Monitoring cloud security in AWS

Monitoring is crucial to maintaining a strong security posture in the cloud, allowing you to detect unusual or unauthorized activities and conditions at a moment's notice. When it comes to AWS, there is a myriad of both native and non-native tools available that are specialized for diverse monitoring needs.

Native tools for monitoring security in AWS

The following are the native tools for monitoring security in AWS:

- **AWS CloudWatch**: This is a built-in monitoring service for AWS resources and applications. CloudWatch collects and tracks metrics, collects and monitors log files, sets alarms, and automatically reacts to changes in your AWS resources.

- **AWS GuardDuty**: This threat detection service continuously monitors malicious activity and unauthorized behavior to protect your AWS accounts and workloads. GuardDuty uses **machine learning (ML)**, anomaly detection, and integrated threat intelligence to identify and prioritize potential threats.

- **AWS Security Hub**: It provides a comprehensive view of the security state of your AWS resources. Security Hub collects security data from various AWS services, such as threat detection findings from GuardDuty and compliance status from AWS Config.

- **AWS Config**: This service provides an inventory of AWS resources and uses rules to evaluate the configuration settings for compliance. Config tracks changes to the configuration over time, enabling security analysis, resource tracking, and compliance auditing.

Non-native tools for monitoring security in AWS

While AWS native tools offer a wide array of security monitoring capabilities, some organizations might prefer or require additional capabilities that are found in non-native tools. Some examples are given as follows:

- **Splunk**: Splunk can ingest and analyze data from various AWS services, offering additional insights and dashboards to visualize your security posture. It can also correlate data across multiple sources, highlighting potentially malicious activity.

- **Datadog**: It is a monitoring service for cloud-scale applications that provides monitoring of servers, databases, tools, and services through a **software as a service (SaaS)** based data analytics platform.

- **Sumo Logic**: This tool provides real-time data insights through dashboards, analytics, and ML capabilities, enabling continuous intelligence for AWS environments.

To choose the right tools, you will need to assess your organizational needs, the complexity of your AWS environment, your budget, and the skills of your security and operations teams. The key to effective security monitoring in AWS (or any cloud environment) is selecting and correctly implementing the tools that provide the visibility and alerting necessary to maintain your security posture.

Monitoring cloud security in Azure

Ensuring the security of cloud environments is vital in today's digital world. In Azure, there are numerous native and non-native tools available to monitor your security posture efficiently.

Native tools for monitoring security in Azure

The following are the native tools for monitoring security in Azure:

- **Azure Monitor**: It maximizes the availability and performance of applications and services by delivering a comprehensive solution for collecting, analyzing, and acting on telemetry from your cloud and on-premises environments. It helps you understand how applications are performing and proactively identifies issues affecting them and the resources they depend on.

- **Azure Security Center**: It provides unified security management and advanced threat protection across hybrid cloud workloads. It allows you to prevent, detect, and respond to threats with increased visibility and control over the security of your Azure resources.

- **Azure Sentinel**: A scalable, cloud-native, **security information and event management (SIEM)** and **security orchestration and automation response (SOAR)** solution. Azure Sentinel delivers intelligent security analytics and threat intelligence across the enterprise, providing a single solution for alert detection, threat visibility, proactive hunting, and threat response.

Non-native tools for monitoring security in Azure

While native tools offer extensive coverage, some organizations might prefer the additional capabilities of non-native tools. The following are some examples:

- **Splunk**: This can ingest and analyze data from various Azure services, providing additional insights and visualization options for understanding your security posture. It can also correlate data from different sources, highlighting potentially malicious activity.

- **Datadog**: A monitoring and analytics platform that can be integrated with Azure. It allows you to view infrastructure metrics, traces, and logs in one place, providing a consolidated view of your cloud environment.

- **Check Point CloudGuard**: This platform offers threat prevention security, compliance, and governance for Azure environments. It offers features such as a firewall, IPS, antivirus, and more for Azure.

In short, the optimal monitoring approach in Azure will depend on several factors, including the complexity of your environment, budget, and the skills of your team. It is essential to choose the tools that align best with your organization's needs, ensuring that you have the necessary visibility and alerting capabilities to maintain a robust security posture.

Monitoring cloud security in IBM Cloud

In IBM Cloud, there are a variety of native and non-native tools that you can use to enhance the security monitoring of your cloud environment.

Native tools for monitoring security in IBM Cloud

The following are the native tools for monitoring security in IBM Cloud:

- **IBM Cloud Activity Tracker**: This records user-initiated activities that change the state of a service in IBM Cloud. This includes **application programming interface (API)** calls, **command line interface (CLI)** commands, and platform events, which can be used to detect unusual or unauthorized activities.

- **IBM Cloud Security Advisor**: This is a centralized dashboard that provides insights into your application and network security. It aggregates, correlates, and visualizes security data from multiple sources, including IBM Cloud services and third-party tools.

- **IBM QRadar on Cloud**: This SIEM system on the IBM Cloud helps security teams accurately detect and prioritize threats across the enterprise. It consolidates log events and network flow data from thousands of devices, endpoints, and applications.

Non-native tools for monitoring security in IBM Cloud

Several third-party tools can also be utilized to monitor IBM Cloud; some of them are explained as follows:

- **Splunk**: A data analytics tool that can be used to analyze security data in real-time. It can be integrated with IBM Cloud to analyze and visualize logs and metrics, thereby enhancing security monitoring.

- **Nagios**: An open-source tool that provides monitoring and alerting services for servers, switches, applications, and services. It alerts users when things go wrong and alerts them again when the problem has been resolved.

- **Tenable.io**: Tenable.io provides a cloud-based vulnerability management platform. It can be integrated with IBM Cloud to discover assets, assess them for vulnerabilities, and provide analytics and visualizations to understand the risks they pose.

Remember, the choice between native and non-native tools will largely depend on your organization's needs and the specific requirements of your workload. Combining both might be the optimal solution to cover all bases, providing comprehensive monitoring for your IBM Cloud environment.

Monitoring cloud security in GCP

GCP offers a wide variety of native and non-native tools for enhancing the monitoring of your cloud environment's security.

Native tools for monitoring security in GCP

Google Cloud provides a range of built-in tools to monitor and enhance security across cloud environments. These native tools enable real-time monitoring, logging, and threat detection, ensuring compliance and robust security postures for cloud-based applications and infrastructure:

- **Google Cloud Operations Suite (formerly Stackdriver):** The Google Cloud Operations Suite is an integrated monitoring, logging, and diagnostics suite that assists in gaining insight into applications running on Google Cloud. It includes features such as error reporting, tracing, and debugging, and it can be used for both real-time monitoring and historical analysis. It integrates with Cloud Monitoring, Cloud Logging, and Cloud Trace to provide full-stack observability.

- **Google Cloud Security Command Center (Cloud SCC):** Cloud SCC is the canonical security and data risk database for GCP. It helps you prevent, detect, and respond to threats from a single pane of glass. It provides asset inventory, discovery, search, and management. Additionally, it integrates with security services such as Google Security Health Analytics, Event Threat Detection, and Container Threat Detection to identify vulnerabilities in applications, misconfigurations, and active threats in workloads.

- **Google Cloud Audit Logs**: Cloud Audit Logs maintain a record of administrative activities in your Google Cloud environment. They help answer the who did what, where, and when? questions within your GCP projects. It categorizes logs into different types, such as Admin Activity logs, Data Access logs, System Event logs, and Policy Denied logs, providing granular visibility into security-related actions.

- **Google Cloud Identity-Aware Proxy** (IAP): IAP helps secure applications and **virtual machines** (**VMs**) by providing identity verification and access control for cloud resources. It ensures that only authorized users and devices can access sensitive applications and services.

- **Google Cloud Forseti Security**: Forseti is an open-source security toolkit for GCP that provides continuous security monitoring and auditing capabilities. It includes policy enforcement, role-based access reviews, firewall rule analysis, and compliance monitoring.

- **Google Cloud Security Posture Management** (CSPM): CSPM tool enables organizations to enforce security best practices and compliance across their GCP environment. It scans resources for misconfigurations and ensures adherence to industry standards such as CIS Benchmarks and ISO 27001 compliance.

- **Google Cloud Threat Intelligence**: Chronicle is a security analytics platform built for large-scale security event analysis. It enables organizations to investigate, detect, and analyze security incidents across cloud and hybrid environments.

- **Google Cloud Data Loss Prevention** (**Cloud DLP**): Cloud DLP helps identify and protect sensitive data within cloud storage, BigQuery, and other GCP services. It detects **personally identifiable information** (**PII**), financial data, and other sensitive information while enforcing security policies.

By leveraging these native tools, organizations can ensure continuous security monitoring, detect and respond to threats proactively, and maintain compliance within the GCP ecosystem.

Non-native tools for monitoring security in GCP

Third-party tools can also provide added security monitoring capabilities in GCP, such as:

- **Splunk**: A popular data analytics tool that can be integrated with GCP to analyze logs and metrics in real-time, providing valuable security insights.

- **Datadog**: A comprehensive monitoring service for cloud-scale applications, providing monitoring of servers, databases, tools, and services through a SaaS-based data analytics platform.

- **Sumo Logic**: This provides advanced cloud log analytics and monitoring and can be integrated with GCP for real-time machine data analytics.

It is important to note that the choice of tools will depend on your organization's specific needs and the requirements of your workload. A combination of native and non-native tools might be ideal to provide a complete and comprehensive monitoring solution for your GCP environment.

Applying encryption in AWS

This section provides a detailed guide on applying encryption in AWS using AWS **Key Management Service** (**KMS**). This is a managed service that makes it easy for you to create and control the encryption keys used to encrypt your data. The steps for applying encryption are as follows:

1. **Sign in to the AWS Management Console**: You need to log in to your AWS Management Console. Make sure you are using an account with the necessary permissions to work with KMS.

2. **Navigate to AWS KMS**: Once you are signed in, navigate to the AWS KMS page.

3. **Create a key**: On the KMS dashboard, select **Customer managed keys**. Click **Create key**.

4. **Configure the key**: You will be taken to a new page where you will setup your new key:

   a. **Alias**: Enter a unique alias for your key. The alias helps you identify the key in lists and drop-down menus.

b. **Advanced options**: KMS keys are regional, but you can choose to make them replicable across regions. The key material origin should be KMS.

c. **Description**: Add an optional description for your key.

d. Click **Next** when finished.

5. **Define key administrative permissions**: Here, you need to select IAM users or roles that have permissions to administer this key (but not use it). Choose from the list and then click **Next**.

6. **Define key usage permissions**: Define who can use this key to encrypt and decrypt data. You may want to give this permission to the roles your applications run under or to specific users responsible for managing data.

7. **Review and finish**: Review your choices and then click **Finish** to create your key. Your new key is now available to use to encrypt and decrypt data.

8. **Use the key for encryption and decryption**: Now, you can use your key for various AWS services that integrate with KMS. For example, you can configure an S3 bucket to automatically encrypt objects when they are stored and decrypt them when they are retrieved using your KMS key. To do this, go to your S3 bucket, navigate to **Properties | Default encryption**, select **AWS-KMS**, and choose the key you just created.

Remember, each AWS service that integrates with KMS has a slightly different process for implementing KMS encryption, so make sure to refer to the specific documentation for each service.

> **Note:** **Managing encryption keys is a critical and sensitive process. Make sure to implement appropriate policies and procedures to control access to your keys. Also note that while encryption helps enhance the security of your data, it is only one aspect of a comprehensive security strategy. Be sure to implement other security measures, such as secure access controls, regular audits of your security configuration, and continuous monitoring of security events.**

Encryption is a critical part of data security, and AWS offers various encryption services to ensure that data is protected in transit and at rest. The following is a detailed look at how to apply encryption in AWS:

1. **Data in transit encryption**: Encryption in transit refers to protecting data while it is being transferred between systems. AWS provides several mechanisms to ensure the protection of data in transit.

a. **AWS Certificate Manager (ACM)**: ACM is a service that simplifies the process of obtaining, managing, and deploying public and private **Secure Sockets Layer/Transport Layer Security (SSL/TLS)** certificates for use with AWS services. SSL/TLS certificates are used to secure network communications and establish the identity of websites over the internet.

b. **AWS virtual private network (VPN)**: VPN connections can be used to establish secure and private sessions with IP networks.

2. **Data at rest encryption**: Encryption at rest is a data protection method that involves encrypting data while it is stored.

a. **AWS KMS**: This allows you to create and manage cryptographic keys and control their use across a wide range of AWS services. It ensures that data at rest is stored in an encrypted form.

b. **AWS Secrets Manager**: Secrets Manager is a secrets management service that enables IT admins to easily rotate, manage, and retrieve database credentials, API keys, and other secrets throughout their lifecycle.

c. **AWS S3 server-side encryption (SSE)**: For data stored in S3 buckets, AWS provides SSE. When you upload an object, Amazon S3 automatically encrypts it. When you access the object, Amazon S3 decrypts it for you. The decryption process is transparent to the end user.

d. **AWS EBS and Amazon RDS**: Also offer options for at-rest encryption. For instance, all EBS volume types support encryption at rest when attached to EC2 instances that support EBS encryption.

3. **Database encryption**:

a. **Amazon RDS**: Amazon RDS supports the use of AWS KMS for encryption at rest and SSL/TLS for encryption in transit.

b. **Amazon DynamoDB**: DynamoDB provides features to encrypt at rest all customer data stored in tables. The encryption at rest includes DynamoDB primary keys and all the attributes for a table.

c. **Amazon Redshift**: It supports the ability to encrypt data at rest and data in transit.

Remember, the correct implementation of encryption is crucial to maintaining the security and integrity of your data. Different AWS services offer unique encryption capabilities that can be tailored to specific security requirements. Make sure to understand these options and leverage them effectively to secure your data.

Applying encryption in Azure

The steps to apply encryption to a VM disk in Microsoft Azure using **Azure Disk Encryption (ADE)** are given as follows:

1. **Sign in to the Azure portal**: First, you need to log in to your Azure portal. Make sure you have the necessary permissions to work with ADE and Key Vault.

2. **Create a Key Vault**: Navigate to the Key Vault service and create a new Key Vault as follows:

    a. **Subscription**: Choose the Azure subscription that you want to use.

    b. **Resource group**: Select or create a resource group.

    c. **Key vault name**: Enter a unique name for the key vault.

    d. **Region**: Choose a region for your key vault.

    e. Click **Review + Create** when finished, and **Create** on the following screen to finalize the creation of the key vault.

3. **Create a key**: Once the Key Vault is created, open the vault and navigate to **Keys**. Click **Generate/Import**. Fill in the form to generate a key.

4. **Set Key Vault advanced access policy**: For ADE to work, you have to allow the Azure platform to access the key vault. Navigate to **Access policies** in the key vault settings and check the box for **Enable access to ADE for volume encryption**.

5. **Enable disk encryption**: Navigate to the VM you want to encrypt. In the VM's settings, find disk encryption. In the disk encryption type, select the appropriate encryption method.

   Then, choose the key vault and key you created earlier and click **Save**.

6. **Validate the encryption**: To validate the encryption status, navigate to **Disks** in the VM settings. The encryption status should now say **Enabled**.

Remember, you can perform these steps on both Linux and Windows VMs. Also, be aware that applying encryption can take a while, depending on the size of your VM's disk. Always follow best practices when working with encryption to ensure the security and integrity of your data.

> **Note:** ADE leverages the BitLocker feature of Windows and the dm-crypt feature of Linux to provide volume encryption for the operating system and the data disks. Also, be sure to implement other security measures in addition to encryption, such as secure access controls, regular audits of your security configuration, and continuous monitoring for security events.

Microsoft Azure provides various ways to implement encryption to protect and secure your data. The following are the key strategies for applying encryption in Azure:

1. **Data in transit encryption**: Azure offers several tools for securing data in transit:

   a. **Azure VPN Gateway**: This service allows you to send encrypted traffic between an Azure **Virtual Network** (**VNet**) and an on-premises location over the public internet.

   b. **Azure Application Gateway**: It provides SSL termination, which removes encryption/decryption overhead from the backend servers and allows them to focus on the application logic.

  c. **Azure Service Bus**: This message broker service provides secure channels for sending data between different parts of your Azure applications with TLS/SSL.

2. **Data at rest encryption**: Azure provides several services for encrypting data at rest:

  a. **Azure Storage Service Encryption**: This service automatically encrypts your data before persisting it to Azure Storage and decrypts it before retrieval. The handling of encryption, encryption at rest, key management, and decryption is transparent to users.

  b. **ADE**: This service leverages the BitLocker feature of Windows and the dm-crypt feature of Linux to provide volume encryption for operating system and data disks.

  c. **Azure SQL Database transparent data encryption**: This encrypts SQL Server, Azure SQL Database, and Azure Synapse Analytics data files, known as **encrypting data at rest**. It performs real-time encryption and decryption of the database, associated backups, and transaction log files at rest without requiring changes to the application.

3. **Database encryption**:

  a. **Azure Cosmos DB**: All data stored in Azure Cosmos DB is automatically encrypted at rest using service-managed keys.

  b. **Azure SQL Database Always Encrypted**: This feature helps protect sensitive data, such as credit card numbers or national identification numbers, stored in Azure SQL Database or SQL Server databases. Always Encrypted allows clients to encrypt sensitive data inside client applications and never reveal the encryption keys to the database engine.

4. **Key management**: Key management is an important aspect of encryption, and Azure provides the following services:

  a. **Azure Key Vault**: Azure Key Vault safeguards cryptographic keys and secrets used by cloud apps and services.

  b. **Azure Managed hardware security module (HSM)**: This fully managed service provides a highly available, secure, and easy-to-use HSM service.

By properly implementing these encryption methods and managing encryption keys, you can ensure that your data remains secure while stored in Azure. Remember, the appropriate use of encryption is vital to maintaining the security and integrity of your data. Different Azure services offer unique encryption capabilities that can be tailored to specific security requirements.

Applying encryption in the IBM Cloud

IBM Cloud uses Key Protect for the IBM Cloud service to manage encryption keys for services in IBM Cloud. The steps required to create and manage encryption keys in IBM Cloud are as follows:

1. **Sign in to the IBM Cloud portal**: Log in to your IBM Cloud account. Make sure you have the necessary permissions to work with Key Protect and the services you wish to encrypt.

2. **Navigate to the Key Protect for IBM Cloud service**: In your dashboard, find the Key Protect for IBM Cloud service. If you do not already have it, you can add it from the IBM Cloud catalog.

3. **Create a Key Protect instance**: Click on the **Create instance** button to create a new Key Protect instance. Give it a name and choose your preferred region and resource group.

4. **Create a key**: Click on the **Get started** button to go to the Key Protect instance. Click on **Create a key**, and fill in the necessary details for your key, including an alias, a description (optional), and whether you want it to be a standard or root key. Then click **Create**.

5. **Use the key for encryption**: You can use your key to encrypt data or manage encryption for other IBM Cloud services. To do this, you would typically pass the key's ID or **Cloud Resource Name** (**CRN**) to the service or application you are configuring.

   The method to apply encryption to a particular service (like a database or storage bucket) depends on that service's capabilities and settings. It generally involves providing the key's CRN and setting an encryption-related configuration option.

   Remember that it is crucial to keep track of your keys and manage their access carefully. Only authorized users and applications should be able to use the keys.

6. **Monitor and manage your keys**: You can monitor the usage of your keys and manage their lifecycle through the Key Protect interface. This includes rotating keys, disabling or enabling keys, and deleting keys.

As an important note, when you delete a key from Key Protect, any data that was encrypted using that key will become unreadable and will effectively be lost unless you have another key with the same cryptographic material or a copy of the data encrypted with a different key. Be extremely careful with key deletion!

Note: **IBM Cloud uses a bring-your-own-key (BYOK) approach, which gives you full control over your encryption keys and helps to meet compliance requirements. Also note that encryption is just one part of a comprehensive security strategy. Be sure to implement other security measures in addition to encryption, such as secure access controls, regular audits of your security configuration, and continuous monitoring for security events.**

IBM Cloud offers a variety of services and features that allow you to encrypt your data and protect your information. The following are the primary methods for applying encryption in the IBM Cloud:

1. **Data in transit encryption**: IBM Cloud provides several services to secure data in transit:

   a. **IBM VPN for VPC**: This service allows the secure transfer of data between your on-premises network, other networks, and your VPC by creating an encrypted VPN connection.

   b. **IBM Cloud Direct Link**: It helps to establish private connectivity between IBM Cloud and your own data center or network, enhancing security for data in transit.

   c. **TLS/SSL certificates**: IBM Cloud provides TLS/SSL certificates, which can be used to encrypt data in transit between client and server.

2. **Data at rest encryption**: IBM Cloud offers several features to secure data at rest:

   a. **IBM Cloud Object Storage**: It encrypts data at rest by default. The encryption keys are managed by IBM Cloud, and the encryption process is transparent to the user.

   b. **IBM Key Protect**: This is a key management service that helps you manage your encryption keys for IBM Cloud services. It lets you store, generate, manage, and destroy your encryption keys, which can be used with data-at-rest encryption for IBM Cloud services.

   c. **IBM Cloud Block Storage and File Storage**: These services offer built-in encryption for data at rest, providing an added layer of data security.

3. **Database encryption**: IBM Cloud offers encryption for various database services:

   a. **IBM Cloud Databases**: All IBM Cloud Databases for PostgreSQL, Elasticsearch, Redis, etcd, RabbitMQ, MySQL, DataStax, and MongoDB automatically encrypt data at rest.

   b. **IBM Db2 on cloud**: It supports native encryption for data at rest. The database encryption is performed at the storage layer and is transparent to applications and users.

4. **Key management**: Key management is crucial to a strong encryption strategy. IBM offers services specifically designed for this task:

   a. **IBM Key Protect**: As mentioned earlier, Key Protect is a cloud-based service designed to manage encryption keys that are used in IBM Cloud services.

   b. **IBM Cloud Hyper Protect Crypto Services**: It is a key management and cloud HSM. It provides exclusive control over your key material and is designed to meet stringent regulatory requirements.

To conclude, IBM Cloud provides a number of encryption and key management services to protect your data in transit, at rest, and during processing. Implementing these encryption methods can help ensure that your data remains secure while stored in the IBM Cloud. It is important to choose the appropriate level of security and key management based on your specific use case and compliance requirements.

Applying encryption in GCP

In GCP, encryption is applied automatically to data at rest and in transit, but you can manage your encryption keys for an additional layer of control. GCP offers a service known as **Cloud KMS** to manage cryptographic keys for your cloud services.

The following are the steps to create and use your encryption keys with Cloud KMS:

1. **Sign in to the GCP Console**: Log in to your Google Cloud account. You will need appropriate permissions to work with Cloud KMS and the services you want to encrypt.

2. **Open the Cloud KMS page**: In the GCP console, go to the navigation menu (three horizontal lines in the top left corner), scroll down to the **Security** section, and click on **Key management**.

3. **Create a key ring**: Click on the **Create key ring** button. Provide a name and location for the key ring. Key rings are used to organize cryptographic keys in GCP. Click **Create** to create the key ring.

4. **Create a key**: Within the key ring you just created, click **Create key** or **Create symmetric key,** depending on your needs. Fill in the necessary details for your key, including its name and purpose (encryption or decryption). You can also set an optional rotation period and the next rotation date for the key.

5. **Use the key for encryption**: Once the key is created, it can be used to encrypt or decrypt data. The method of applying this key to a specific service will vary based on the service's capabilities and settings. Generally, it involves providing the key's resource ID and enabling an encryption-related setting.

6. **Monitor and manage your keys**: You can monitor the usage of your keys and manage their lifecycle through the Cloud KMS interface. This includes rotating keys, disabling or enabling keys, and destroying keys.

As an important note, when you destroy a key in Cloud KMS, any data that was encrypted with that key becomes unreadable. Be extremely careful with key deletion!

Note: **GCP uses a BYOK approach, which gives you full control over your encryption keys and helps to meet compliance requirements. Also, remember that encryption is just one part of a comprehensive security strategy. Be sure to implement other security measures in addition to encryption, such as secure access controls, regular audits of your security configuration, and continuous monitoring for security events.**

GCP ensures the safety and privacy of data by implementing automatic encryption at rest and in transit. Let us explore further to understand the various encryption capabilities of GCP:

1. **Data in transit encryption**: GCP ensures that data is encrypted when it is traveling from one point to another, be it over the internet, within Google Network, or even between data centers.

   a. **Google Cloud load balancer**: Supports SSL/TLS for secure data transmission.

   b. **Google Cloud VPN**: Creates an encrypted VPN tunnel between your on-premises network and your Google VPC network.

   c. **Google Cloud Interconnect**: Provides private communication between your on-premises network and your VPC network.

2. **Data at rest encryption**: GCP automatically encrypts all data before it is written to disk. Google uses several layers of encryption, depending on the type of storage and service.

   a. **Google Cloud Storage**: Each object's data and metadata are encrypted under the 256-bit **Advanced Encryption Standard** (AES).

   b. **Google Compute Engine**: Persistent Disks, SSD Persistent Disks, and snapshots are encrypted under AES-256.

   c. **Google Kubernetes Engine (GKE)**: For GKE clusters, Cloud KMS can be used to manage the keys used to encrypt and decrypt the secrets stored in etcd.

3. **Database encryption**: For data stored in various databases, Google Cloud provides automatic encryption.

   a. **Cloud SQL**: All Cloud SQL data is encrypted at rest.

   b. **Bigtable**: Bigtable data is encrypted at rest using AES0256.

   c. **Firestore**: All data in Firestore is encrypted at rest and in transit.

4. **Key Management**: Google offers several services to manage encryption keys:

   a. **Google Cloud KMS**: A fully managed service to generate, use, rotate, and destroy symmetric encryption keys for protecting sensitive data.

   b. **Cloud HSM**: A fully managed, highly available service for hosting and using your private keys in hardware security modules.

   c. **Cloud EKM**: Provides external control of your cryptographic keys used by Google Cloud resources.

   d. **Cloud Key Access Justifications**: This service provides a detailed justification each time a request is made to use your key, which gives you greater control and visibility into key use.

Overall, encryption is a core part of Google's data security. When implemented correctly, it can provide a strong line of defense against unauthorized access to your data. Always remember to apply best practices for managing and storing your encryption keys to maximize your data protection.

Preparation/testing the security configurations in AWS

Preparation and testing of security configurations in AWS involves a series of steps that focus on ensuring the correct and secure deployment of resources, as well as the readiness of your infrastructure to respond to potential security threats. These steps involve identifying potential vulnerabilities, taking steps to mitigate those vulnerabilities, and testing to ensure your defenses are adequate.

The following is a step-by-step guide to preparing and testing your security configurations in AWS:

1. **Setting up IAM roles and policies**: Ensure that your AWS account is properly configured with the least privilege access policies. Use IAM to create users, roles, and assign policies that grant only the necessary permissions.

2. **Secure your AWS resources**: Secure your AWS resources, such as EC2 instances and S3 buckets, by enabling appropriate security controls. Use security groups and **network access control lists** (**NACLs**) to control inbound and outbound traffic to your EC2 instances.

3. **Enable logging and monitoring**: Activate AWS CloudTrail to log, continuously monitor, and retain account activity related to actions across your AWS infrastructure. Also, use AWS CloudWatch to collect and track metrics and set alarms for your AWS resources.

4. **Apply encryption**: Encrypt your data at rest and in transit. Use AWS KMS to create and manage cryptographic keys and control their use across a wide range of AWS services.

5. **Configure Amazon VPC**: Use Amazon VPC to launch AWS resources in a VNet that you define. Create a VPC, setup subnets, and configure route tables and network gateways.

6. **Testing your security configuration**: Testing your security configurations is crucial. AWS provides several tools to assist you:

   a. **AWS Security Hub**: Gives you a comprehensive view of your high-priority security alerts and compliance status. It can run automated security checks based on AWS best practices.

   b. **AWS Inspector**: An automated security assessment service that helps improve the security and compliance of applications deployed on AWS.

    c. **AWS Trusted Advisor**: An online resource to help you reduce cost, increase performance, and improve security by optimizing your AWS environment.

    d. Always remember that testing is an iterative process, and the objective is to identify and address vulnerabilities in your security configurations.

7. **Regularly audit and update your security configuration**: Security needs are constantly evolving, so regular audits and updates of your security configurations are essential. You can schedule regular security audits and follow AWS security advisories and recommendations.

Remember, the idea is not only to prepare but also to continuously monitor and iterate on your security configurations, adapting to new requirements and threats as they arise. The process is not linear but cyclical.

Security testing and preparation in AWS consists of configuring security measures and validating them to ensure your data and resources are well protected. Let us walk through the process:

1. **Preparation**: Before we move into testing, we must first prepare the security configurations. This involves:

    a. **IAM**: Configure IAM users, roles, and permissions to secure access to your AWS services and resources.

    b. **Security groups and NACLs**: Configure security groups and NACLs to control inbound and outbound traffic to your instances and subnets.

    c. **VPC configurations**: Setup your VPC with the required subnet, route table, internet gateway, and NAT gateway configurations.

    d. **Encryption**: Implement encryption at rest and in transit where necessary using AWS services like KMS and ACM.

    e. **Data protection**: Enable data protection measures like enabling versioning in S3, RDS snapshots, EBS snapshots, etc.

    f. **Logging and monitoring**: Enable AWS CloudTrail for API activity monitoring, AWS Config for resource inventory, AWS CloudWatch for performance monitoring.

2. **Testing**: Once the configurations are prepared, testing should be carried out to ensure their effectiveness.

    a. **Penetration testing**: AWS allows and provides guidelines for penetration testing of your EC2 instances, RDS, CloudFront, API Gateways, Lambda, and many more to identify any vulnerabilities. Remember, you need prior approval from AWS for conducting penetration testing.

    b. **Security scanners**: Tools like AWS Inspector can be used to run automated security assessment service to help improve the security and compliance of applications deployed on AWS.

    c. **Compliance checking**: AWS Config can be used to assess, audit, and evaluate the configurations of your AWS resources. It can check for deviations from prescribed configurations, visualize compliance levels, and dive into configuration details of a resource at any point in time.

    d. **IAM Analyzer**: AWS IAM Access Analyzer helps you identify the resources in your organization and accounts, such as Amazon S3 buckets or IAM roles, that are shared with an entity outside of your account.

Remember, testing is not a one-time process but should be an integral part of your application lifecycle. The security landscape is constantly evolving, and regular testing helps to identify and remediate new vulnerabilities and ensure continuous security of your AWS environment.

Preparation/testing the security configurations in Azure

Preparing and testing security configurations in Azure involves a series of steps to ensure that your resources are deployed securely and that your infrastructure is ready to respond to potential security threats. The following is a step-by-step guide:

1. **Setup of Azure AD and RBAC**: Ensure that your Azure account is properly configured with the principle of least privilege. Use Azure AD for identity management and RBAC to assign permissions to users, groups, and applications at a certain scope.

2. **Secure your Azure resources**: Secure your Azure resources, such as VM instances and storage accounts, by enabling appropriate security controls. Use **network security groups** (**NSGs**) to control inbound and outbound traffic to your instances.

3. **Enable logging and monitoring**: Enable Azure Monitor and Azure Log Analytics to collect, analyze, and act on telemetry data from your Azure and on-premises environments.

4. **Apply encryption**: Encrypt your data at rest and in transit. Use Azure Key Vault to manage and control the cryptographic keys used for cloud-scale applications.

5. **Configure VNets**: Use Azure VNets to represent your own network in the cloud. It is a logical isolation of the Azure cloud dedicated to your subscription. Define a VNet, setup subnets, and configure route tables and network gateways.

6. **Testing your security configuration**: Testing your security configurations is crucial. Azure provides several tools to assist you:

    a. **Azure Security Center**: Provides unified security management and advanced threat protection. It can also provide a security score, which helps you understand your security posture.

    b. **Azure Advisor**: A personalized cloud consultant that helps you follow best practices to optimize your Azure deployments. It includes a security assistance feature.

7. **Regularly audit and update your security configuration**: Perform regular audits and updates of your security configurations as security needs are continually evolving. You can schedule regular security audits and follow Azure security advisories and recommendations.

Keep in mind that security in the cloud is an ongoing task. It involves regular assessment, tuning, and reiteration of your security configurations to adapt to new requirements and potential threats.

Security testing and preparation in Azure is about establishing proper security measures and verifying them to ensure that your data and resources are adequately safeguarded. The following steps provide a walk-through of this process:

1. **Preparation**: Preparing security configurations often involves several key steps, including:

    a. **IAM**: Use Azure AD to manage users and groups, setup **multi-factor authentication (MFA)**, and apply RBAC.

    b. **Network security**: Setup NSGs to manage inbound and outbound traffic to your resources, such as VMs and subnets.

    c. **Encryption**: Implement encryption at rest and in transit where needed. Azure Key Vault can be used to safeguard cryptographic keys and other secrets used by cloud apps and services.

    d. **Data protection**: Protect your data by enabling features like Azure Backup and Azure Site Recovery.

    e. **Monitoring**: Enable Azure Monitor and Log Analytics for tracking performance and logs.

2. **Testing**: After the security configurations are established, it is essential to test them to ensure they are functioning as intended:

    a. **Security Center**: Azure Security Center provides unified security management and advanced threat protection. It can assess your environment and provide recommendations to optimize your security posture.

    b. **Azure Advisor**: Azure Advisor can provide personalized recommendations based on best practices, including for security.

    c. **Compliance checking**: Azure Policy helps you manage and prevent IT issues with policy definitions that enforce rules and effects for your resources.

    d. **Penetration testing**: Azure provides guidelines for penetration testing. This can help identify potential vulnerabilities. You do not need prior approval for most testing, but some types of testing, such as DDoS, do require approval.

Remember, security testing should be ongoing, not a one-time event. Regular testing can help to detect and fix new vulnerabilities, ensuring the continuous security of your Azure environment.

Preparation/testing the security configurations in IBM Cloud

IBM Cloud has a variety of tools and services to help you prepare and test your security configurations. The following steps will guide you through some key tasks:

1. **Setup and configure IAM**: As in other cloud services, IBM Cloud uses IAM to control who has access to your resources. Assign users and groups to roles that determine what actions they can perform.

2. **Secure your IBM Cloud resources**: Secure your IBM Cloud resources such as virtual instances, containers, and databases. This may involve configuring security groups to control inbound and outbound traffic, setting up private endpoints for secure connectivity, or using secrets managers to handle sensitive data.

3. **Enable logging and monitoring**: Use IBM Cloud's monitoring and logging services to keep track of what happens in your environment. Setup alerts for suspicious activity and regularly review log data for signs of potential security issues.

4. **Apply encryption**: Protect your data at rest and in transit using encryption. IBM Cloud provides key management services that you can use to handle encryption keys.

5. **Configure VNets**: Setup VPCs and subnets to control how your resources are networked together. Apply security groups and ACLs to regulate traffic at the subnet level.

6. **Testing your security configuration**: Testing your security configurations is a crucial step to ensure that they function as expected. IBM Cloud provides several tools for this, including:

   a. **IBM Security Verify**: This tool can perform access risk assessments, giving you insight into potential vulnerabilities in your IAM setup.

   b. **IBM Cloud Security Advisor**: This service helps you understand your overall security posture and provides recommendations for improvements.

7. **Regularly audit and update your security configuration**: As with all aspects of security, maintaining your security configuration is an ongoing process. Regularly review your settings, and stay informed about new features or changes in IBM Cloud's security offerings.

Remember, security in the cloud requires a proactive approach and regular attention to changes in your environment, as well as the broader threat landscape. Regular assessment and updating of your security configurations to adapt to new requirements and threats is essential.

IBM Cloud offers a robust set of tools and services to help you prepare and test your security configurations. The following is a step-by-step guide on how to approach these tasks in IBM Cloud:

1. **Preparation**: Here are some steps to ensure the proper security setup in your IBM Cloud environment:

   a. **IAM**: With IBM Cloud IAM, you can create access policies to secure your resources. Use the principle of least privilege when assigning roles and responsibilities to your users and groups.

   b. **Network security**: IBM Cloud provides security groups and network ACLs to secure your network traffic. You can also leverage private networks to isolate your resources.

   c. **Data protection**: Use key management services and secret management services provided by IBM Cloud to handle encryption keys and secrets. Consider implementing IBM Cloud Hyper Protect Services for highly sensitive workloads.

   d. **Monitoring and logging**: Use IBM Cloud Activity Tracker with LogDNA to monitor user activity in your account. IBM Cloud Log Analysis with LogDNA can help you manage and analyze log data.

2. **Testing**: Once your security configurations are in place, you should test them:

   a. **IBM Cloud Security and Compliance Center**: This service helps you define your security posture, manage security and compliance throughout your digital transformation, and mitigate risks by using a security program that can adapt to business changes.

   b. **IBM Cloud Vulnerability Advisor**: This tool scans your instances for vulnerabilities and insecure configurations and helps to remediate them.

   c. **IBM Cloud Schematics**: Schematics uses Terraform to define and deploy your cloud resources in an automated, repeatable manner. Use this to spin up test environments and validate your security configurations.

   d. **Penetration testing**: IBM Cloud has a policy for penetration testing. Prior to conducting any penetration tests, you need to complete the penetration testing permission request form to obtain approval.

Remember that security in the cloud is an ongoing process. Regular auditing, updating of security configurations, and responding promptly to security alerts are crucial steps in maintaining a secure environment. As your organization grows and evolves, so too should your security practices.

Preparation/testing the security configurations in GCP

GCP offers numerous ways to prepare and test security configurations for your cloud environment. These range from access control to data encryption, as well as network and application security.

The following is a step-by-step guide to get you started:

1. **Setup and configure IAM**: GCP's IAM service allows you to control who has access to which resources in your environment. You can define roles with different permissions and assign them to users, groups, or service accounts.

2. **Enable security controls**: Apply security controls to your GCP resources to minimize risk. For example, use VPC Service Controls to secure your APIs and services, or use Security Command Center to gain visibility into your security posture.

3. **Configure network security**: Use VPC and firewall rules to protect your network. You can define private IP address ranges, create subnets, configure routing, and control inbound and outbound traffic.

4. **Apply encryption**: GCP encrypts customer data stored at rest by default. However, for certain types of data, you may want to manage your own encryption keys or use **customer-managed encryption keys (CMEK)**.

5. **Enable logging and monitoring**: Use Google Cloud's operations suite (formerly **Stackdriver**) for logging, monitoring, and alerting. These tools can help you detect unusual activity and troubleshoot issues.

6. **Regularly test your security configurations**: Google Cloud Web Security Scanner identifies security vulnerabilities in your Google App Engine applications. Additionally, consider performing penetration testing and vulnerability scanning. Note that some forms of testing may require authorization from Google.

7. **Keep your configurations up-to-date**: Cloud security is not a one-time task. Make sure to continuously review and update your configurations. Subscribe to GCP's security notifications to stay updated on any new features or changes.

This guide provides a general idea of preparing and testing security configurations in GCP. Keep in mind that security is a broad field, and what you need to do can vary significantly depending on the specifics of your project and your organization's requirements. Always refer to GCP's best practices and guidelines when securing your cloud environment.

GCP provides numerous tools and services to prepare and test your security configurations. Here is a detailed guide:

1. **Preparation**: Setting up a secure environment in GCP involves several steps:

    a. **IAM:** With GCP IAM, define who (identity) has what access (role) to which resource. Follow the principle of least privilege grant only necessary permissions to your resources.

    b. **Network security**: Use GCP's VPC for networking. Utilize tools such as firewall rules, Security Groups, and VPC Service Controls to secure your network traffic.

    c. **Data protection**: Google Cloud's KMS and Cloud HSM allow you to generate, use, rotate, and destroy symmetric and asymmetric cryptographic keys. Use these tools for managing encryption keys.

    d. **Monitoring and logging:** GCP's operations suite (formerly Stackdriver) provides monitoring, logging, and diagnostics. Use this to gain insight into how your application runs and troubleshoot faster.

2. **Testing**: After configuring your security setup, it is crucial to test it:

    a. **Security Command Center**: This is Google Cloud's comprehensive security and data risk platform for data and applications. Use this for gaining insights, identifying threats, and ensuring you are complying with data use policies.

    b. **Cloud Security Scanner**: Google Cloud's security scanner identifies security vulnerabilities in your Google App Engine web applications. It can automatically scan and detect four common vulnerabilities, including **cross-site scripting (XSS)**, Flash injection, mixed content (HTTP in HTTPS), and outdated/insecure libraries.

    c. **Penetration testing**: Google allows and encourages users to conduct penetration testing on their GCP environments. However, you are required to adhere to the Acceptable Use Policy and Terms of Service, and there is no need for prior approval for a wide range of testing activities.

Implementing security is a continuous process, not a one-time task. Keep reviewing your security configurations, perform regular audits, and always stay updated with the latest security practices.

This guide provides a high-level overview. Always refer to the detailed documentation provided by Google Cloud for comprehensive, up-to-date information and instructions.

Illustration

Let us imagine you have a company called *TechNova*. TechNova has recently decided to migrate its services to AWS. They have multiple teams with varied levels of access required. As a part of the migration, the TechNova team has to setup IAM for their teams, enabling encryption for their data, and having a monitoring solution to watch their AWS resources.

Case study

The TechNova team starts by reviewing the AWS security best practices. They then setup their IAM roles, use MFA for added security, and configure their VPCs. They also configure their security groups and NACLs. The TechNova team enables AWS CloudTrail, Amazon CloudWatch, and VPC Flow Logs for logging and monitoring. They also regularly audit their AWS environment using AWS Config and AWS Trusted Advisor. For encryption, they use AWS KMS. They also setup AWS Shield for DDoS protection.

For testing, the team performs penetration testing, uses AWS Inspector for automated security assessment, and employs third-party tools for assessing their security posture.

Conclusion

In this chapter, we have explored the concept of monitoring, applying encryption, and preparing/testing security configurations across different cloud platforms, including AWS, Azure, IBM, and GCP. Each of these platforms offers native tools for monitoring and encryption as well as preparation and testing of security configurations. We explored the native and non-native tools and understood how to apply encryption and prepare/test security configurations.

In the next chapter, we will be focusing on demystifying **security as code (SaC)**, emphasizing its significance and application in modern cloud-centric technology, and providing a comprehensive understanding of how security can be seamlessly integrated into the cloud infrastructure lifecycle.

Key takeaways

- Continuous monitoring is essential for maintaining cloud security, enabling early detection of threats and anomalies using tools like AWS CloudWatch, Azure Monitor, IBM QRadar, and GCP Operations Suite.

- Encryption plays a pivotal role in protecting data at rest and in transit across all major cloud platforms. Native tools like AWS KMS, Azure Key Vault, IBM Key Protect, and GCP Cloud KMS help manage keys securely.

- Preparation and security testing ensure that configurations are correctly implemented. This includes validating encryption setups, monitoring alerts, and enforcing compliance standards.

- All four cloud platforms offer native and third-party integrations to automate monitoring, incident response, and security assessments.

- A well-structured monitoring and testing strategy reduces risk exposure and helps maintain compliance with industry regulations such as ISO, HIPAA, and GDPR.

Key terms

- **Cloud security**: The practice of protecting cloud resources, data, and services from unauthorized access, data breaches, and other security threats.

- **Monitoring**: The process of continuously observing and collecting data on cloud resources and activities to identify and respond to security incidents.

- **Encryption**: The process of converting data into a coded or unreadable format to protect it from unauthorized access. This can be applied to data at rest and data in transit.

- **AWS**: Amazon provides a popular cloud computing platform that offers a wide range of cloud services.

- **Azure**: Microsoft's cloud computing platform, providing a variety of cloud services and solutions.

- **IBM Cloud**: IBM's cloud computing platform offers infrastructure and services for cloud computing.

- **GCP**: Google's cloud computing platform provides cloud services and products.

- **Shared responsibility model**: A framework that defines the division of security responsibilities between a cloud service provider and its customers.

- **IAM**: A set of policies and technologies for controlling and managing user access to cloud resources.

- **Penetration testing**: A security assessment technique in which ethical hackers simulate real-world attacks to identify vulnerabilities in a system.

- **Vulnerability scanning**: The process of scanning cloud resources and infrastructure to identify known **security vulnerabilities**.

- **SIEM**: A system that collects and analyzes security event data to provide real-time threat detection and incident response.

- **Data encryption in transit**: The practice of encrypting data as it is transmitted between a client and a server, ensuring its confidentiality during transmission.

- **Data encryption at rest**: The practice of encrypting data when it is stored in a persistent state, such as in databases or on disk.

- **Security Audit**: A systematic review of cloud infrastructure and configurations to assess compliance with security policies and best practices.

- **Least privilege**: The principle of granting users or systems the minimum level of access or permissions needed to perform their tasks.

- **Compliance monitoring**: The ongoing process of ensuring that cloud infrastructure and practices comply with relevant industry regulations and standards.

- **Serverless computing**: A cloud computing model in which cloud providers manage the infrastructure, allowing developers to focus on writing and deploying code without managing servers.

- **Zero Trust security**: A security model that assumes no trust in any user or system, requiring verification and authentication for every access request.

- **Threat Intelligence**: Information about potential cyber threats and vulnerabilities that can be used to proactively defend against security incidents.

- **Incident response**: A structured approach to addressing and managing security incidents, including preparation, detection, containment, eradication, recovery, and lessons learned.

- **Encryption key management**: The practice of securely generating, storing, and managing encryption keys used to protect data.

- **RBAC**: A method of managing access to cloud resources by assigning specific permissions to roles rather than individual users.

- **ELB**: A service that automatically distributes incoming application traffic across multiple targets, such as Amazon EC2 instances, in the AWS cloud.

- **Continuous compliance monitoring**: The ongoing process of monitoring and enforcing compliance with security policies and standards in real-time.

Solved exercises

1. **What is the purpose of GCP's IAM?**

   Answer: GCP's IAM allows you to control who has access to which resources in your environment. You can define roles with different permissions and assign them to users, groups, or service accounts.

2. **Does GCP encrypt customer data stored at rest by default?**

   Answer: Yes, GCP encrypts customer data stored at rest by default.

3. **Which service in GCP helps identify security vulnerabilities in your Google App Engine applications?**

   Answer: Google Cloud Security Scanner.

4. **What principle should you follow when granting permissions to resources in GCP?**

   Answer: The principle of least privilege.

5. **Which GCP service offers monitoring, logging, and diagnostics?**

   Answer: Google Cloud's operations suite (formerly known as Stackdriver).

6. **Name one tool in GCP that allows you to manage encryption keys.**

   Answer: Google Cloud's Key Management Service.

7. **Can users conduct penetration testing on their GCP environments without prior approval from Google?**

   Answer: Yes, however, they must adhere to Google's Acceptable Use Policy and Terms of Service.

8. **Which platform in GCP provides insights, identifies threats, and ensures compliance with data use policies?**

   Answer: Security Command Center.

9. **What are VPC Service Controls used for in GCP?**

   Answer: They are used to secure APIs and services within GCP.

10. **For what kind of data might a user want to manage their encryption keys in GCP?**

    Answer: For certain types of sensitive data or for adhering to specific regulatory or compliance requirements.

Unsolved exercises

1. How can you integrate third-party tools with GCP's IAM for enhanced identity management?

2. What are the key differences between CSEK and CMEK in GCP?

3. Name some of the common vulnerabilities that the Google Cloud Web Security Scanner can detect.

4. How do firewall rules in GCP's VPC help improve the security of your cloud resources?

5. Describe a scenario where the principle of least privilege can prevent potential security breaches in GCP.

6. Which GCP service would you use to generate, rotate, and destroy symmetric and asymmetric cryptographic keys?

7. How do GCP's Operations Suite (formerly Stackdriver) alerts help in proactive threat detection?

8. In which situations might you need prior authorization from Google before performing certain forms of testing on GCP?

9. How does GCP ensure data integrity and security when transferring data between its services?

10. What measures should be taken in GCP to secure a multi-regional deployment?

Join our Discord space

Join our Discord workspace for latest updates, offers, tech happenings around the world, new releases, and sessions with the authors:

https://discord.bpbonline.com

## CHAPTER 9

Security as Code

Introduction

In this chapter, we will take a transformative approach to integrating security into infrastructure management. This paradigm shift leverages tools like Terraform and Ansible to automate and codify security policies, ensuring a dynamic and robust defense mechanism in the fluid landscape of cloud computing. The chapter aims to demystify **security as code (SaC)**, emphasizing its significance and application in modern cloud-centric technology.

The chapter is tailored for professionals and students with foundational cloud computing knowledge. It aims to provide a comprehensive understanding of how security can be seamlessly integrated into the cloud infrastructure lifecycle. Through practical examples and exercises, readers will learn to implement and manage security configurations using code, thus enhancing the security and efficiency of cloud environments.

Structure

The chapter covers the following topics:

- Configurations for security and infrastructure as code
- Compliance as code
- Case study

Objectives

By the end of this chapter, you will have a comprehensive understanding of SaC in cloud environments. You will learn the significance of automating security practices using code and the transformation from traditional security approaches. You will gain proficiency in using tools like Terraform and Ansible for security management, differentiating their roles and applications. The chapter will equip you with the skills to implement security configurations and compliance requirements through coding, preparing you to create more secure and efficient cloud infrastructures.

Prerequisites

Readers should come prepared with a basic understanding of cloud computing, including familiarity with common cloud platforms and services. Additionally, a foundational knowledge of programming or scripting is essential as it will aid in grasping the implementation of security policies and configurations through code. A general awareness of fundamental security principles is also beneficial, setting the stage for more advanced discussions on security measures specific to cloud environments. These prerequisites are crucial for fully engaging with the chapter's content, which focuses on integrating advanced security practices into cloud computing through coding and automation.

Configurations for security and infrastructure as code

This section focuses on using coding practices to manage and automate security and infrastructure in cloud environments. This approach involves:

- **Infrastructure as code (IaC)** is a key practice in DevOps that involves managing and provisioning computing infrastructure through machine-readable definition files, rather than physical hardware configuration or interactive configuration tools. This approach enables teams to automatically manage, monitor, and provision resources in the cloud, leading to more efficient and error-free operations. IaC promotes consistency in server configurations, enhances scalability, and facilitates better management and tracking of infrastructure changes. It is closely tied to automation and is essential for achieving the speed and agility required in modern cloud environments. Tools like Terraform and AWS CloudFormation are commonly used to implement IaC.

Benefits of managing security through code

Managing security through code offers several benefits, such as:

- **Automation and efficiency**: Automating security tasks reduces human error and increases efficiency.

- **Consistency**: Code-based management ensures uniform security configurations across all environments.

- **Scalability**: Easily scale security measures as infrastructure grows.

- **Rapid response**: Quick adaptation to emerging threats through code changes.

- **Version control and audit trails**: Tracking and auditing changes in security policies becomes easier with version-controlled code.

- **Integration with DevOps**: Seamless integration with existing **continuous integration/continuous deployment (CI/CD)** pipelines for continuous security.

- **Compliance assurance**: Consistently enforce compliance standards.

This approach aligns security management with modern cloud and software development practices, ensuring robust, scalable, and agile security in dynamic IT environments.

Overview of Terraform and Ansible

Terraform and Ansible are pivotal tools in implementing IaC. They are discussed as follows:

- **Terraform**: An open-source tool created by *HashiCorp*, Terraform enables users to define and provision a datacenter infrastructure using a high-level configuration language. It is known for its ability to manage both cloud and on-premises resources and supports multiple cloud service providers. Terraform works by creating an execution plan to determine what actions are necessary to achieve the desired state specified in the configuration files, and then it executes the plan to build the described infrastructure.

- **Ansible**: Developed by *Red Hat*, Ansible is an open-source tool for software provisioning, configuration management, and application deployment. Unlike Terraform, Ansible focuses more on the automation of the software deployment and configuration side of things. It uses YAML for its playbook configurations, making it highly readable and easy to use. Ansible works by connecting to nodes and pushing out small programs called **Ansible modules** to them. These modules are executed, and then they report back to the Ansible server.

Both tools are integral in modern DevOps practices, with Terraform excelling in infrastructure provisioning and Ansible in automating software configuration and deployment.

Terraform for security management

Terraform, an IaC tool, is adept at managing cloud infrastructure, including aspects of security management. It allows for defining both infrastructure and security policies as code, enabling automated deployment and consistent security configurations across diverse environments. Terraform's approach ensures that security is an integral part of the infrastructure setup process from the beginning rather than being retroactively applied. This method enhances security consistency, reduces manual errors, and simplifies compliance with security standards. By using Terraform, organizations can efficiently manage security settings for cloud resources, aligning them with the overall infrastructure in a unified and automated manner.

Terraform basics and its role in security

Terraform, a key tool in IaC, plays a significant role in managing and provisioning infrastructure in cloud environments. Its basic functionality involves writing configurations in a human-readable language, which Terraform then uses to create an execution plan and manage infrastructure accordingly. In terms of security, Terraform's strength lies in its ability to define security configurations as part of the infrastructure code. This integration ensures that security measures are automatically and consistently applied across all infrastructure deployments. By treating security rules and policies as code, Terraform facilitates more secure, predictable, and efficient infrastructure management, reducing the risk of human error and inconsistencies in security implementations.

Writing Terraform scripts for security settings involves several steps, which are explained as follows:

1. **Define resources**: Start by defining the infrastructure resources (like servers, networks, databases) in Terraform configuration files (**.tf**). Each resource's security settings are specified in these definitions.

2. **Set security groups and rules**: For instance, in AWS, you define security groups and rules within these groups. This includes inbound and outbound rules, specifying ports, protocols, and source/destination IPs.

3. **Implement role-based access control (RBAC)**: Define roles and assign specific permissions to these roles for accessing and modifying cloud resources.

4. **Encryption settings**: Specify encryption settings for data storage and transmission. For example, setting up encrypted AWS S3 buckets or RDS databases.

5. **Compliance as code**: Codify compliance requirements into the Terraform scripts. This ensures that the infrastructure automatically adheres to certain standards and policies.

6. **Use modules for reusability**: Create modules for common security patterns to ensure consistency and reusability across different projects.

7. **Version control**: Store your Terraform scripts in a version control system to track changes and maintain a history of your security configurations.

8. **Testing and validation**: Before deploying, test the scripts using Terraform's plan and apply commands to ensure they perform as expected.

By following these steps, you can effectively use Terraform scripts to manage and enforce security settings in a cloud environment.

Use cases for automated compliance checks, security group management are as follows:

- **Automated compliance checks**: Terraform can be used to ensure that infrastructure deployments adhere to compliance standards. By defining compliance requirements as code, Terraform scripts automatically check and enforce these requirements during deployment, simplifying compliance management and reducing manual oversight.

- **Security group management**: Terraform scripts manage cloud security groups and their rules, allowing for the precise control of access to resources. This enables organizations to automate the creation and maintenance of security groups, ensuring consistent and secure access configurations across their cloud environments.

Ansible for security automation

Ansible is a powerful tool for automating security tasks, providing efficient and consistent security configurations across diverse environments. It uses simple YAML syntax for its playbooks, making it accessible for defining security automation tasks. Key use cases include:

- **Automated patch management**: Ansible can automate the process of updating software and systems, ensuring that security patches are applied promptly across all servers.

- **Configuration management**: It ensures that all system configurations meet specified security standards, reducing the risk of misconfigurations that could lead to vulnerabilities.

- **Compliance enforcement**: With Ansible, compliance with security standards and policies can be automated, ensuring that systems are always compliant with industry or regulatory requirements.

Ansible's agentless architecture and idempotent nature make it ideal for security automation, allowing for scalable and repeatable security practices.

Understanding Ansible Playbooks for security tasks

Ansible Playbooks are YAML files used to define automation tasks, including security operations. They allow for the scripting of complex processes, such as patch management, configuration enforcement, and security checks, in a readable format. Each playbook consists of one or more plays, targeting specific hosts with a set of tasks to execute. For security tasks, playbooks can automate the deployment of security configurations, enforce security policies, and ensure systems comply with required standards, making them essential for maintaining a secure and consistent environment across all managed nodes.

Writing Ansible scripts for automated security deployment

Writing Ansible scripts for automated security deployment involves creating Ansible Playbooks that define the desired security configurations and tasks. These scripts can automate the deployment of security measures, such as firewall rules, system updates, and application settings, ensuring that all systems in your infrastructure comply with your security standards. The process typically includes defining tasks to install security updates, configure system settings according to security policies, and ensure that only necessary services are running. By leveraging Ansible's capabilities, organizations can automate their security deployments, reducing the risk of human error and ensuring consistent security postures across their environments.

Use cases for automated patch management, configuration enforcement, that are crucial for maintaining security are as follows:

- **Automated patch management**: Ansible can automate the process of applying security patches across numerous systems, ensuring all devices are up-to-date with the latest security fixes. This reduces vulnerabilities and enhances security without manual intervention.

- **Configuration enforcement**: Ansible ensures systems adhere to defined security configurations, automatically correcting any deviations. This consistent enforcement helps maintain compliance with security policies and standards, reducing the risk of security breaches caused by misconfigurations.

Compliance in code

Compliance in code involves detailing how organizations can embed compliance and regulatory requirements directly into their infrastructure and security configurations through code. This method leverages IaC and SaC practices, ensuring that all infrastructure provisioning and security operations automatically meet compliance standards. The approach facilitates automated, continuous compliance monitoring and enforcement, which is crucial for maintaining adherence to regulatory standards in a scalable, efficient manner. It also allows for rapid adjustments to compliance policies in response to regulatory changes, ensuring that compliance is an integral, seamlessly managed aspect of the infrastructure lifecycle. This concept is pivotal for organizations looking to streamline compliance processes and reduce the risk of non-compliance in dynamic cloud environments.

Role of compliance in cloud security

Compliance plays a critical role in cloud security by ensuring that cloud services and operations adhere to established regulations and standards. It involves the implementation of controls and policies that protect data and maintain privacy, aligning cloud operations with legal, regulatory, and business requirements. Effective compliance strategies help organizations avoid legal penalties, safeguard customer data, and enhance trust. In the cloud, where resources are dynamically allocated and scaled, maintaining compliance requires continuous monitoring and automation to adapt to the changing environment and regulatory landscape.

Implementing compliance as code

Implementing compliance as code deeply integrates regulatory and compliance checks within the automation scripts that manage cloud infrastructure and security configurations. This method relies on defining compliance requirements in a structured format that can be interpreted by automation tools like Terraform and Ansible. Doing so ensures that every piece of infrastructure deployed complies with relevant standards, such as the *Payment Card Industry Data Security Standard* (*PCI DSS*) for payment processing or the *Health Insurance Portability and Accountability Act* (*HIPAA*) for healthcare data. This proactive approach allows for continuous compliance verification, significantly reducing the manual burden of audits and checks, and enabling a more dynamic response to changes in compliance requirements or the infrastructure itself. It transforms compliance from a reactive, manual checklist into a dynamic, integrated component of the continuous integration and deployment pipeline, enhancing overall security posture and compliance adherence of cloud-based systems.

The steps for implementing compliance as code are as follows:

1. **Define compliance requirements**: Start by identifying the specific regulatory standards and compliance requirements relevant to your organization and infrastructure.

2. **Audit existing infrastructure**: Assess your current infrastructure against these compliance requirements to identify gaps.

3. **Codify compliance policies**: Translate the compliance requirements into code using tools like Terraform for infrastructure provisioning and Ansible for configuration management.

4. **Integrate into CI/CD pipelines**: Incorporate these compliance checks into your CI/CD pipelines to ensure that compliance is evaluated with every change.

5. **Automate monitoring and reporting**: Implement automated systems to continuously monitor compliance and generate reports for internal and external audits.

6. **Iterate and improve**: Regularly review and update your compliance code to adapt to changes in regulations or business needs.

By following these steps, organizations can ensure that their cloud environments remain compliant with relevant regulations through automated, codified processes.

Tools and methods for ensuring compliance through code

Ensuring compliance through code involves using specialized tools and methods:

- **IaC tools**: Terraform and CloudFormation allow for the definition of cloud infrastructure in code, including compliance requirements.

- **Configuration management tools**: Ansible, Chef, and Puppet can enforce and maintain system configurations as per compliance standards.

- **Compliance as code frameworks**: **Open Policy Agent** (**OPA**) enables policy definition and enforcement across the cloud stack.

- **Security and compliance scanners**: Tools like SonarQube, Checkov, and Inspec can automatically scan code and infrastructure for compliance with defined policies.

These tools and methods facilitate the automation of compliance checks and enforcement in a consistent, repeatable manner across all infrastructure deployments.

Case study

A relevant case study for implementing SaC involves a financial services company transitioning to cloud services while needing to maintain strict compliance with financial regulations. The company adopted Terraform to manage its cloud infrastructure and Ansible for configuration management, ensuring that all deployed resources met compliance and security standards from the outset. They codified security policies, such as encryption protocols for data at rest and in transit, and automated compliance checks against industry standards. This approach significantly reduced manual compliance efforts, accelerated deployment cycles, and enhanced the security posture by integrating compliance and security measures directly into the CI/CD pipeline.

Conclusion

In this chapter, we explored the transformative concept of SaC, emphasizing its significance in automating and integrating security within cloud infrastructure management. We discussed tools like Terraform and Ansible in detail, showing how they enable the codification of security configurations and compliance, thereby ensuring scalable, efficient, and consistent security practices. The chapter provides a comprehensive guide for applying SaC principles through practical examples, automated compliance checks, and security group management. This chapter lays the foundation for adopting modern cloud security practices, underlining the importance of automation and codification in achieving robust security and compliance.

In the next chapter, we will be focusing on best practices for cloud-native implementations while considering key compliance aspects, including Zero Trust, data protection policies, attack surface reduction, and architecture considerations.

Key takeaways

- SaC automates and integrates security policies into the cloud infrastructure lifecycle using tools like Terraform and Ansible, enhancing consistency and efficiency.

- Terraform is ideal for provisioning infrastructure and embedding security configurations (e.g., security groups, RBAC, encryption) directly in code to enable compliance and auditability.

- Ansible supports configuration management and automates security tasks like patching, policy enforcement, and compliance checks using simple YAML playbooks.

- Compliance as Code enables organizations to codify and continuously enforce regulatory standards (like HIPAA or PCI DSS), transforming compliance into an automated, scalable practice.

- By embedding security and compliance rules into CI/CD pipelines, SaC aligns security with DevOps, enabling faster deployments while maintaining a strong security posture across environments.

Key terms

- **SaC**: The practice of managing and implementing security policies and configurations through code, integrating security measures into the infrastructure management process.

- **IaC**: A method for managing and provisioning computer data centers through machine-readable definition files, rather than physical hardware configuration or interactive configuration tools.

- **Terraform**: An open-source tool developed by HashiCorp that allows for the building, changing, and versioning of infrastructure safely and efficiently in the cloud.

- **Ansible**: An open-source software tool by Red Hat for automating software provisioning, configuration management, and application deployment.

- **Compliance as code**: The process of embedding compliance and regulatory requirements directly into the code that manages infrastructure and security, ensuring automatic adherence to these standards.

- **Automated compliance checks**: The use of scripts or code to automatically verify that infrastructure configurations meet specific compliance or regulatory standards.

- **Security group management**: The process of creating and managing virtual firewalls that control inbound and outbound traffic to cloud resources.

- **Configuration management**: The practice of handling changes systematically so that a system maintains its integrity over time, particularly in ensuring that all systems are configured to a desired and secure state.

- **Patch management**: The process of distributing and applying updates to software to fix vulnerabilities, improve functionality, or increase security.

- **Cloud security**: The collection of procedures, technologies, policies, and controls employed to protect cloud-based systems, data, and infrastructure.

- **Compliance standards**: Specific guidelines or regulations that organizations must follow to protect information and remain in legal and regulatory compliance.

- **YAML**: A human-readable data serialization standard that can be used in conjunction with all programming languages and is often used for writing Ansible Playbooks.

- **CI/CD pipeline**: CI/CD a method to frequently deliver apps to customers by introducing automation into the stages of app development.

- **Idempotence**: The property of certain operations in computing whereby they can be applied multiple times without changing the result beyond the initial application.

- **OPA**: An open-source, general-purpose policy engine that enables unified, context-aware policy enforcement across the entire stack.

Solved exercises

1. **What is SaC?**

   Answer: SaC involves integrating security practices directly into the infrastructure management and deployment processes, automating and codifying security policies to ensure consistent and efficient security across cloud resources.

2. **How does Terraform contribute to SaC?**

   Answer: Terraform allows for the definition and provisioning of cloud IaC, including security configurations, enabling automated deployment and management of secure cloud environments.

3. **Explain the role of Ansible in automating security deployments.**

   Answer: Ansible automates the deployment and management of security configurations across infrastructure, using playbooks to apply security updates, enforce configurations, and ensure systems are compliant with security standards.

4. **What are the benefits of managing security through code?**

   Answer: Benefits include automation and efficiency in deploying security measures, consistency across deployments, scalability of security practices, and enhanced compliance through automated checks.

5. **How can Terraform be used for automated compliance checks?**

   Answer: Terraform scripts can define compliance requirements as part of the infrastructure code, automatically checking and enforcing these requirements during deployment to ensure compliance with industry standards.

6. **Describe a practical use case of Ansible for security automation.**

   Answer: A practical use case involves using Ansible to automate patch management, where Ansible Playbooks are written to update systems with the latest security patches across multiple servers, ensuring all devices are consistently protected against vulnerabilities.

7. **What is the importance of compliance in cloud security?**

   Answer: Compliance ensures that cloud services and operations adhere to established regulations and standards, protecting data, maintaining privacy, and enhancing trust by aligning cloud operations with legal and business requirements.

8. **How does implementing compliance as code streamline regulatory adherence?**

   Answer: By embedding compliance requirements directly into code, organizations can automate the enforcement and monitoring of compliance standards, making compliance an integrated part of the development and deployment process.

9. **Give an example of how Terraform can manage security groups.**

   Answer: Terraform can define security groups and rules within its configuration files, specifying inbound and outbound rules, ports, protocols, and source/destination IPs to manage access control to resources automatically.

10. **What is a key advantage of using Ansible for configuration enforcement?**

    Answer: Ansible ensures that all system configurations meet specified security standards, automatically correcting any deviations. This continuous enforcement helps maintain compliance with security policies and reduces the risk of security breaches caused by misconfigurations.

Unsolved exercises

1. Define SaC and explain how it changes the traditional approach to security in cloud environments.

2. How does Terraform enable SaC, and what specific security configurations can it manage? Provide examples.

3. Describe the role of Ansible in SaC. How can it be used to automate security tasks across different environments?

4. List and explain the benefits of managing security through code. How does this approach improve compliance and operational efficiency?

5. With Terraform, how can automated compliance checks be implemented within IaC? Outline the steps involved.

6. Present a use case where Ansible is used for security automation, specifically focusing on automated patch management. Detail the process and expected outcomes.

7. Discuss the significance of compliance in cloud security. How does achieving compliance differ in a cloud environment compared to traditional IT settings?

8. Explain the concept of compliance as code and how it can be implemented within a cloud infrastructure. What challenges might organizations face in this implementation?

9. Provide an example of managing security groups using Terraform. What considerations should be made to ensure these configurations enhance security posture?

10. What are the advantages and potential limitations of using Ansible for configuration enforcement in a dynamic cloud environment?

Join our Discord space

Join our Discord workspace for latest updates, offers, tech happenings around the world, new releases, and sessions with the authors:

https://discord.bpbonline.com

CHAPTER 10

Best Practices for Cloud-native Implementations

Introduction

In recent years, cloud-native technologies have revolutionized the way organizations design, develop, and deploy applications. In today's digital landscape, cloud-native implementations have become a cornerstone for organizations looking to achieve scalability, agility, resilience, and cost efficiency that were previously unattainable with traditional methods. However, as businesses transition to cloud-native environments, they must also ensure that compliance requirements are met to maintain data security, privacy, and regulatory adherence. Cloud providers like **Amazon Web Services (AWS)**, Google Cloud, Azure, and IBM Cloud offer powerful tools and services that can help organizations build robust and secure cloud-native applications. However, to ensure the success of these implementations, it is crucial to follow best practices that address compliance considerations, Zero Trust, data protection policies, attack surface reduction, architecture design, patching, and vulnerability assessment.

This chapter will cover best practices for cloud-native implementations while considering key compliance aspects, including Zero Trust, data protection policies, attack surface reduction, and architecture considerations.

Structure

In this chapter, we will discuss the following topics:

- Introduction to cloud-native implementations

- Protocols

- Identity and Access Management

- Security compliance in cloud technology

- Logging and monitoring

- Incident response

- Security training and awareness

Objectives

As you delve into the comprehensive exploration of cloud-native security, your objectives focus on acquiring a holistic understanding and actionable insights to effectively safeguard your cloud-native implementations. Your goals encompass mastering key areas, such as compliance considerations, Zero Trust principles, data protection policies, attack surface reduction, architecture design, patching strategies, and vulnerability management.

One crucial aspect of cloud security is compliance expertise. You will gain a deep understanding of compliance requirements, standards, and frameworks relevant to cloud-native environments. By equipping yourself with this knowledge, you will be able to navigate the intricate landscape of regulations and ensure that your applications meet industry-specific compliance needs.

Understanding the Zero Trust model is another key objective. This approach is fundamental in modern security paradigms, requiring robust identity verification, access controls, and least privilege access. By mastering Zero Trust principles, you will establish a strong security foundation within cloud-native architectures, minimizing unauthorized access and potential breaches.

A vital component of cloud security is data protection proficiency. You will explore policies related to data classification, encryption, access controls, and masking. Developing expertise in these areas will help you implement effective security measures to safeguard sensitive information across various cloud platforms.

Another critical focus area is attack surface reduction. You will gain insights into understanding and mitigating vulnerabilities in cloud-native applications. By implementing strategies such as network segmentation and minimizing exposure points, you can effectively reduce the risk of cyber threats in dynamic cloud environments.

Building architectural insight is essential for designing secure, scalable, and resilient cloud-native applications. Learning best practices and reference frameworks from major cloud providers will enable you to create optimized applications that adhere to security standards while leveraging cloud-native capabilities.

An effective patch management strategy is necessary to maintain the security and stability of cloud applications. You will master techniques for automated patch deployment, testing, and prioritization to ensure timely updates and proactive security maintenance.

Lastly, vulnerability management expertise is crucial for identifying and mitigating security weaknesses. By developing a thorough understanding of vulnerability scanning and penetration testing, you will learn how to assess risks, conduct security evaluations, and strengthen the overall security posture of cloud environments.

By achieving these objectives, you will be well-equipped to implement robust security strategies that protect cloud-native applications from evolving threats.

Introduction to cloud-native implementations

Compliance considerations are crucial in ensuring the security and trustworthiness of cloud-native applications. Organizations transitioning to the cloud must adhere to various regulations, standards, and industry best practices to safeguard sensitive data, maintain customer trust, and avoid legal liabilities. In this chapter, we will explore the intricacies of compliance considerations for cloud-native implementations, the importance of compliance, common compliance frameworks, and strategies to achieve and maintain compliance in leading cloud platforms.

Understanding cloud-native

Cloud-native is an approach to building and running applications that fully embraces the advantages of cloud computing. At its core, cloud-native is a set of practices that enable organizations to build more reliable, scalable, and agile applications, thus responding faster to market demands and enhancing customer experiences.

Microservices architecture

Unlike monolithic architectures, where everything is intertwined in a single codebase, cloud-native applications use a microservices architecture. This structure breaks down the application into smaller, independent components, each responsible for a specific function. This modularity allows for easier updates, quicker scaling, and better fault isolation.

Containerization

Cloud-native heavily relies on containerization. Containers encapsulate an application and its dependencies in a lightweight, standalone package. This ensures consistency across various computing environments, be it development, testing, or production. Tools like Docker and Kubernetes have become synonymous with this practice, streamlining the deployment and management of containers.

Dynamic orchestration

Dynamic orchestration is a critical component of cloud-native architecture. Orchestration tools, like Kubernetes, manage the lifecycle of containers in a cloud-native environment.

They handle the deployment, scaling, and networking of containers automatically, making the system more efficient and resilient.

DevOps integration

Cloud-native is deeply integrated with DevOps practices. It emphasizes **continuous integration/continuous deployment (CI/CD)**, where code changes are automatically built, tested, and deployed. This integration accelerates the development cycle, reduces manual intervention, and increases the quality of the software.

Advantages over traditional architectures

Cloud-native applications offer several benefits compared to traditional architectures. The following are some key advantages:

- **Scalability**: Cloud-native applications can scale out (or in) automatically depending on the demand, which is a stark contrast to the scaling limitations of traditional architectures.

- **Resilience**: The distributed nature of microservices enhances the overall resilience of the application. Failure in one component does not bring down the entire system.

- **Agility**: The combination of microservices and DevOps practices allows teams to be more agile, rapidly iterating on products and responding to customer needs.

- **Cost-effectiveness**: Pay-as-you-go pricing models of cloud services, along with the efficient use of resources, make cloud-native more cost-effective.

Fundamental differences from past architectures

Modern cloud-native architectures differ significantly from traditional approaches. The following are some key distinctions:

- **Architecture**: Past architectures often relied on tightly-coupled, monolithic designs, making changes cumbersome and risky.

- **Deployment**: Traditional deployment methods were often manual and prone to errors, unlike the automated and consistent deployments in cloud-native.

- **Scaling**: Scalability in traditional architectures was often a challenge, requiring significant foresight and investment.

Cloud-native represents a paradigm shift in how applications are developed, deployed, and managed. It leverages the full potential of cloud computing, offering unparalleled flexibility, efficiency, and speed. As businesses continue to evolve in a digital-first world, cloud-native is not just an option; it is a necessity for staying competitive and meeting the dynamic demands of modern software development and deployment.

Overview of cloud service providers

In the realm of cloud-native computing, the selection of a cloud service provider is a crucial decision that can significantly impact the architecture, capabilities, and performance of your applications. The following section is an analysis of the major cloud service providers: AWS, **Google Cloud Platform (GCP)**, Microsoft Azure, and IBM Cloud.

Amazon Web Services

AWS is one of the most widely adopted cloud platforms in the world. Known for its robustness, scalability, and broad service offerings, AWS is often the go-to choice for enterprises seeking a comprehensive and reliable cloud solution, as follows:

- **Strengths**:
  - **Extensive service offerings**: AWS provides a vast array of services covering computing, storage, databases, **machine learning (ML)**, analytics, and more. Its comprehensive service catalog is well-suited for enterprises that demand a wide range of capabilities.

  - **Mature ecosystem**: Being the oldest among its peers, AWS has a mature ecosystem with extensive documentation, a large community, and a broad range of third-party integrations.

  - **Global reach**: AWS has an extensive global network, offering high availability and redundancy across numerous geographic locations.

- **Use cases**: AWS is particularly beneficial for large-scale enterprises needing a broad range of services, high scalability, and a global presence.

Google Cloud Platform

GCP has carved a niche for itself with its strong focus on data analytics, artificial intelligence, and seamless open-source integration. It is an excellent choice for organizations looking to leverage advanced analytics and scalable ML solutions backed by Google's infrastructure, as discussed:

- **Strengths**:
  - **Data analytics and ML**: GCP excels in offering cutting-edge data analytics and ML services. It integrates seamlessly with popular open-source tools and offers **artificial intelligence (AI)** and ML solutions that are highly scalable and easy to use.

  - **Open-source integration**: GCP is known for its strong commitment to open-source technologies, making it a preferred choice for organizations relying on open-source solutions.

- o **Networking capabilities**: Google's private global fiber network provides fast and reliable connectivity, which is a significant advantage for data-intensive applications.

- **Use cases**: Ideal for organizations focusing on data analytics, AI, ML, and those who prefer open-source integration.

Microsoft Azure

Microsoft Azure is a powerful cloud platform known for its seamless enterprise integration, particularly for organizations already invested in Microsoft technologies. Its strong hybrid capabilities and developer-friendly tools make it an appealing choice for enterprises seeking flexibility and productivity, as discussed:

- **Strengths**:

  - o **Enterprise integration**: Azure offers seamless integration with Microsoft's software products such as Windows Server, Active Directory, and SQL Server. This makes it a natural fit for businesses heavily invested in Microsoft products.

  - o **Hybrid capabilities**: Azure provides strong support for hybrid cloud environments, allowing a more flexible approach in integrating on-premises data centers with cloud services.

  - o **Developer tools**: It offers a range of developer tools and services that enhance productivity and support various programming languages and frameworks.

- **Use cases**: Azure is well-suited for businesses that require tight integration with other Microsoft products and services, and those looking for robust hybrid cloud solutions.

IBM Cloud

IBM Cloud is recognized for its strong hybrid and multi-cloud capabilities, AI-driven services, and a focus on enterprise-grade security. It is particularly well-suited for organizations operating in highly regulated industries and those pursuing complex, distributed cloud strategies, as discussed:

- **Strengths**:

  - o **Hybrid and multi-cloud focus**: IBM Cloud places a strong emphasis on hybrid and multi-cloud solutions, offering tools and services that allow businesses to manage complex cloud environments effectively.

  - o **AI and cognitive services**: Leveraging its Watson platform, IBM Cloud offers powerful AI and cognitive computing capabilities, making it a strong contender for AI-driven applications.

o **Strong security and compliance**: Known for its focus on security and compliance, IBM Cloud appeals to industries that have stringent regulatory requirements.

- **Use cases**: IBM Cloud is ideal for enterprises requiring strong hybrid and multi-cloud management, AI capabilities, and those in regulated industries.

Choosing the right cloud service provider depends on your specific needs and strategic goals. AWS is a comprehensive, all-around player with a global reach. GCP stands out in data analytics and open-source integration. Azure is the go-to for businesses embedded in the Microsoft ecosystem and seeking hybrid solutions. IBM Cloud caters to those with a focus on AI, security, and regulatory compliance. Understanding the unique strengths of each provider will help align your cloud-native strategy with the provider that best fits your organizational needs.

Cloud-native implementation steps

This part of the chapter breaks down the practical steps involved in implementing cloud-native strategies across different cloud platforms. You will find detailed guides for each provider:

- **In AWS**: You will learn the steps to implement a cloud-native architecture in AWS, including setting up the AWS environment, deploying microservices using Amazon **Elastic Kubernetes Service** (**EKS**), implementing CI/CD pipelines with AWS CodePipeline and CodeBuild, and ensuring monitoring and security with Amazon CloudWatch and AWS Shield.

- **In GCP**: This subsection guides you on leveraging Google Cloud for cloud-native applications. It covers setting up the environment, deploying applications using **Google Kubernetes Engine** (**GKE**), managing data with BigQuery, and integrating AI capabilities using Google AI Platform.

- **In Azure**: Here, the focus is on using Azure for cloud-native solutions. You will learn about setting up the Azure environment, deploying applications with **Azure Kubernetes Service** (**AKS**), implementing Azure DevOps for CI/CD, and securing and ensuring compliance with Azure Security Center.

- **In IBM Cloud**: This part explores using IBM Cloud for cloud-native applications. It discusses setting up IBM Cloud, deploying applications with IBM Cloud Kubernetes Service, integrating AI with IBM Watson, and managing data with IBM Cloud Databases.

Considerations specific to each cloud provider

The chapter concludes by discussing considerations unique to each cloud provider. This includes understanding cost management and security in AWS, leveraging hybrid cloud and Microsoft ecosystem integration in Azure, taking advantage of data analytics and network infrastructure in Google Cloud, and utilizing AI and ML capabilities in IBM Cloud. This section will be particularly important for you to tailor your cloud-native approach to the specific strengths and features of each cloud service provider.

Protocols

Protocols are critical in establishing secure communication channels and maintaining data integrity within cloud environments. In this section, we will cover essential protocols used in cloud security, provide implementation examples, and share related code snippets to demonstrate their usage.

Protocols like **Hypertext Transfer Protocol Secure (HTTPS)**, **Secure Shell (SSH)**, and **Message Queuing Telemetry Transport (MQTT)** are instrumental in securing communication and data transfer within cloud environments. By using these protocols with appropriate libraries and tools, organizations can establish secure connections, access remote resources, and exchange data with confidence, ensuring the confidentiality and integrity of their information.

Hypertext Transfer Protocol Secure

HTTPS is the standard for secure communication on the web, combining HTTP with **Secure Sockets Layer/ Transport Layer Security (SSL/TLS)** encryption to protect data in transit. Here is a Python example illustrating how to make an HTTPS request using the **requests** library:

```
import requests


# Define the URL with HTTPS
url = "https://api.example.com/data"


# Send an HTTPS GET request
response = requests.get(url)


# Process the HTTPS response
if response.status_code == 200:
    encrypted_data = response.content
    # Decrypt the data if necessary
    # ...
else:
    print("Error:", response.status_code)
```

Secure Shell

SSH is a cryptographic network protocol used for secure remote access to servers and data transfer. The following is an example of using SSH with Python's **paramiko** library to establish an SSH connection and execute a command on a remote server:

```
import paramiko

# Initialize an SSH client
ssh_client = paramiko.SSHClient()
ssh_client.set_missing_host_key_policy(paramiko.AutoAddPolicy())

# Connect to the remote server
ssh_client.connect('remote-server.example.com', username='your_username',
password='your_password')

# Execute a command on the remote server
stdin, stdout, stderr = ssh_client.exec_command('ls -l')

# Print the output
print(stdout.read().decode())

# Close the SSH connection
ssh_client.close()
```

Message Queuing Telemetry Transport

MQTT is a lightweight, publish-subscribe protocol commonly used in IoT and cloud applications for efficient message exchange. The following is a Python example using the **paho.mqtt** library to publish and subscribe to MQTT messages:

```
import paho.mqtt.client as mqtt

# Define MQTT broker and topic
broker_address = "mqtt.example.com"
topic = "my_topic"

# Create an MQTT client
client = mqtt.Client()

# Connect to the MQTT broker
```

```
client.connect(broker_address)

# Publish a message
message = "Hello, MQTT!"
client.publish(topic, message)

# Subscribe to a topic
def on_message(client, userdata, message):
    print(f"Received message: {message.payload.decode()}")

client.on_message = on_message
client.subscribe(topic)

# Start the MQTT loop
client.loop_forever()
```

Identity and Access Management

Identity and Access Management (IAM) is a fundamental concept in cloud security that revolves around managing user identities and controlling their access to cloud resources. In this section, we will explore IAM principles, provide implementation examples, and share related code snippets to demonstrate how IAM can be effectively applied in cloud environments.

IAM is a cornerstone of cloud security, ensuring that the right users have the right access to resources. By effectively implementing IAM solutions provided by cloud service providers like AWS, GCP, and Azure, organizations can maintain strict control over access permissions, enforce security policies, and protect their cloud assets from unauthorized access or misuse.

IAM fundamentals

IAM encompasses user authentication, authorization, and permissions management. Proper IAM implementation ensures that only authorized users can access specific resources or perform defined actions.

Amazon Web Services Identity and Access Management

AWS IAM is a widely used IAM service that allows you to control access to AWS resources. Here is an example using AWS IAM in Python to create a new user and assign permissions:

```python
import boto3

# Initialize the IAM client
iam = boto3.client('iam')

# Create a new IAM user
user_name = 'new_user'
iam.create_user(UserName=user_name)

# Define a policy for the user
policy_document = {
    "Version": "2012-10-17",
    "Statement": [
        {
            "Effect": "Allow",
            "Action": "s3:ListBucket",
            "Resource": "arn:aws:s3:::example-bucket"
        },
        {
            "Effect": "Allow",
            "Action": [
                "s3:GetObject",
                "s3:PutObject"
            ],
            "Resource": "arn:aws:s3:::example-bucket/*"
        }
    ]
}

# Attach the policy to the user
policy_name = 's3-access-policy'
iam.put_user_policy(UserName=user_name, PolicyName=policy_name,
PolicyDocument=json.dumps(policy_document))
```

Google Cloud Identity and Access Management

Google Cloud IAM is used to manage access to GCP resources. Here is an example using GCP IAM in Python to grant a user permission to a GCP project:

```
from google.oauth2 import service_account
from googleapiclient import discovery

# Define the service account key file
key_file_path = 'path/to/service_account_key.json'

# Initialize the IAM API client
credentials = service_account.Credentials.from_service_account_file(key_file_
path, scopes=['https://www.googleapis.com/auth/cloud-platform'])
iam = discovery.build('iam', 'v1', credentials=credentials)

# Define the user's email
user_email = 'user@example.com'

# Grant the user the roles/editor role on the project
project_id = 'my-project-id'
policy = iam.projects().getIamPolicy(resource=project_id).execute()
policy['bindings'].append({'role': 'roles/editor', 'members': ['user:' +
user_email]})
iam.projects().setIamPolicy(resource=project_id, body={'policy': policy}).
execute()
```

Azure Identity and Access Management

Azure IAM is used to manage access to Azure resources. Here is an example using Azure IAM in Python to create a new user and assign them a role:

```
from azure.identity import DefaultAzureCredential
from azure.management.resources import ResourceManagementClient

# Initialize the Azure Resource Management client
credential = DefaultAzureCredential()
resource_client = ResourceManagementClient(credential, 'your-subscription-id')

# Define the user's details
user_principal_name = 'user@example.com'
role_name = 'Contributor'
scope = '/subscriptions/your-subscription-id'

# Create a new user and assign the role
resource_client.role_assignments.create(scope,role_name, user_principal_name)
```

Security compliance in cloud technology

Ensuring security compliance is a crucial aspect of cloud technology, especially for organizations subject to regulatory requirements. In this section, we will explore the concept of security compliance, provide implementation examples, and share related code snippets to help organizations meet industry-specific standards and regulations.

Security compliance is essential for organizations to protect sensitive data and maintain trust with customers and partners. By using the compliance tools and resources provided by cloud service providers like AWS, GCP, and Azure, organizations can assess, enforce, and report on compliance with regulatory frameworks, ensuring that their cloud deployments meet industry-specific standards and best practices.

Security compliance involves adhering to industry-specific regulations, standards, and best practices to protect data and maintain trust. Common regulatory frameworks include the *General Data Protection Regulation (GDPR)*, the *Health Insurance Portability and Accountability Act (HIPAA)*, *Payment Card Industry Data Security Standard (PCI DSS)*, and more.

Example of implementing compliance in AWS

AWS offers various compliance tools and resources to help organizations meet regulatory requirements. Here is an example of using AWS Config to monitor and enforce compliance rules:

```
import boto3

# Initialize the AWS Config client
config = boto3.client('config')

# Define a custom AWS Config rule for compliance
rule_name = 'my-custom-compliance-rule'
description = 'Ensure EC2 instances are properly tagged'
scope = {
    'ComplianceResourceTypes': ['AWS::EC2::Instance']
}
input_parameters = {
    'tagKey': 'Environment',
    'tagValue': 'Production'
}

# Create the AWS Config rule
```

```
config.put_config_rule(
    ConfigRuleName=rule_name,
    Description=description,
    Scope=scope,
    Source={
        'Owner': 'AWS',
        'SourceIdentifier': 'EC2_INSTANCE_PROPERLY_TAGGED'
    },
    InputParameters=input_parameters
)
```

Implementing compliance in GCP

GCP provides compliance solutions to assist organizations in adhering to regulations. Here is an example using the GCP Security Command Center to assess compliance with *Center for Internet Security (CIS) Benchmarks*:

```
from google.cloud import securitycenter

# Initialize the Security Command Center client
client = securitycenter.SecurityCenterClient()

# Define the CIS benchmark finding filter
filter_ = 'resource.type="gce_instance" AND source_properties.cis-benchmark-
compliance="FAILED"'

# Query Security Command Center for non-compliant resources
findings = client.list_findings(parent="organizations/your-organization-id",
filter_=filter_)

# Process and remediate non-compliant resources
for finding in findings:
    resource_name = finding.resource_name
    # Remediate the non-compliance as needed
```

Implementing compliance in Azure

Microsoft Azure offers compliance solutions and tools to help organizations meet regulatory requirements. Here is an example of using Azure Policy to enforce compliance rules:

```
from azure.identity import DefaultAzureCredential
from azure.management.policyinsights import PolicyInsightsClient
from azure.management.policyinsights.models import ComplianceStateType

# Initialize the Azure Policy Insights client
credential = DefaultAzureCredential()
policy_client = PolicyInsightsClient(credential)

# Define the compliance state filter
filter_ = "policyAssignmentId eq '/subscriptions/your-subscription-id/
providers/Microsoft.Authorization/policyAssignments/your-policy-assignment-
id' and complianceState eq 'NonCompliant'"

# Query Azure Policy Insights for non-compliant resources
non_compliant_resources = list(policy_client.query_results.
list(query=filter_))

# Remediate non-compliant resources as needed
for resource in non_compliant_resources:
    resource_id = resource.policy_assignment_id
    # Remediate the non-compliance as needed
```

Logging and monitoring

Logging and monitoring are essential components of cloud security, enabling organizations to detect and respond to security incidents promptly. In this section, we will understand the significance of logging and monitoring, provide implementation examples, and share related code snippets to demonstrate their application in cloud environments.

Logging and monitoring are indispensable for detecting and responding to security incidents in cloud environments. By using cloud-native services like AWS CloudWatch, GCP Cloud Monitoring and Logging, and Azure Monitor, organizations can gain visibility into their resources, setup alerts for suspicious activities, and respond swiftly to security threats, enhancing their overall security posture.

Logging involves recording events and activities within a cloud environment, while monitoring is the real-time analysis of these logs for anomalies and security threats. Combined, they provide the visibility needed to identify and respond to security incidents effectively.

AWS CloudWatch for logging and monitoring

Amazon CloudWatch is a comprehensive service for logging and monitoring AWS resources. Here is an example of setting up CloudWatch Logs and alarms using Python's **boto3** library:

```python
import boto3


# Initialize the CloudWatch client
cloudwatch = boto3.client('cloudwatch')


# Create a CloudWatch Log Group
log_group_name = 'my-log-group'
cloudwatch.create_log_group(logGroupName=log_group_name)


# Create a CloudWatch Log Stream
log_stream_name = 'my-log-stream'
cloudwatch.create_log_stream(logGroupName=log_group_name,
logStreamName=log_stream_name)


# Put a log event into the Log Stream
log_event = 'Error: Unauthorized access attempt'
cloudwatch.put_log_events(
    logGroupName=log_group_name,
    logStreamName=log_stream_name,
    logEvents=[
        {
            'timestamp': 1234567890,
            'message': log_event
        }
    ]
)


# Create a CloudWatch Alarm
alarm_name = 'my-alarm'
cloudwatch.put_metric_alarm(
    AlarmName=alarm_name,
    AlarmDescription='Unauthorized access alarm',
    ActionsEnabled=True,
```

```
    AlarmActions=['arn:aws:sns:us-east-1:123456789012:my-topic'],
    MetricName='Errors',
    Namespace='LogMetrics',
    Statistic='Sum',
    Period=60,
    EvaluationPeriods=1,
    Threshold=1,
    ComparisonOperator='GreaterThanOrEqualToThreshold'
)
```

GCP Cloud Monitoring and Logging

Google Cloud Monitoring and Logging provide comprehensive observability for GCP resources. Here is an example of setting up logs and alerts using the Google Cloud SDK:

```
# Create a new Log Sink
gcloud logging sinks create my-log-sink pubsub.googleapis.com/projects/my-
project-id/topics/my-topic --log-filter='severity>=ERROR'


# Create an alert policy
gcloud monitoring alert-policies create my-alert-policy --notification-
channels='projects/my-project-id/notificationChannels/my-notification-
channel' --conditions=metric.type="logging.googleapis.com/user/my-log-sink"
AND metric.label.severity="ERROR"
```

Azure Monitor and Azure Log Analytics

Azure Monitor and Azure Log Analytics provide robust monitoring and logging capabilities for Azure resources. Here is an example of creating an Azure Log Analytics workspace and configuring alerts using Azure CLI:

```
# Create a Log Analytics workspace
az monitor log-analytics workspace create --resource-group my-resource-
group --workspace-name my-log-analytics-workspace --location eastus


# Configure a diagnostic setting to send logs to Log Analytics
az monitor diagnostic-settings create --name my-diagnostic-settings
--resource my-resource-id --workspace my-log-analytics-workspace --logs
'[{"category": "SecurityEvents", "enabled": true}]'


# Create an action group for alerts
az monitor action-group create --name my-action-group --resource-group my-
```

```
resource-group --short-name my-action-group --email-action email@example.com
```

```
# Create an alert rule
az monitor metrics alert create --name my-alert-rule --resource my-
resource-id --resource-group my-resource-group --condition "count >= 1"
--window-size 5m --action my-action-group --description "Security alert"
--severity 3
```

Incident response

Incident response is a critical aspect of cloud security, ensuring that organizations can effectively detect, contain, and mitigate security incidents. In this section, we will explore the principles of incident response, provide implementation examples, and share related code snippets to demonstrate how to respond to security incidents in cloud environments.

Incident response fundamentals

Incident response is a structured approach to addressing and managing security incidents. It involves several key phases, including detection, analysis, containment, eradication, recovery, and lessons learned.

Incident detection in AWS

AWS offers various tools and services for incident detection, such as AWS CloudTrail for logging and AWS Config for resource tracking. Here is an example of setting up AWS CloudTrail and configuring an S3 bucket to store logs:

```python
import boto3

# Initialize the CloudTrail client
cloudtrail = boto3.client('cloudtrail')

# Create a new CloudTrail trail
trail_name = 'my-cloudtrail-trail'
cloudtrail.create_trail(
    Name=trail_name,
    S3BucketName='my-cloudtrail-logs-bucket',
)

# Start the trail
cloudtrail.start_logging(Name=trail_name)
```

Incident analysis in GCP

GCP offers tools like Google **Cloud Security Command Center** (**Cloud SCC**) for incident analysis. Here is an example of using Cloud SCC to analyze security findings:

```
from google.cloud import securitycenter

# Initialize the Security Command Center client
client = securitycenter.SecurityCenterClient()

# List all security findings
findings = list(client.list_findings(parent="organizations/your-organization-
id"))

# Analyze and respond to security findings
for finding in findings:
    # Analyze the finding and take appropriate action
```

Incident containment and mitigation in Azure

Microsoft Azure provides resources like Azure Security Center for incident containment and mitigation. Here is an example of using Azure Security Center to initiate a **virtual machine** (**VM**) remediation:

```
# Trigger a VM remediation using Azure Security Center
az vm remediate --name my-vm --resource-group my-resource-group
```

Incident recovery and lessons learned

Incident recovery involves restoring affected systems and data to their normal state, while lessons learned involve evaluating the incident response process to improve future responses.

Incident response playbooks

Incident response playbooks are predefined procedures that guide incident responders through the steps to take during an incident. These playbooks can be implemented using various automation tools and scripts tailored to your organization's specific needs.

Security training and awareness

Security training and awareness are critical components of cloud security, helping organizations educate their employees and users to recognize and prevent security threats are vital for organizations to strengthen their security posture and reduce the risk of security breaches. By providing employees and users with the knowledge and tools to recognize and respond to security threats, organizations can create a security-conscious culture and minimize the human factor in security incidents.

In this section, we will explore the importance of security training and awareness, provide implementation examples, and share related resources to help organizations create effective security education programs.

Importance of security training and awareness

Security training and awareness are essential for fostering a security-conscious culture within an organization. They empower employees and users to understand security best practices, recognize threats, and respond appropriately.

Security training programs

Organizations should establish security training programs that cover a range of topics, including:

- **Phishing awareness**: Training employees to identify phishing emails and avoid falling victim to phishing attacks.

- **Password management**: Educating users on creating strong passwords and using password managers.

- **Data handling**: Teaching proper data handling procedures, especially when dealing with sensitive or confidential information.

- **Device security**: Promoting secure device usage, including laptops, mobile devices, and IoT devices.

- **Cloud security**: Providing guidance on securely using cloud services, configuring security settings, and recognizing cloud-related threats.

Security training implementation example

Here is an example of implementing a simple security training module in Python, covering the topic of password management:

```python
def password_training():
    print("Welcome to Password Management Training!")
    print("You will learn how to create strong passwords.")

    while True:
        password = input("Enter a new password: ")
```

```
        if len(password) < 8:
            print("Password is too short. It should be at least 8
characters.")
        elif not any(char.isupper() for char in password):
            print("Password should contain at least one uppercase letter.")
        elif not any(char.islower() for char in password):
            print("Password should contain at least one lowercase letter.")
        elif not any(char.isdigit() for char in password):
            print("Password should contain at least one digit.")
        else:
            print("Congratulations! Your password is strong.")
            break

if __name__ == "__main__":
    password_training()
```

Security awareness programs

In addition to formal training, organizations should create ongoing security awareness programs. These programs can include:

- **Regular security newsletters**: Providing employees with security updates, best practices, and tips through newsletters.

- **Simulated phishing campaigns**: Running simulated phishing campaigns to test employees' awareness and training effectiveness.

- **Security awareness events**: Hosting events or webinars to raise awareness about emerging threats and best practices.

- **Reporting mechanisms**: Establishing a clear process for reporting security incidents or suspicious activities.

Security awareness implementation example

Here is an example of implementing a simulated phishing campaign using Python and the **smtplib** library to send simulated phishing emails to employees:

```
import smtplib

# Simulated phishing email content
subject = "Urgent: Verify Your Account"
```

```
body = "Click the link below to verify your account:\nhttps://phishingsite.
com/verify"
sender_email = "phishing@example.com"
recipient_email = "employee@example.com"

# Send the simulated phishing email
with smtplib.SMTP("smtp.example.com") as server:
    server.login(sender_email, "password")
    server.sendmail(sender_email, recipient_email, f"Subject: {subject}\n\
n{body}")
```

Conclusion

Securing cloud-native environments requires a holistic approach, covering compliance, Zero Trust, data protection, attack surface reduction, architecture design, and vulnerability management. Adhering to compliance standards ensures data integrity and trust, while a Zero Trust model enforces continuous verification and access controls. Strong data protection policies and attack surface reduction enhance resilience against cyber threats. Well-architected, scalable designs and effective patch management further strengthen security. Cloud providers like AWS, Google Cloud, and Azure offer tools to streamline these efforts. Continuous monitoring and adaptability are key to maintaining a robust and secure cloud-native ecosystem.

In the next chapter, we will be focusing on the strategic application of security and compliance measures outside the cloud, fortifying the security posture of non-cloud architectures through well-defined strategies and robust policies.

Key takeaways

The important takeaways from this chapter are as follows:

- **Holistic approach**: Cloud-native security requires a comprehensive approach that encompasses compliance, Zero Trust, data protection, attack surface reduction, architecture design, patching, and vulnerability management.

- **Compliance awareness**: Understanding and adhering to compliance standards such as GDPR, HIPAA, PCI DSS, and SOC 2 is crucial to maintaining data integrity and legal requirements.

- **Zero Trust fundamentals**: Implementing a Zero Trust architecture emphasizes continuous verification, strong access controls, and context-based access to enhance security.

- **Data protection prioritization**: Data classification, encryption at rest and in transit, data masking, and retention policies are vital to protect sensitive information.

- **Attack surface awareness**: Reducing the attack surface through network segmentation, microservices design, and API security helps minimize potential vulnerabilities.

- **Architecture for security**: Scalable, resilient, and stateless architecture designs, coupled with CI/CD integration, create a strong foundation for cloud-native security.

- **Patching best practices**: Automation, regular testing, prioritization, and phased rollouts are essential for effective patch management in dynamic cloud environments.

- **Vulnerability management**: Regular vulnerability scanning and penetration testing identify weaknesses, allowing timely mitigation and improved security measures.

- **Platform-specific tools**: Leading cloud platforms like AWS, Google Cloud, Azure, and IBM Cloud provide specialized tools for security, compliance, and vulnerability management.

- **Continuous improvement**: Ongoing monitoring, adaptation, and learning from experiences ensure that cloud-native security remains robust and responsive.

- **Reader objectives**: As a reader, your objectives are to master compliance standards, embrace Zero Trust principles, implement data protection policies, reduce attack surfaces, design resilient architectures, prioritize patching, and execute effective vulnerability management.

By embracing these takeaways, organizations can confidently navigate the complexities of cloud-native security, mitigating risks and building resilient systems that protect data, applications, and users in the ever-changing landscape of technology and threats.

Key terms

- **Compliance considerations**:
  - **Compliance**: Adherence to regulatory standards and policies.
  - **GDPR**: European Union data protection law.
  - **HIPAA**: Healthcare data protection law.
  - **PCI DSS**: Credit card data security requirements.
  - **SOC 2**: Framework for security, availability, processing integrity, confidentiality, and privacy.

- **Zero Trust**:
  - **Zero Trust architecture**: A security approach based on continuous verification and limited trust.
  - **Identity verification**: Confirming user or device identity before granting access.

- o **Context-based access**: Allowing access based on user context, regardless of location.
- **Data protection policies**:
  - o **Data classification**: Categorizing data based on sensitivity.
  - o **Encryption at rest**: Data encryption when stored in databases or storage.
  - o **Data masking**: Replacing sensitive data with fictitious values for protection.
  - o **Data retention**: Defining data storage duration based on legal or business requirements.
- **Attack surface reduction**:
  - o **Attack surface**: Points of vulnerability in a system or application.
  - o **Network segmentation**: Isolating network components to reduce attack opportunities.
- **Architecture design**:
  - o **Microservices architecture**: Application design using small, independent services.
  - o **Scalability**: Ability to handle increased workloads.
  - o **Resilience**: System's ability to recover from failures.
  - o **CI/CD**: An automated software delivery process.
- **Patching**:
  - o **Patch management**: Applying updates to software to address vulnerabilities.
  - o **Automation**: Automated processes for patch deployment and management.
- **Vulnerability scans/vulnerability assessment and penetration testing**:
  - o **Vulnerability scanning**: Identifying vulnerabilities in software and systems.
  - o **Penetration testing**: Simulating real-world attacks to find security weaknesses.
- **Cloud platforms**:
  - o **AWS**: Cloud computing platform by Amazon.
  - o **Google Cloud**: Cloud services and infrastructure by Google.
  - o **Microsoft Azure**: Cloud computing platform by Microsoft.
  - o **IBM Cloud**: Cloud services and solutions by IBM.
- **Continuous improvement**:
  - o **Continuous monitoring**: Ongoing observation and assessment of security measures.
  - o **CI/CD integration**: Integrating security practices into the CD process.

- **Security posture**:
  - ○ **Security resilience**: Ability to withstand and recover from security incidents.
  - ○ **Threat management**: Strategies to detect and mitigate cybersecurity threats.

Solved exercises

1. **What is the core principle of the Zero Trust security model?**

   Answer: The Zero Trust security model is based on continuous verification and least privilege access. It assumes that no user or device should be trusted by default—access is granted only after verifying identity and context.

2. **What is the purpose of data masking in cloud security?**

   Answer: Data masking replaces sensitive information with fictitious but realistic values to protect the actual data during testing, development, or exposure to untrusted environments.

3. **Which cloud platform provides the Well-Architected Framework for guiding secure cloud design?**

   Answer: AWS provides the AWS Well-Architected Framework to help design secure, high-performing, resilient, and efficient cloud infrastructure.

4. **What does vulnerability scanning help detect in a cloud-native environment?**

   Answer: Vulnerability scanning identifies and assesses known security weaknesses in software, infrastructure, and configurations to prevent potential exploitation.

5. **What is the benefit of using a microservices architecture in cloud-native applications?**

   Answer: Microservices architecture allows applications to be broken into smaller, independent services, enabling better scalability, resilience, and isolated security control for each service.

6. **Why are phased rollouts important in patch management?**

   Answer: Phased rollouts help minimize disruption by gradually deploying patches across environments, allowing early detection of issues before full-scale implementation.

7. **What is the function of CI/CD pipelines in secure cloud development?**

   Answer: CI/CD pipelines automate testing and deployment, enabling frequent code changes while integrating security checks, ensuring faster and safer delivery of updates.

8. **How does penetration testing differ from vulnerability scanning?**

   Answer: While vulnerability scanning identifies potential weaknesses, penetration testing simulates real-world attacks to exploit those weaknesses and demonstrate the potential impact.

9. **What is the role of continuous monitoring in cloud-native environments?**

   Answer: Continuous monitoring ensures real-time visibility into systems, enabling early detection of threats, compliance enforcement, and adaptive responses to security incidents.

10. **Why are reference architectures like the AWS Well-Architected Framework valuable?**

    Answer: They provide best practices and guidelines for building secure, scalable, and resilient applications, reducing design errors and aligning solutions with industry standards.

Unsolved exercises

1. Explain the core principles of the Zero Trust security model and how it differs from traditional perimeter-based security.

2. Discuss the significance of compliance considerations in cloud-native environments. Can you provide examples of compliance standards relevant to cloud computing?

3. What are some key components of an effective data protection policy for cloud-native applications? How do data classification, encryption, and access controls contribute to data security?

4. Describe the concept of network segmentation and its role in reducing the attack surface. How can network segmentation be implemented effectively in a cloud-native architecture?

5. Explain the benefits of adopting a microservices architecture for cloud-native applications. How does a microservices approach contribute to security, scalability, and resilience?

6. Discuss the challenges of patch management in cloud-native environments. How can organizations overcome these challenges and ensure effective patching?

7. What is the purpose of vulnerability scanning in cloud-native security? How does continuous vulnerability monitoring contribute to maintaining a secure cloud environment?

8. Differentiate between penetration testing and vulnerability scanning. Can you provide examples of scenarios where each practice is valuable?

9. How can organizations ensure a proactive approach to security in cloud-native environments? What strategies and best practices can be employed for continuous security improvement?

10. Explain the role of reference architectures provided by cloud platforms in designing secure and reliable cloud-native applications. How can organizations benefit from incorporating these frameworks into their design processes?

## CHAPTER 11

Best Practices for Non-cloud-native Implementations

Introduction

In this chapter, we will focus on the strategic application of security and compliance measures outside the cloud. As organizations continue to manage and operate within non-cloud-native environments, understanding how to effectively implement security frameworks, such as the Zero Trust model, and maintain rigorous compliance standards is paramount. This chapter unpacks these practices, aiming to fortify the security posture of non-cloud architectures through well-defined strategies and robust policies.

Tailored for both professionals and students, this chapter bridges foundational security principles with advanced practices essential for protecting non-cloud infrastructures. By integrating theoretical concepts with practical applications, including data protection policies and vulnerability assessments, readers are equipped to design, enhance, and secure their non-cloud environments effectively. Through engaging case studies and interactive exercises, this chapter not only educates but also empowers readers to apply these best practices in real-world scenarios, thereby enhancing both their understanding and their ability to act in non-cloud settings.

Structure

The chapter covers the following topics:

- Zero Trust

- Data protection policies
- Attack surface
- Architecture
- Patching
- Vulnerability scans and VAPT

Objectives

By the end of this chapter, you will have a comprehensive understanding of best practices for non-cloud-native implementations. You will learn the significance of applying rigorous security measures and compliance standards in environments not hosted in the cloud. You will gain proficiency in frameworks such as Zero Trust, understand how to secure a perimeter-less architecture, and become adept at implementing robust data protection and vulnerability management strategies. The chapter will equip you with the skills to design secure architectures, conduct effective patch management, and carry out thorough vulnerability assessments, preparing you to enhance the security and compliance of non-cloud infrastructures.

Prerequisites

Readers should come prepared with a basic understanding of network security, including familiarity with common security protocols and mechanisms. Additionally, foundational knowledge of IT infrastructure-both hardware and software-is crucial, as it will aid in grasping the best practices for securing non-cloud-native environments.

A general awareness of compliance requirements and standards is also beneficial, setting the stage for more detailed discussions on adhering to legal and regulatory frameworks. These prerequisites are crucial for fully engaging with the chapter's content, focused on implementing rigorous security measures and compliance standards in non-cloud environments.

Zero Trust

Zero Trust is a strategic approach to cybersecurity that eliminates the traditional concept of a trusted internal network and an untrusted external network. Instead, it requires all users, whether inside or outside the organization's network, to be authenticated, authorized, and continuously validated for security configuration and posture before being granted access to applications and data.

Significance of Zero Trust in non-cloud environments

In non-cloud-native environments, where resources may reside within a fixed and controllable perimeter, the Zero Trust model is especially pertinent. It addresses the vulnerabilities that arise from assuming that everything inside an organization's network can be trusted. This assumption often leads to exploitable security gaps, particularly when dealing with sophisticated threats and insider risks.

Core principles of Zero Trust

The Zero Trust security model is based on several core principles that help organizations minimize risks and protect sensitive data. The following key principles outline the fundamental aspects of Zero Trust:

- **Least privilege access**: Each user and device are given the minimum access required to perform their tasks. This principle reduces the potential damage from breaches and insider threats.

- **Microsegmentation**: The network is divided into secure zones. Each zone requires separate access permissions, and communication between zones is strictly controlled, limiting the spread of breaches.

- **Multi-factor authentication (MFA)**: MFA is enforced on all access points to verify the identity of users and devices, enhancing the security of sensitive resources.

- **Continuous monitoring and validation**: Regular checks are performed on the user's and device's security posture to ensure compliance with the organization's security policies. This ongoing verification helps detect and respond to threats in real-time.

Implementing Zero Trust

Implementing Zero Trust in non-cloud-native architectures require a structured approach to securing critical data and controlling access. The following steps outline key strategies to effectively apply Zero Trust principles in such environments:

- **Identify sensitive data and resources**: Begin by identifying which data, assets, and services are critical and require protection under the Zero Trust model.

- **Map the transaction flows**: Understand how traffic moves across the network, which helps in designing a microsegmentation strategy to protect these flows.

- **Enforce strict, access controls**: Implement strict access control policies using an **Identity and Access Management (IAM)** framework to ensure that only authenticated and authorized users and devices can access your resources.

- **Deploy security technologies**: Utilize technologies such as firewalls, **intrusion detection systems (IDS)**, and **data loss prevention (DLP)** tools to monitor and control access points and segment networks.

- **Educate and train employees**: Regular training on the principles of Zero Trust and safe security practices is essential for maintaining security awareness and compliance.

Challenges and considerations

While Zero Trust offers significant security benefits, its implementation comes with challenges that organizations must carefully consider. The following are key obstacles and factors to keep in mind when adopting a Zero Trust approach:

- **Legacy systems**: Integrating Zero Trust into older, non-cloud architectures can be challenging due to the inflexibility and vulnerability of legacy systems.

- **Complexity in implementation**: Designing and maintaining a Zero Trust architecture requires a deep understanding of network layouts and rigorous management of access controls, which can be complex and resource-intensive.

- **Continuous improvement**: Zero Trust is not a set it and forget it solution. It requires ongoing assessment and adaptation to new threats and evolving technologies.

Implementing Zero Trust in non-cloud-native implementations enhance security by rigorously verifying everything attempting to connect to an organization's systems before access is granted. By adopting a Zero Trust framework, businesses can significantly mitigate the risk of data breaches and build a robust defense against both external and internal threats. This proactive approach is fundamental in creating a secure operational environment for non-cloud-native systems.

Data protection policies

Data protection policies are essential guidelines that dictate how an organization's data is managed, secured, and preserved to ensure confidentiality, integrity, and availability. In non-cloud-native environments, where data may reside on physical servers or in-house databases, these policies play a critical role in safeguarding sensitive information from unauthorized access and breaches.

Importance of data protection

In non-cloud-native settings, direct control over physical systems and data storage can offer advantages in terms of data security customization and compliance with regulations. However, it also entails the responsibility of manually securing the infrastructure and applying comprehensive data protection policies to prevent data loss and mitigate threats.

Core elements of data protection policies

Implementing effective data protection policies in non-cloud environments requires a structured approach to safeguarding sensitive information. The following core elements are essential for ensuring data security and compliance in such architectures:

- **Data classification**: Identify and classify data based on its sensitivity and importance to the organization. This classification helps in applying appropriate security measures and compliance protocols.

- **Access control**: Define who can access different types of data based on their role within the organization. Implementing **role-based access control (RBAC)** ensures that employees only access data necessary for their duties.

- **Data encryption**: Encrypt sensitive data both at rest and in transit to protect it from unauthorized access. Encryption is vital in preventing data breaches, especially for sensitive information such as personal identification numbers, financial details, and health records.

- **Physical security**: Since non-cloud environments often involve on-premises data storage, physical security measures are crucial. This includes secure facilities, controlled access, and surveillance systems to protect against unauthorized physical access.

- **Data retention and disposal**: Establish policies for how long different types of data are retained and the methods for safely disposing of data that is no longer needed. This is important for compliance with legal and regulatory requirements and for protecting against data leakage.

Implementing data protection policies

Implementing data protection policies in non-cloud architectures requires a comprehensive strategy to safeguard sensitive information and ensure compliance. The following key steps outline best practices for developing and maintaining effective data protection policies:

- **Policy development**: Collaborate with stakeholders, including IT, legal, and compliance teams, to develop policies that address all aspects of data protection specific to the organization's needs.

- **Regular audits**: Conduct regular audits to ensure that data protection policies are being followed and to identify any areas of improvement. Audits help in maintaining compliance and improving data security practices.

- **Incident response planning**: Develop and implement an incident response plan that includes procedures for responding to data breaches. This plan should outline roles and responsibilities, as well as steps for containing and mitigating incidents.

- **Training and awareness**: Regular training programs for employees on the importance of data protection, understanding the organization's policies, and recognizing security threats. This helps in building a culture of security awareness within the organization.

- **Update and adaptation**: Data protection policies should be dynamic, adapting to new threats, technological advancements, and changes in regulatory requirements. Regularly update the policies to reflect these changes.

Challenges and considerations

When implementing data protection policies in non-cloud environments, organizations must navigate several challenges. The following are key considerations to address for effective policy enforcement and security management:

- **Complexity in enforcement**: Enforcing data protection policies in non-cloud environments can be challenging due to the need for extensive manual processes and monitoring.

- **Integration with modern technologies**: Integrating traditional data protection methods with newer technologies and systems can be complex but necessary to ensure comprehensive security.

- **Compliance with multiple regulations**: Organizations may need to comply with multiple regulatory bodies, making it essential to design flexible yet stringent data protection policies.

For non-cloud-native implementations, data protection policies are foundational to securing sensitive information and ensuring operational integrity. By effectively applying these policies, organizations can safeguard their data against the evolving landscape of cyber threats while complying with legal and regulatory standards.

Attack surface

The attack surface of an organization refers to the sum of all possible points (digital and physical) where an unauthorized user can try to enter data or extract data from an environment. In non-cloud-native implementations, managing the attack surface involves understanding and mitigating risks associated with all hardware, software, network services, and data that are accessible to unauthorized entities.

Significance of attack surface management

Non-cloud-native environments typically involve a range of legacy systems, on-premises hardware, and other integrated systems that may not inherently benefit from the automated security controls and configurations available in cloud-based resources. Managing the attack surface in such environments is crucial to protect against external and internal threats, minimize vulnerabilities, and ensure data integrity and system availability.

Key components of attack surface management

Effective attack surface management is crucial for minimizing security risks and protecting organizational assets. The following key components help in identifying, reducing, and mitigating potential attack vectors:

- **Asset discovery and management**: Comprehensive inventory and management of all physical and digital assets. This includes keeping track of what devices are connected to the network, what software is installed and ensuring that unauthorized devices and software are not present.

- **Network segmentation**: Dividing the network into smaller, controlled segments or zones can significantly reduce the attack surface. Each segment can have its own unique security settings and access controls, isolating critical systems from one another to prevent lateral movement by attackers.

- **Regular vulnerability assessments**: Systematic and regular checks for vulnerabilities in the system, including outdated software, missing patches, or configuration errors that could be exploited by attackers. This also involves prioritizing vulnerabilities to address those that pose the greatest risk first.

- **Patch management**: Developing and implementing a robust patch management strategy to ensure that all software and systems are up-to-date with the latest security patches. This reduces the risk of vulnerabilities that can be exploited by cyber-attackers.

- **Least privilege access control**: Implementing strict access controls that limit user access to the minimum necessary to perform their job functions. This reduces the potential for damage if an account is compromised.

Implementing attack surface reduction strategies

Reducing the attack surface in non-cloud architectures requires a proactive approach to security. The following strategies help organizations minimize vulnerabilities and strengthen their overall security posture:

- **Enhanced monitoring and detection**: Deploy advanced monitoring tools to continuously observe network traffic and system activities for unusual behavior that may indicate a security breach.

- **Security configuration management**: Maintain standard security configurations for all systems. Utilize security configuration management tools to automate the process of securing hardware and software configurations against established benchmarks and standards.

- **Employee training and awareness**: Regular training for employees to recognize phishing attacks, social engineering tactics, and other common threats that could expand the attack surface.

- **Physical security measures**: Since non-cloud-native systems often involve significant on-premises components, physical security controls are critical. This includes secure access to buildings, server rooms, and data centers.

- **Third-party risk management**: Manage risks associated with third-party vendors and service providers, including conducting security assessments of their practices and ensuring that they adhere to the organization's security standards.

Challenges and considerations

When reducing the attack surface in non-cloud environments, organizations must navigate several challenges. The following key considerations highlight potential obstacles and factors to address for effective security management:

- **Complexity of legacy systems**: Older systems may not support the latest security practices, making it difficult to reduce the attack surface effectively.

- **Resource constraints**: Limited budget and staffing resources can impede the thorough implementation of attack surface reduction strategies.

- **Balancing usability and security**: Tightening security often comes at the expense of usability or operational efficiency, requiring careful planning to strike the right balance.

Effectively managing the attack surface in non-cloud-native implementations is critical to minimizing potential entry points for attackers. By comprehensively understanding and implementing strategies to reduce the attack surface, organizations can enhance their overall security posture, protect sensitive data, and ensure system integrity in increasingly complex IT environments.

Architecture

Architecture in non-cloud-native implementations involves designing and organizing systems that reside primarily on-premises or in privately managed data centers. This architectural approach dictates how data, applications, and security are integrated and managed across physical servers and infrastructure without the scalable, elastic features typically provided by cloud environments.

Significance of architecture in non-cloud environments

The architecture of non-cloud-native systems is pivotal for ensuring operational efficiency, security, and resilience. Unlike cloud environments, non-cloud architectures often face constraints related to scalability, redundancy, and dynamic resource allocation. Therefore, careful planning and strategic design are crucial to optimize performance and ensure robust security measures are embedded within the fabric of the IT landscape.

Core components of non-cloud architecture

Non-cloud architectures rely on a solid foundation of core components to ensure performance, security, and reliability. The following elements are essential for building and maintaining robust on-premises systems:

- **Scalability and flexibility**: Designing systems that can scale effectively within the limitations of physical hardware. This may involve clustering, load balancing, and the use of scalable storage solutions.

- **Redundancy and fault tolerance**: Implementing redundancy at various levels of the architecture to ensure high availability and fault tolerance. This includes using redundant hardware, RAID configurations for storage, and backup power solutions.

- **Security architecture**: Integrating comprehensive security controls directly into the infrastructure architecture. This includes firewalls, intrusion detection systems, and data encryption, alongside physical security measures to protect hardware and facilities.

- **Network design**: Structuring the network to optimize performance and security. This includes segmenting the network to create secure zones, deploying appropriate routing and switching configurations, and ensuring adequate bandwidth for business operations.

- **Maintenance and upgradability**: Designing systems with future maintenance and upgrades in mind to minimize downtime and disruption. This involves standardizing hardware components, using modular software applications, and planning for easy access to critical components for maintenance.

Implementing effective non-cloud architectures

Building an effective non-cloud architecture requires careful planning, integration, and ongoing management. The following key strategies help ensure a secure, efficient, and scalable on-premises infrastructure:

- **Thorough planning and design**: Begin with comprehensive planning to understand business needs, technological requirements, and security considerations. This includes selecting the right hardware and software that align with the organization's long-term goals.

- **Best practices in system integration**: Ensure that all components of the IT infrastructure are compatible and can integrate seamlessly. This reduces complexities and potential security vulnerabilities associated with disparate systems.

- **Regular system evaluations**: Periodically review the architecture to identify bottlenecks, inefficiencies, or outdated components that may need optimization or replacement.

- **Adherence to standards and compliance**: Design architectures that comply with relevant industry-standards and regulatory requirements. This ensures that the systems are not only secure but also legally compliant.

- **Collaboration across departments**: Encourage ongoing collaboration between IT, security, and operational teams to ensure the architecture continues to meet the evolving needs of the organization.

Challenges and considerations

Implementing and maintaining non-cloud architectures comes with unique challenges that organizations must address to ensure efficiency and security. The following considerations highlight key obstacles and factors to keep in mind:

- **Legacy systems integration**: Integrating new solutions with legacy systems can be challenging but is often necessary to protect investments and ensure continuity of operations.

- **Cost constraints**: Non-cloud architectures may involve significant upfront investment in hardware and infrastructure, necessitating careful budget management and **return on investment (ROI)** analysis.

- **Complex disaster recovery planning**: Developing effective disaster recovery plans in non-cloud environments typically requires more complex considerations due to the physical nature of the infrastructure.

The architecture of non-cloud-native implementations plays a crucial role in how effectively an organization can operate and secure its IT environment. By emphasizing strategic design, security integration, and continuous evaluation, businesses can ensure their non-cloud architectures are robust, secure, and capable of supporting their operational goals. This foundational stability allows organizations to navigate the complexities of non-cloud environments confidently.

Patching

Patching refers to the process of updating software and systems with code changes that are primarily intended to fix vulnerabilities, bugs, or enhance functionalities. In non-cloud-native environments, where infrastructure may not benefit from the automated scaling and updating features of cloud services, effective patch management is crucial for maintaining system security and functionality.

Significance of patch management

The architecture of non-cloud environments often includes a variety of legacy systems, bespoke applications, and dedicated hardware setups that require a more hands-on approach to maintenance and updates. Effective patch management ensures these systems remain secure against known vulnerabilities and operate efficiently, mitigating risks that could lead to data breaches or system failures.

Core components of patch management strategy

A well-structured patch management strategy is essential for maintaining system security, stability, and compliance. The following core components ensure an effective approach to identifying, testing, and deploying patches across an organization's infrastructure:

- **Inventory of assets**: A comprehensive inventory that lists all assets within the infrastructure, detailing their operating systems, applications, and other relevant software. This inventory helps in identifying which systems need updates and the priority of these updates.

- **Standardized patch testing**: Before deployment, patches should be tested in a controlled environment. This helps ensure that they do not introduce new issues into the live environment, particularly incompatibilities or functionality problems.

- **Prioritization of patches**: Not all patches are of equal importance; some fix critical security vulnerabilities while others might enhance features or fix minor bugs. Prioritizing patches based on the risk assessment helps in addressing the most critical vulnerabilities first.

- **Automated patch deployment**: Where possible, automating the deployment of patches can help maintain consistency and reduce the time to patch across the network, minimizing windows of vulnerability.

- **Patch compliance and auditing**: Regular audits to ensure that all systems are compliant with the organization's patch management policy. This should include checks to ensure that patches have been successfully applied and are functioning as expected.

Implementing effective patch management

Effective patch management in non-cloud architectures requires a structured approach to ensure security, system stability, and minimal disruption. The following best practices help organizations streamline the patching process and maintain a secure IT environment:

- **Develop a patch management policy**: Establish a formal policy that outlines how patches are managed, tested, approved, and documented. This policy should be communicated across all IT teams.

- **Leverage patch management tools**: Utilize tools that can help automate the patch management process, from detection and testing to deployment. These tools can also offer valuable reporting features for audit purposes.

- **Regular schedule and maintenance windows**: Establish and adhere to a regular schedule for patch management activities. Set maintenance windows during off-peak hours to minimize impact on business operations.

- **Training and awareness**: Ensure that all IT staff are trained on the importance of patch management and understand the organization's processes and tools. This includes training on how to handle exceptions and emergency patches.

- **Emergency patching procedures**: Develop procedures for emergency patching in response to critical vulnerabilities that are being actively exploited. This process should be expedited and bypass normal testing to protect systems from imminent threats.

Challenges and considerations

Implementing patch management in non-cloud environments comes with unique challenges that must be carefully addressed to ensure system security and stability. The following considerations highlight key obstacles and factors to manage effectively:

- **Compatibility issues**: Especially in environments with legacy systems, patches may not always be fully compatible with older hardware or software, necessitating additional customization or consideration.

- **Resource allocation**: Effective patch management can be resource-intensive, requiring dedicated time and personnel to implement properly.

- **Change management**: Each patch can potentially change the environment in significant ways. Managing these changes to prevent disruption is crucial, particularly in tightly integrated non-cloud environments.

In non-cloud-native implementations, robust patch management is essential for maintaining the security and integrity of the system infrastructure. By implementing structured and proactive patch management practices, organizations can protect themselves against the exploitation of known vulnerabilities and ensure the longevity and reliability of their IT systems. This proactive approach to system maintenance is critical for safeguarding data and maintaining operational stability.

Vulnerability scans and VAPT

Vulnerability scans and **vulnerability assessment and penetration testing (VAPT)** are critical components of a comprehensive security strategy, particularly in non-cloud-native environments. These practices involve the systematic identification, analysis, and testing of security vulnerabilities in an organization's infrastructure, which includes both software and hardware components.

Significance of VAPT in non-cloud environments

In non-cloud-native settings, where infrastructures might not benefit from the continuous updates and centralized security management typical of cloud services, VAPT plays a crucial role. It ensures that existing and potential security vulnerabilities within on-premises systems are identified, assessed, and mitigated. This proactive approach is essential to defend against external attacks and internal security breaches.

Core elements of VAPT for non-cloud architectures

To build a strong security foundation, it is important to regularly assess risks in traditional systems. The following points explain key steps involved in VAPT for non-cloud setups:

- **Vulnerability scanning**: Automated tools are used to scan systems, networks, and applications for known vulnerabilities. These scans provide a snapshot of potential security weaknesses that need to be addressed.

- **Penetration testing**: Unlike automated scans, penetration testing involves simulating real-world attacks in a controlled manner to evaluate the effectiveness of existing security measures. It helps identify vulnerabilities that could be exploited and tests the organization's incident response capabilities.

- **Assessment frequency**: Regular scheduling of vulnerability assessments and penetration tests is crucial. The frequency should align with the risk level of the organization's assets and compliance requirements.

- **Scope and coverage**: Defining the scope is critical to ensure that all relevant systems and applications are tested. This includes network devices, servers, endpoints, and applications, particularly those that handle sensitive or critical data.

- **Remediation and follow-up**: Once vulnerabilities are identified, they must be promptly remediated based on their risk severity. This process should also include a follow-up assessment to ensure that the remediation was effective.

Implementing effective VAPT strategies

A comprehensive VAPT strategy is crucial for identifying and mitigating security risks in non-cloud architectures. The following core elements help ensure a proactive approach to safeguarding systems and data:

- **Develop a VAPT policy**: Establish a formal VAPT policy that outlines the process, responsibilities, scope, and frequency of tests. Ensure that the policy is aligned with industry best practices and compliance requirements.

- **Select appropriate tools and resources**: Utilize industry-standard tools for vulnerability scanning and penetration testing. Consider the specific needs of non-cloud environments, such as the ability to test physical controls and older systems.

- **Engage qualified personnel**: Ensure that the team performing VAPT is qualified and experienced. This may involve in-house experts or external consultants, depending on the organization's capabilities.

- **Comprehensive reporting**: Generate detailed reports that not only highlight vulnerabilities but also provide actionable recommendations for remediation.

Reports should be accessible to relevant stakeholders and used to guide security improvements.

- **Integration with risk management**: Integrate findings from VAPT into the organization's overall risk management strategy. This helps prioritize security efforts based on the potential impact of identified vulnerabilities.

Challenges and considerations

Conducting VAPT in non-cloud environments comes with unique challenges that must be carefully managed. The following key considerations highlight potential obstacles and best practices for effective implementation:

- **Resource-intensive**: Both vulnerability scanning and penetration testing are resource-intensive processes, requiring significant time and specialized skills.

- **Impact on business operations**: Tests, especially penetration testing, can impact system performance or availability. It is crucial to plan these activities during low-impact hours and ensure proper backup processes are in place.

- **Keeping pace with evolving threats**: As new types of threats emerge, the tools and techniques used in VAPT must also evolve. Staying updated with the latest security trends and threat intelligence is essential.

For non-cloud-native environments, effective implementation of vulnerability scans and VAPT is indispensable. These practices not only help identify and mitigate vulnerabilities but also enhance the overall security posture by preparing the organization to handle real-world security challenges effectively. By integrating regular VAPT activities into their security framework, organizations can ensure the ongoing integrity and security of their non-cloud infrastructures.

Conclusion

This chapter covers essential strategies for enhancing security and compliance in non-cloud-native environments, outlining critical areas such as the implementation of Zero Trust principles, development of robust data protection policies, management of the attack surface, and thoughtful architectural design. It highlights the importance of rigorous patch management and regular vulnerability assessments VAPT to preemptively address potential security weaknesses. Specific topics covered include designing non-cloud systems with scalability and redundancy in mind, integrating security directly into infrastructure, and automating patch processes to reduce vulnerabilities. The chapter also emphasizes the significance of ongoing employee training in security best practices and the necessity for regular compliance checks and audits to ensure systems adhere to regulatory standards. By applying these comprehensive best practices, organizations can significantly fortify their non-cloud-native systems against emerging threats while maintaining high operational efficiency and compliance with regulatory requirements.

In the next chapter, we will be focusing on how to integrate security seamlessly into DevOps practices, particularly within cloud environments. Utilizing tools like Jenkins and other automation engines, we explore how to setup effective DevSecOps pipelines that enhance security without sacrificing speed or efficiency.

Key takeaways

- **Zero Trust is essential**: Even in on-premise environments, never assume any user or device is trustworthy. Apply strict access controls, microsegmentation, and continuous verification to limit internal and external risks.

- **Data protection starts with policy**: Develop strong data classification, access control, encryption, and retention policies to secure sensitive information stored on local servers.

- **Know and reduce your attack surface**: Identify every entry point into your systems (devices, applications, users), then reduce exposure using segmentation, regular scans, and access restrictions.

- **Design architecture with security in mind**: Build non-cloud systems with scalability, redundancy, fault tolerance, and embedded security controls like firewalls and IDS to ensure operational resilience.

- **Patching is non-negotiable**: Timely patching of all systems prevents exploitation of known vulnerabilities. Use automated tools, defined policies, and clear schedules to stay current.

- **VAPT strengthens defense**: Regularly conduct vulnerability scans and penetration tests to find and fix weak points before attackers do. This is crucial for systems without cloud's built-in protections.

- **Train your people**: Employees play a key role in security. Continuous training helps them spot threats like phishing and follow proper data handling procedures.

- **Plan for legacy challenges**: Older systems cannot always support modern security tools. Customize solutions and integrate them cautiously while preparing for eventual upgrades.

- **Compliance is an ongoing process**: Maintain alignment with legal and regulatory standards through audits, documentation, and regular updates to your policies and practices.

- **Physical security still matters**: On-premise environments require strong physical protections—secure server rooms, access control, and surveillance are vital.

Key terms

- **Zero Trust**: A security model that eliminates the concept of trust from an organization's network architecture. It is based on the principle of never trust, always verify, requiring strict identity verification for every person and device trying to access resources on a private network, regardless of whether they are inside or outside the network perimeter.

- **Data protection policies**: Guidelines and protocols established by an organization to manage the security of its data, including how it is processed, shared, stored, and destroyed, to ensure compliance with regulatory requirements and protect against data breaches.

- **Attack surface**: The total number of points or attack vectors where an unauthorized user can try to enter or extract data from an environment. Managing the attack surface involves reducing the number of possible entry points and vulnerabilities.

- **Architecture**: The structural design of systems and networks in an IT environment. In non-cloud-native implementations, architecture refers to the arrangement and interconnections of physical and virtual components, including servers, storage devices, network equipment, and software systems.

- **Patching**: The process of updating software and systems with modifications like bug fixes or security enhancements to correct known vulnerabilities and improve performance or usability.

- **Vulnerability scans**: Automated processes that inspect the security weaknesses in an organization's systems and software. These scans identify known vulnerabilities that could potentially be exploited by attackers.

- **VAPT**: A comprehensive evaluation process involving the identification, quantification, and prioritization of vulnerabilities in a system, combined with simulated attacks (penetration testing) to assess the security of the system.

- **Patch management**: The systematic notification, identification, deployment, installation, and verification of patches in an IT environment. Effective patch management helps mitigate security risks and maintain system integrity.

- **Compliance**: Adherence to laws, regulations, guidelines, and specifications relevant to the organization's business processes. In the context of IT security, compliance often refers to following standards that protect data privacy and integrity.

- **Microsegmentation**: A security technique that involves dividing a network into separate, secure zones, each with its own set of access controls and security measures. This limits the ability of an attacker to move laterally across a network if they gain access to one part.

- **Legacy systems**: Outdated computing systems or applications that continue to be used, despite the availability of newer technologies. Legacy systems may not support newer security practices, making them vulnerable to cyber threats.

- **Redundancy**: The duplication of critical components or functions of a system with the intention of increasing reliability of the system, usually in the form of a backup or fail-safe.

- **Network segmentation**: The practice of splitting a computer network into subnetworks, each being a network segment or network layer. This enhances performance and improves security.

Solved exercises

1. **What is Zero Trust, and how is it implemented in non-cloud environments?**

   Answer: Zero Trust is a security model that operates on the principle of never trust, always verify, regardless of the user's network location. In non-cloud environments, it is implemented by enforcing strict access controls, segmenting the network into secure zones, and continuously verifying the security posture of all devices and users accessing the system.

2. **Why are data protection policies crucial in non-cloud-native implementations?**

   Answer: Data protection policies are crucial because they ensure the integrity, confidentiality, and availability of data. They help comply with legal and regulatory standards, protect sensitive information from unauthorized access, and mitigate the risks of data breaches.

3. **Describe how attack surface management can be optimized in a non-cloud environment.**

   Answer: Attack surface management in non-cloud environments can be optimized by maintaining a detailed asset inventory, regularly performing vulnerability scans, implementing network segmentation, and enforcing least privilege access controls to minimize potential entry points for attackers.

4. **What role does architecture play in securing non-cloud-native systems?**

   Answer: Architecture plays a crucial role by ensuring systems are designed with security in mind. This includes incorporating elements like redundancy for fault tolerance, secure network design, and scalable configurations that can support security updates and defensive strategies effectively.

5. **How does patch management contribute to cybersecurity in non-cloud environments?**

   Answer: Patch management helps maintain system security by regularly updating software and systems with the latest patches that fix vulnerabilities, thus preventing attackers from exploiting known security gaps.

6. **Explain the importance of conducting regular VAPT in non-cloud architectures.**

   Answer: Regular VAPT allows organizations to proactively discover and fix security vulnerabilities, test the effectiveness of existing security measures, and ensure compliance with cybersecurity standards, thereby reducing the risk of cyberattacks.

7. **What are some challenges of integrating modern security practices with legacy systems in non-cloud environments?**

   Answer: Challenges include compatibility issues, where modern security solutions may not be directly applicable to older systems, resource constraints in updating or replacing outdated technology, and the complexity of managing a mixed environment with varying security capabilities.

8. **How can organizations ensure compliance with data protection regulations in non-cloud-native systems?**

   Answer: Organizations can ensure compliance by implementing strict data protection policies, conducting regular security audits, ensuring all data handling practices meet legal requirements, and maintaining transparent data processing and storage procedures.

9. **What is the significance of employee training in maintaining security in non-cloud-native implementations?**

   Answer: Employee training is significant as it raises awareness about security best practices, equips employees with the skills to recognize and respond to security threats, and fosters a culture of security within the organization, reducing the risk of insider threats and human error.

10. **Describe the process of network segmentation in a non-cloud-native environment.**

    Answer: Network segmentation in a non-cloud-native environment involves dividing the network into smaller, controlled segments or zones. Each segment has its own security settings and access controls, which isolate critical systems from each other, limiting the potential for widespread access in case of a breach.

Unsolved exercises

1. How can Zero Trust architectures be tailored to accommodate legacy applications in a non-cloud-native environment?

2. What strategies can be employed to ensure data encryption in legacy systems that do not support modern encryption methods?

3. Identify the key factors to consider when conducting a risk assessment for a non-cloud-native environment.

4. Discuss the potential impacts of not regularly updating patch management protocols in non-cloud systems.

5. How can microsegmentation be effectively implemented in a complex, non-cloud-native network?

6. What are the best practices for managing third-party risks in non-cloud-native systems?

7. Examine the implications of failing to perform regular VAPT on organizational security and compliance.

8. Propose methods to overcome resource constraints when upgrading security in non-cloud-native systems.

9. What measures can be taken to enhance physical security in non-cloud data centers?

10. Discuss the challenges and solutions for maintaining compliance with international data protection laws in multinational non-cloud environments.

Join our Discord space

Join our Discord workspace for latest updates, offers, tech happenings around the world, new releases, and sessions with the authors:

https://discord.bpbonline.com

CHAPTER 12
DevSecOps

Introduction

In this chapter, we will enter the transformative world of DevSecOps, focusing on how to integrate security seamlessly into DevOps practices, particularly within cloud environments. Utilizing tools like Jenkins and other automation engines, we explore how to setup effective DevSecOps pipelines that enhance security without sacrificing speed or efficiency. This chapter provides a comprehensive guide on planning, building, and managing DevSecOps pipelines, highlighting best practices and common pitfalls.

Designed for early to mid-career professionals and students with a basic understanding of DevOps and cloud computing, this chapter aims to equip readers with the knowledge and skills to implement DevSecOps successfully. Through practical examples, illustrations, and real-life case studies, you will learn to appreciate the critical role of security in the development lifecycle and discover strategies to integrate it seamlessly into your workflows.

Structure

The chapter covers the following topics:

- Jenkins and other engines
- Best practices

- Setting up a secure DevSecOps pipeline
- Planning a pipeline
- Components of pipeline
- Case study

Objectives

By the end of this chapter, you will have a comprehensive understanding of DevSecOps within cloud environments. You will learn the importance of integrating security practices seamlessly into DevOps pipelines using tools like Jenkins and other engines. You will gain proficiency in planning, setting up, and managing DevSecOps pipelines, ensuring they align with both security protocols and business objectives. The chapter will equip you with the skills to identify and implement the necessary components of an effective pipeline, enhancing both security and efficiency in development processes.

Prerequisites

Before starting this chapter, readers should come prepared with a foundational understanding of cloud computing, including familiarity with common cloud platforms and services. Additionally, a basic knowledge of DevOps concepts and practices is essential, as it will aid in understanding the integration of security within these processes. Familiarity with general IT security principles and some experience with automation tools such as Jenkins or similar would also be beneficial. These prerequisites are crucial for fully engaging with the chapter's content, which focuses on advancing these foundational skills into a comprehensive approach to DevSecOps in cloud environments.

Jenkins and other engines

Jenkins is one of the most popular open-source automation servers used in DevOps for **continuous integration/continuous delivery (CI/CD)**. It excels in managing and controlling development processes involving builds, tests, and deployment. In the context of DevSecOps, Jenkins can be configured to include security measures as a fundamental part of these processes, thereby embedding security into the very fabric of the application lifecycle.

Other notable engines

Besides Jenkins, several other CI/CD tools play significant roles in DevSecOps practices, including GitLab CI/CD, CircleCI, Bamboo, and Travis CI. Each tool offers unique features that can support or enhance security integrations within different stages of software development.

Jenkins in DevSecOps

Jenkins plays a crucial role in integrating security into the DevSecOps pipeline. The following key features help enhance security and streamline the development process:

- **Security plugins**: Jenkins supports numerous plugins that enhance security, such as the OWASP Dependency-Check plugin to analyze dependencies for known vulnerabilities, or *Aqua Security Trivy* to scan for vulnerabilities in container images.

- **Automated testing**: Jenkins can automate the execution of static and dynamic security tests, integrating results directly into the development pipeline, which helps in identifying and addressing security issues early in the development cycle.

- **Configuration as code**: Jenkins pipelines can be defined as code, which itself can be version-controlled and reviewed for security compliance, ensuring that security configurations are consistent and under scrutiny.

Capabilities of other engines

The following are some widely used alternatives and their key features:

- **GitLab CI/CD**: Integrates directly with GitLab's **version control systems** (**VCSs**) to provide a seamless CI/CD experience. It includes features for security such as built-in static and dynamic application security testing and dependency scanning.

- **CircleCI**: Known for its high customization capabilities, CircleCI can integrate a variety of security tools into the workflow and is often praised for its performance and ease of use in complex environments.

- **Bamboo**: Created by *Atlassian*, Bamboo is particularly effective for enterprises deeply embedded into the Atlassian ecosystem. It supports various security and compliance features tailored for larger organizations.

- **Travis CI**: Popular in open-source projects, Travis CI facilitates easy integration with GitHub and supports several security extensions to ensure secure software development practices.

Implementing Jenkins and other tools in DevSecOps

To effectively use Jenkins and other engines in DevSecOps, several key practices should be considered, as follows:

- **Continuous security feedback**: Implement tools and plugins that provide real-time security feedback to developers. This helps in addressing vulnerabilities as soon as they are introduced.

- **Integration with security tools**: Ensure that the CI/CD pipeline integrates seamlessly with specialized security tools to perform automated security scans, audits, and checks at each stage of software delivery.

- **Customizable workflows**: Utilize the flexibility of these tools to create customized workflows that match the specific security needs of the organization while maintaining speed and efficiency in the CI/CD process.

Challenges and considerations

The following are some critical factors to address for a successful DevSecOps strategy:

- **Complexity in integration**: Integrating security into existing CI/CD pipelines using Jenkins or other tools can be complex, requiring a deep understanding of both tooling and security.

- **Balancing speed and security**: There is often a tension between the speed of development and the thoroughness of security practices. Finding the right balance is crucial for successful DevSecOps implementation.

- **Keeping up with evolutions**: As both security threats and CI/CD technologies evolve rapidly, continuous learning and adaptation of tools and practices are necessary.

Jenkins and other automation engines are pivotal in implementing DevSecOps by facilitating the integration of security into the development pipeline, enhancing the security posture without compromising the speed or quality of software delivery. These tools, when effectively utilized, can transform the security landscape of software development, ensuring that security is a continuous and integral part of the development process.

Best practices

DevSecOps integrates security into the CI/CD pipeline of DevOps. This approach ensures that security considerations are an inherent part of development, operations, and release processes, rather than being tacked on at the end. Best practices in DevSecOps are designed to automate core security tasks by embedding them into daily operations, thereby improving overall security posture without sacrificing speed or efficiency.

Core best practices in DevSecOps

To build a secure and resilient development pipeline, organizations must adopt key DevSecOps best practices. The following are some essential strategies to integrate security seamlessly into the software development lifecycle:

- **Shift left on security**:
  - **Concept**: Incorporate security early and often in the development lifecycle. By shifting left, security checks and controls are implemented from the very beginning of the software development process.

- **Implementation**: Integrate automated security tools into the VCSs where developers commit their code. Use **static application security testing (SAST)** and **dynamic application security testing (DAST)** tools to catch vulnerabilities early.

- **Automate security processes**:

  o **Concept**: Automation is key in DevSecOps to ensure that security practices keep pace with rapid deployment cycles.

  o **Implementation**: Deploy tools that automatically scan for vulnerabilities in code, dependencies, and even running applications in real-time. Automate the response to common security incidents to speed up resolution times.

- **Continuous security monitoring**:

  o **Concept**: Continuous monitoring of applications and infrastructure to detect and respond to threats in real-time.

  o **Implementation**: Use tools that provide continuous monitoring and alerting for security anomalies. This includes monitoring network traffic, user activities, and access logs to quickly identify potentially malicious activity.

- **Integrate compliance as code**:

  o **Concept**: Compliance requirements are codified to ensure they are automatically applied and validated throughout the development and deployment process.

  o **Implementation**: Use configuration management tools to enforce compliance policies. These tools can check configurations against predefined compliance rules and automatically correct deviations.

- **Foster a collaborative security culture**:

  o **Concept**: Security is a shared responsibility in DevSecOps. Encouraging a culture that promotes close collaboration between development, operations, and security teams is crucial.

  o **Implementation**: Regular training and workshops to update teams on the latest security threats and practices. Encourage security teams to participate in development meetings and vice versa.

- **Use immutable infrastructure**:

  o **Concept**: Immutable infrastructure treats infrastructure elements as replaceable and disposable rather than something to be updated and patched directly.

  o **Implementation**: Use containerization and orchestration tools like Docker and Kubernetes to deploy applications in containers that can be replaced entirely with new versions rather than patched in place.

- **Security incident management and response**:
  - o **Concept**: Develop and implement a robust incident response plan that can handle the security issues effectively and swiftly.
  - o **Implementation**: Automate certain responses to common security incidents. For instance, if an intrusion is detected, the system could automatically isolate affected systems or roll back to a secure state.

Challenges in implementing DevSecOps best practices

While DevSecOps enhances security and efficiency, its implementation comes with several challenges. Organizations must navigate the following obstacles to successfully integrate security into their development workflows:

- **Balancing speed and security**: Developers are often under pressure to deliver features rapidly, which can lead to shortcuts in security. Ensuring that security does not slow down development is a key challenge.

- **Complexity of tools and integration**: With a plethora of tools available, choosing the right ones and integrating them into existing systems can be complex and resource-intensive.

- **Up-skilling teams**: DevSecOps requires a blend of development, operations, and security knowledge. Training teams and fostering interdisciplinary skills are essential but challenging.

Implementing best practices in DevSecOps not only enhances the security of applications but also contributes to a more robust and efficient development pipeline. By embedding security deeply into the CI/CD process, organizations can ensure continuous compliance, reduce vulnerabilities, and foster a proactive security culture that keeps pace with rapid development cycles. These practices are fundamental in building a resilient, secure, and competitive software delivery environment in today's digital landscape.

Setting up a secure DevSecOps pipeline

Setting up a DevSecOps pipeline involves integrating security tools and practices throughout the software development and deployment lifecycle. This process ensures that security is embedded at every stage, from initial design through integration, testing, deployment, and software delivery.

The steps to setup a DevSecOps pipeline are given as follows:

1. **Planning and assessment**:
   a. **Initial planning**: Identify the specific security needs and compliance requirements of the project. Assess the current state of development and operations practices to integrate security smoothly.

b. **Tool selection**: Choose the appropriate tools that can automate security checks and tasks. Tools should be compatible with existing development environments and robust enough to handle required security measures.

2. **Integration of security tools**:

    a. **SAST**: Integrate SAST tools into the VCS so that code is automatically scanned for vulnerabilities upon commit. Tools like SonarQube, Checkmarx, or Fortify can be used for this purpose.

    b. **DAST**: Configure DAST tools to perform automated tests on running applications in pre-production environments. Tools such as OWASP ZAP or Burp Suite are commonly used.

3. **Automate the security pipeline**:

    a. **CI/CD integration**: Integrate security tools within the CI/CD pipeline using platforms like Jenkins, GitLab CI, or CircleCI. This ensures that security scans and tests are part of the build and deployment processes.

    b. **Security as code**: Codify security configurations and policies using **infrastructure as code (IaC)** tools like Terraform or Ansible. This helps maintain consistent security settings across all environments.

4. **Continuous monitoring and feedback**:

    a. **Real-time monitoring**: Implement monitoring tools to continuously track the application and infrastructure health for any security anomalies. Tools like Splunk, Elastic Stack, or Prometheus can provide insights into ongoing operations and potential security issues.

    b. **Feedback mechanisms**: Establish a feedback loop that brings security insights back to development teams quickly. Incorporate automated alerts and dashboards that help developers understand the security context and implications of their code.

5. **Security review and compliance checks**:

    a. **Regular security audits**: Schedule periodic security reviews and compliance checks to ensure that the pipeline and its outputs adhere to established security standards and regulations.

    b. **Compliance as code**: Use compliance scanning tools to audit environments automatically. Tools like Chef InSpec or Aqua Security can validate the security posture against compliance standards.

6. **Training and education**:

    a. **Developer training**: Conduct regular training sessions for developers on secure coding practices and awareness of the latest security threats and vulnerabilities.

b. **Cross-disciplinary collaboration**: Foster a culture of collaboration where security teams are involved in the development process from the start, and developers are made part of security planning and incident response activities.

Challenges in pipeline setup

Setting up a secure and efficient pipeline comes with several challenges that organizations must navigate:

- **Complex integration**: Integrating multiple tools and ensuring they work harmoniously can be complex and time-consuming.

- **Resistance to change**: Cultural resistance from teams accustomed to traditional development practices can impede the adoption of integrated security practices.

- **Maintaining pipeline performance**: Ensuring that the introduction of security checks does not significantly slow down the development and deployment processes.

Setting up a DevSecOps pipeline is a strategic process that enhances security without compromising on efficiency or speed. By automating security tasks, continuously monitoring applications and infrastructure, and fostering a culture of security awareness and collaboration, organizations can protect against evolving cybersecurity threats while maintaining rapid development cycles. This integrated approach not only secures applications but also aligns with modern agile and DevOps practices, ensuring that security and development go hand in hand.

Planning a pipeline

Planning a DevSecOps pipeline is crucial for integrating security seamlessly into the software development lifecycle. This initial planning stage sets the foundation for building a robust, secure, and efficient pipeline that aligns with organizational goals and compliance requirements.

The key steps in planning a DevSecOps pipeline are as follows:

1. **Define security and business objectives**:

    a. **Objective alignment**: Establish clear security goals that align with the organization's business objectives. This might include ensuring data protection, meeting regulatory compliance, or reducing the risk of security breaches.

    b. **Stakeholder involvement**: Engage stakeholders from security, development, operations, and business units early in the planning process to ensure their needs and concerns are addressed.

2. **Assess current infrastructure and capabilities**:

   a. **Infrastructure review**: Conduct a thorough assessment of the existing IT infrastructure, development practices, and security measures. This review helps identify gaps that the DevSecOps pipeline needs to address.

   b. **Capability evaluation**: Evaluate the team's current capabilities in terms of skills, technologies, and processes. Determine if additional training, hiring, or technology acquisitions are necessary.

3. **Select tools and technologies**:

   a. **Tool compatibility**: Choose tools that integrate well with each other and with the existing development environment. Consider tools for continuous integration, continuous delivery, security automation, and monitoring.

   b. **Security integration**: Select security tools that can be integrated throughout the development stages, from code analysis tools for developers to dynamic scanning tools for the **quality assurance (QA)** and operations teams.

4. **Design the pipeline architecture**:

   a. **Workflow design**: Map out the workflow of the pipeline, detailing each stage of the development process from code commit to deployment, and where security checks will be integrated.

   b. **Automation points**: Identify points within the pipeline where processes can be automated, such as code commits, build approvals, security scans, testing, and deployments.

5. **Develop a security policy integration plan**:

   a. **Policy codification**: Develop a plan to codify security policies and compliance requirements into the pipeline, ensuring they are automatically enforced at appropriate stages.

   b. **Compliance checks**: Plan for regular compliance checks within the pipeline to ensure ongoing adherence to standards and regulations.

6. **Plan for monitoring and feedback loops**:

   a. **Continuous monitoring**: Integrate tools that provide continuous monitoring of the deployed applications and infrastructure to detect and respond to threats in real-time.

   b. **Feedback mechanisms**: Establish feedback loops that enable quick communication of security issues back to development teams, facilitating rapid remediation.

7. **Establish risk management and response strategies**:

   a. **Risk assessment**: Regularly assess risks associated with new code, third-party components, and other changes within the pipeline.

b. **Incident response**: Develop and integrate an incident response plan within the pipeline to quickly handle potential security incidents without disrupting the overall workflow.

Challenges in planning a DevSecOps pipeline

Successfully planning a DevSecOps pipeline requires addressing several key challenges as follows:

- **Balancing speed and security**: Finding the right balance between maintaining fast development cycles and integrating thorough security measures.

- **Cultural changes**: Overcoming resistance to new workflows or tools, particularly from teams that are accustomed to less integrated security practices.

- **Resource allocation**: Allocating sufficient resources, both human and technological, to support the implementation and ongoing operation of the pipeline.

Effective planning of a DevSecOps pipeline is a strategic process that requires careful consideration of security, business objectives, existing capabilities, and technological needs. By systematically addressing these areas in the planning phase, organizations can build a DevSecOps pipeline that not only secures their applications and data but also supports efficient and agile development practices. This foundation enables organizations to respond swiftly to security threats and adapt to changing business and regulatory environments.

Components of pipeline

A DevSecOps pipeline integrates various components that work together to ensure that security is a part of the software development lifecycle from inception to deployment. Each component plays a critical role in automating processes, enforcing security policies, and ensuring continuous integration and delivery with an emphasis on security.

Key components of a DevSecOps pipeline

A DevSecOps pipeline consists of several essential components that work together to ensure secure and efficient software development and deployment:

- **Source code repository**:
  - **Function**: Serves as the starting point where all application code is stored and managed. It is crucial for version control and tracking changes.
  - **Security Integration**: Integration with security tools for scanning code upon check-in, ensuring that vulnerabilities are identified and addressed early in the development process.

- **CI server**:

  - **Function**: Automates the building and testing of code every time a change is made to the source code repository. This helps in identifying integration issues early.

  - **Security integration**: Executes security tests alongside other tests, such as SAST, to detect potential security flaws in the code.

- **Configuration management tools**:

  - **Function**: Manages the configuration of servers and other infrastructure components, ensuring they are setup consistently and in compliance with defined policies.

  - **Security integration**: Enforces security configurations and compliance settings automatically across all environments, reducing the risk of human error.

- **Container orchestration tools**:

  - **Function**: Manages the deployment, scaling, and operation of containerized applications, commonly using tools like Kubernetes.

  - **Security integration**: Includes security controls to manage container security, such as ensuring containers are only running approved images and implementing network policies to isolate applications.

- **Artifact repository**:

  - **Function**: Stores built versions of code (artifacts) that are ready to be deployed, ensuring they are retrievable for deployment to different environments.

  - **Security integration**: Scans and stores artifacts safely, ensuring that only secure and approved artifacts are deployed to production environments.

- **Deployment automation tools**:

  - **Function**: Automates the deployment process, ensuring that code moves smoothly from development to production environments without manual intervention.

  - **Security integration**: Includes security checks and gates that must be passed before code is deployed, ensuring compliance with security policies.

- **Monitoring and logging tools**:

  - **Function**: Provides ongoing visibility into the application and infrastructure health by collecting, monitoring, and analyzing logs and metrics.

  - **Security integration**: Monitors for security anomalies and potential threats in real-time, providing alerts and enabling quick response to incidents.

- **Feedback tools**:
  - ○ **Function**: Collects feedback from the operation of applications in production, including user feedback and automated crash reports.
  - ○ **Security integration**: Feeds security incident data back to development teams, facilitating continuous improvement in security practices.

Challenges in integrating pipeline components

Integrating various tools and technologies within a DevSecOps pipeline comes with several challenges:

- **Tool compatibility**: Ensuring that all components of the pipeline integrate seamlessly can be challenging, especially when involving a mix of old and new technologies.
- **Complexity management**: As more tools and processes are integrated, managing the complexity of the pipeline can become difficult, requiring specialized skills and knowledge.
- **Security at scale**: Ensuring that security measures are scalable and do not become bottlenecks as the application and user base grow.

The components of a DevSecOps pipeline are designed to work together to automate the integration, deployment, and security of software applications. By understanding and effectively integrating these components, organizations can ensure that security is not an afterthought but a fundamental aspect of all phases of the development lifecycle. This approach not only improves security outcomes but also enhances the speed and quality of software development, deployment, and maintenance.

Case study

A relevant case study for implementing security as code involves a financial services company transitioning to cloud services while needing to maintain strict compliance with financial regulations. The company adopted Terraform to manage its cloud infrastructure and Ansible for configuration management, ensuring that all deployed resources met compliance and security standards from the outset. They codified security policies, such as encryption protocols for data at rest and in transit, and automated compliance checks against industry standards. This approach significantly reduced manual compliance efforts, accelerated deployment cycles, and enhanced the security posture by integrating compliance and security measures directly into the CI/CD pipeline.

Conclusion

In this chapter, we explored the crucial strategies for setting up and managing a DevSecOps pipeline, particularly within non-cloud environments. Key components like Jenkins and other CI/CD tools, combined with best practices for integrating security into every stage of software development, ensure that security is a fundamental aspect rather than an afterthought. We delved into the significance of planning a pipeline, integrating security tools seamlessly, and employing continuous monitoring to safeguard applications. By understanding how to effectively embed security practices from the start and maintaining vigilant monitoring, organizations can fortify their defenses against emerging threats while fostering a culture that values proactive security measures. This approach not only secures the software development lifecycle but also enhances operational efficiency and compliance, illustrating the transformative potential of DevSecOps in today's digital landscape.

The next chapter is on understanding key standards such as ISO, CMMI, HIPAA, and other significant regulations that impact various aspects of cloud computing. We will explore how these frameworks guide the security measures, data handling practices, and overall governance of cloud services, ensuring that organizations meet legal, ethical, and technical standards.

Key takeaways

- **Security built into DevOps**: DevSecOps integrates security directly into the CI/CD pipeline, ensuring that applications are secure from the first line of code to production release—without slowing down development.

- **Tools like Jenkins power the pipeline**: Jenkins and other automation engines (e.g., GitLab CI, CircleCI, Bamboo) help embed automated security checks (SAST, DAST, dependency scanning) into every phase of development.

- **Best practices drive results**: Strategies like shift left, automating security, using immutable infrastructure, and compliance as code make DevSecOps both secure and efficient.

- **Pipeline setup matters**: Planning and building a secure DevSecOps pipeline involves selecting the right tools, codifying policies, and embedding real-time monitoring and feedback to catch issues early.

- **Culture is key**: Success depends on cross-functional collaboration, continuous upskilling, and treating security as a shared responsibility across development, operations, and security teams.

- **Real-world success**: Case studies show that codifying security and compliance (e.g., using Terraform + Ansible) improves deployment speed, reduces risk, and simplifies audits.

Key terms

- **DevSecOps**: An approach to culture, automation, and platform design that integrates security as a shared responsibility throughout the entire IT lifecycle.

- **Jenkins**: An open-source automation server used to automate parts of software development related to building, testing, and deploying, facilitating continuous integration and continuous delivery.

- **Continuous integration**: A development practice where developers integrate code into a shared repository frequently, preferably several times a day. Each integration can then be verified by an automated build and automated tests.

- **Continuous delivery**: A software development practice where code changes are automatically built, tested, and prepared for a release to production.

- **Static application security testing**: A set of technologies designed to analyze source code, byte code, and binaries for coding and design conditions that are indicative of security vulnerabilities.

- **Dynamic application security testing**: A process of testing an application or software product in an operating state. It is performed from the outside in by attacking the application while it is running.

- **Container orchestration**: The automated arrangement, coordination, and management of computer systems, middleware, and services as part of providing an application or microservice architecture using containers.

- **Kubernetes**: An open-source system for automating deployment, scaling, and management of containerized applications.

- **Artifact repository**: A server that stores artifacts like binaries and dependencies, which are necessary to manage a software release lifecycle.

- **Configuration management**: The process of systematically handling changes to a system in a way that it maintains integrity over time, often involving tools and practices to manage code, automate scripts, and other tasks.

- **Infrastructure as code**: The management of infrastructure (networks, virtual machines, load balancers, and connection topology) in a descriptive model, using the same versioning as DevOps team uses for source code.

- **Shift left**: A practice in software development where teams focus on quality, work on problem prevention instead of detection, and begin testing earlier than traditional methods.

- **Compliance as code**: The principle of coding compliance and regulatory requirements directly into the processes of infrastructure configuration and management.

- **Monitoring and logging tools**: Tools used to continuously monitor applications and infrastructure for performance and security issues, and to capture, store, and analyze log data for further insights.

- **Feedback tools**: Systems and practices used to gather and relay feedback on software performance and security back to development and operations teams to aid in improvement.

Solved exercises

1. **What is DevSecOps and why is it important in modern software development?**

   Answer: DevSecOps integrates security practices within the DevOps process, ensuring that security is a continuous focus from the initial stages of development to deployment. It is important because it reduces the risk of security issues discovered late in the lifecycle, thus maintaining the pace of DevOps without compromising on security.

2. **How does Jenkins facilitate DevSecOps?**

   Answer: Jenkins supports DevSecOps by automating security tasks within the CI/CD pipeline. It can integrate various security tools for static and dynamic analysis, enforce security gates before proceeding to subsequent stages, and automate responses to security issues detected during the build or deployment phases.

3. **What is the role of automated testing in a DevSecOps pipeline?**

   Answer: Automated testing in DevSecOps includes running automated security tests alongside functional tests to catch vulnerabilities early. This helps ensure that security is tested consistently and automatically, reducing the chances of human error and oversight.

4. **Describe how to integrate a SAST tool within the Jenkins pipeline.**

   Answer: A SAST tool can be integrated into the Jenkins pipeline using plugins or scripts that trigger scans automatically when code is committed or as part of scheduled builds. The results are then reviewed, and builds can be failed or flagged if critical vulnerabilities are found, ensuring issues are addressed promptly.

5. **What are the benefits of container orchestration tools in DevSecOps?**

   Answer: Container orchestration tools like Kubernetes enhance DevSecOps by providing automated deployment, scaling, and management of containerized applications, including security aspects. They help enforce consistent security policies across all containers and can automatically handle container security at scale.

6. **Explain the concept of shift left in DevSecOps.**

   Answer: Shift left refers to the practice of integrating security early in the software development process rather than treating it as an afterthought. This approach involves incorporating security reviews and testing early in the development stages to identify and mitigate risks sooner.

7. **How does continuous monitoring support DevSecOps practices?**

   Answer: Continuous monitoring in DevSecOps involves using tools to continuously scan and analyze the security state of applications and infrastructure. It helps identify and respond to security threats in real-time, ensuring ongoing compliance and security even after deployment.

8. **What steps are involved in planning a DevSecOps pipeline?**

   Answer: Planning a DevSecOps pipeline involves defining security and business objectives, assessing current infrastructure, selecting appropriate tools, designing the workflow and integration points for security tools, developing a security policy integration plan, and establishing mechanisms for monitoring and feedback.

9. **Why is it important to have feedback mechanisms in a DevSecOps pipeline?**

   Answer: Feedback mechanisms are crucial in a DevSecOps pipeline because they ensure that any security issues detected during or after deployment are quickly relayed back to the development team for remediation. This promotes a continuous improvement cycle and helps prevent similar issues in the future.

10. **How do compliance checks integrate into a DevSecOps pipeline?**

    Answer: Compliance checks in a DevSecOps pipeline are automated as much as possible and integrated at various stages of the CI/CD process. Tools can scan for compliance with security policies and regulatory requirements during code commits, builds, and deployments, ensuring that every release adheres to the necessary standards.

Unsolved exercises

1. How can a DevSecOps team effectively manage the integration of new security tools without disrupting existing workflows?

2. What are the best strategies for maintaining security when deploying microservices using container orchestration tools like Kubernetes in a DevSecOps environment?

3. Discuss the potential security risks associated with the automated deployment processes in DevSecOps pipelines. How can these risks be mitigated?

4. What are the key considerations for selecting a DAST tool for integration into a Jenkins pipeline?

5. How can DevSecOps practices be tailored to comply with specific industry regulations, such as GDPR in the EU or HIPAA in the healthcare sector?

6. What metrics should be used to measure the effectiveness of a DevSecOps pipeline? How can these metrics drive continuous improvement?

7. Evaluate the role of AI and ML in enhancing security within DevSecOps practices. What are the potential benefits and challenges?

8. How can organizations ensure that security findings from tools integrated within the DevSecOps pipeline are prioritized and addressed appropriately?

9. Discuss the impact of using IaC on security in DevSecOps. What specific security practices should be implemented to secure IaC configurations?

10. How can DevSecOps teams foster a culture that effectively balances speed, innovation, and security in software development and deployment processes?

CHAPTER 13

Compliance and Regulatory Considerations

Introduction

In this chapter, we will enter into the complex world of compliance and regulatory considerations crucial for operating in cloud environments. The focus will be on understanding key standards, such as **International Organization for Standardization (ISO)**, **Capability Maturity Model Integration (CMMI)**, **Health Insurance Portability and Accountability Act (HIPAA)**, and other significant regulations that impact various aspects of cloud computing. We will explore how these frameworks guide the security measures, data handling practices, and overall governance of cloud services, ensuring that organizations meet legal, ethical, and technical standards.

Designed for early to mid-career professionals and students with a basic understanding of cloud computing concepts, this chapter aims to equip readers with the knowledge to navigate the regulatory landscape effectively. Through real-life examples, best practices, and clear explanations, you will learn how to implement compliance strategies that not only meet but exceed the required standards, enhancing both trust and security in cloud deployments.

Structure

The chapter covers the following topics:

- List of top compliances

- Best practices
- Case study: GDPR compliance
- Case study: HIPAA standards
- Case study: PCI DSS in hybrid cloud environment

Objectives

By the end of this chapter, you will have a thorough understanding of the various compliance and regulatory frameworks that are crucial for cloud computing, such as ISO standards, CMMI, and HIPAA. You will learn how these regulations influence cloud architecture, security measures, and business processes. You will gain expertise in implementing best practices for maintaining compliance in the cloud, ensuring that your cloud services are not only efficient but also fully compliant with necessary legal and ethical standards. The chapter will equip you with the skills to effectively prepare for audits and manage compliance documentation, empowering you to uphold and exceed regulatory requirements in your cloud deployments.

Prerequisites

Before diving into this chapter, readers should come prepared with:

- **A foundational understanding of cloud computing**, including familiarity with common cloud platforms and services. This background will aid in understanding how compliance standards apply to different cloud architectures and services.

- **Basic knowledge of general compliance and regulatory frameworks**, which will help in grasping the specifics of how such frameworks impact cloud operations. Awareness of privacy, data protection, and sector-specific compliance issues is beneficial.

- **An introductory level of IT security knowledge** is crucial as it underpins many compliance requirements. Understanding basic security concepts like encryption, authentication, and threat management will enhance comprehension of how these are integrated into compliance strategies.

These prerequisites are essential for fully engaging with the chapter's content, allowing readers to effectively understand and implement compliance and regulatory practices in cloud environments.

List of top compliances

In cloud computing, adhering to compliance and regulatory standards is crucial for ensuring data security, privacy, and trust. Compliance standards can vary widely depending on industry, region, and the type of data handled. This section outlines the top compliance standards that organizations deploying cloud services should be aware of.

Key compliance frameworks

Compliance frameworks play a critical role in ensuring data security, privacy, and regulatory adherence in cloud computing. Organizations must align with these standards to protect sensitive information, maintain trust, and avoid legal or financial penalties. The following are some of the most widely recognized compliance frameworks:

- **ISO/IEC 27001**:

  - **Overview**: An international standard that provides requirements for an **information security management system (ISMS)** to help organizations secure their information assets.

  - **Cloud relevance**: ISO/IEC 27001 is crucial for cloud providers and users to establish, implement, maintain, and continuously improve their security management.

- **ISO/IEC 27017**:

  - **Overview**: A code of practice for information security controls based on ISO/IEC 27002 for cloud services.

  - **Cloud relevance**: This standard provides guidelines on the security aspects of cloud computing, recommending controls and implementation guidance for both cloud service providers and cloud service users.

- **ISO/IEC 27018**:

  - **Overview**: A code of practice that focuses on protection of personal data in the cloud.

  - **Cloud relevance**: It addresses cloud-specific aspects of data privacy, complementing the existing ISO/IEC 27001 standard by adding privacy controls to the mix thereby ensuring that the data is handled securely.

- **HIPAA**:

  - **Overview**: U.S. legislation that provides data privacy and security provisions for safeguarding medical information.

  - **Cloud relevance**: Cloud service providers that handle **protected health information (PHI)** must comply with HIPAA requirements to ensure that patient data is protected.

- **GDPR**:

  - **Overview**: Regulation in EU law on data protection and privacy in the EU and the *European Economic Area (EEA)*.

  - **Cloud relevance**: It impacts cloud storage, processing, and handling practices for personal data of EU citizens, requiring cloud providers to ensure data protection by design and by default.

- **PCI DSS**:
  - o **Overview**: A set of security standards designed to ensure that all companies that accept, process, store, or transmit credit card information maintain a secure environment.
  - o **Cloud relevance**: Any cloud service used to store, process, or transmit credit card information must be PCI DSS compliant.

- **FedRAMP**:
  - o **Overview**: A U.S. government program that provides a standardized approach to security assessment, authorization, and continuous monitoring for cloud products and services.
  - o **Cloud relevance**: Cloud service providers that want to work with U.S. federal agencies must have FedRAMP authorization, ensuring their offerings meet stringent security requirements.

- **SOX**:
  - o **Overview**: A U.S. law that sets requirements for all U.S. public company boards, management, and public accounting firms, focusing on improving the accuracy and reliability of corporate disclosures.
  - o **Cloud relevance**: Affects how cloud services are used to manage and store financial data, with implications for compliance and data integrity.

Understanding these top compliance standards is essential for any organization using cloud computing services. By ensuring compliance with these standards, organizations can protect their data, meet legal obligations, and build trust with their customers and partners. Moreover, compliance is not just about avoiding penalties but also about securing data and leveraging it safely to drive business value in the cloud.

Best practices

In the context of cloud computing, adhering to compliance and regulatory frameworks is not just about fulfilling legal obligations but also about safeguarding data and maintaining trust with stakeholders. Best practices in compliance help organizations manage their regulatory responsibilities efficiently and effectively, minimizing risks and enhancing operational integrity.

Key best practices for compliance in cloud computing

Maintaining compliance in cloud computing requires a proactive approach that aligns with industry regulations and security standards. Organizations must adopt best practices to mitigate risks, protect sensitive data, and meet legal obligations. The following are the key strategies for achieving and maintaining compliance in the cloud:

- **Understand your compliance landscape**:
  - o **Detail**: It is crucial for organizations to fully understand the specific compliance requirements that apply to their industry, the type of data they handle, and the jurisdictions in which they operate.
  - o **Implementation**: Conduct regular compliance audits and assessments. Use compliance mapping tools to align your cloud operations with relevant laws and standards.

- **Choose the right CSPs**:
  - o **Detail**: Selecting CSPs that have a strong compliance track record is vital. Ensure that they comply with the necessary regulatory standards that apply to your data and operations.
  - o **Implementation**: Evaluate CSPs based on their certifications and compliance reports (e.g., SOC 2, ISO 27001). Negotiate terms that align with your compliance needs in **service level agreements (SLAs)**.

- **Data governance and classification**:
  - o **Detail**: Effective data governance ensures that data is managed properly and remains compliant throughout its lifecycle.
  - o **Implementation**: Implement robust data classification schemes to identify sensitive or regulated data and apply appropriate controls based on data sensitivity.

- **Implement strong access control**:
  - o **Detail**: Controlling who has access to what data is fundamental to maintaining compliance, especially in multi-tenant cloud environments.
  - o **Implementation**: Utilize IAM solutions that support granular access controls and integration with existing corporate directories. Regularly review and adjust access permissions.

- **Encryption and data protection**:
  - o **Detail**: Protecting data at rest and in transit using encryption is often a requirement under various compliance frameworks.
  - o **Implementation**: Deploy encryption technologies that meet or exceed industry standards. Manage encryption keys securely.

- **Regular training and awareness programs**:
  - o **Detail**: Keeping staff informed about compliance responsibilities and current data protection strategies reduces risks of non-compliance.
  - o **Implementation**: Conduct ongoing training sessions on compliance requirements, security awareness, and best practices. Simulate phishing attacks and other common threats to educate employees.

- **Incident response and reporting**:
  - o **Detail**: Being prepared to handle and report security incidents properly is required under regulations like GDPR and HIPAA.
  - o **Implementation**: Develop an incident response plan that includes procedures for containment, investigation, and notification within timelines mandated by applicable laws.

- **Continuous monitoring and compliance auditing**:
  - o **Detail**: Continuous monitoring of compliance controls and regular audits are necessary to ensure ongoing adherence to regulatory requirements.
  - o **Implementation**: Use automated tools to continuously monitor compliance posture and conduct regular internal and external audits.

- **Documentation and record keeping**:
  - o **Detail**: Maintaining thorough documentation is crucial for proving compliance during audits and investigations.
  - o **Implementation**: Keep detailed logs of data processing activities, access controls, and compliance efforts. Use automated solutions where possible to ensure accuracy and completeness.

Adopting these best practices in compliance not only helps organizations meet regulatory requirements but also builds a foundation for robust data security and risk management. By integrating these practices into their cloud strategy, organizations can navigate the complex landscape of compliance with confidence, ensuring their cloud deployments are secure, compliant, and optimized for performance.

Case study: GDPR compliance

Background: A multinational retail corporation faced significant challenges in aligning its cloud operations with the stringent requirements of the GDPR due to its diverse customer base across Europe.

Objective: To implement comprehensive GDPR compliance measures across all cloud services, ensuring data protection, privacy, and consent mechanisms are in place and auditable.

Implementation:

- **Data mapping and classification**: Conducted a thorough audit of data flows across international borders and classified data according to sensitivity and regulatory requirements.

- **Privacy by design**: Integrated privacy controls directly into the development of cloud-based applications, ensuring data minimization and purpose limitation.

- **Consent management**: Deployed a centralized consent management platform to manage user preferences seamlessly across multiple channels.

Outcome: The corporation successfully met GDPR compliance, significantly reducing the risk of penalties and enhancing customer trust through transparent data practices.

Case study: HIPAA standards

Background: A U.S.-based healthcare provider needed to migrate patient data to the cloud while ensuring compliance with the HIPAA.

Objective: To secure patient data in the cloud, maintain high availability, and ensure all access, audit, and data integrity requirements of HIPAA are met.

Implementation:

- **Risk assessment and management**: Performed a detailed risk assessment to identify potential security vulnerabilities in the cloud setup.

- **Encryption and access controls**: Implemented AES-256 encryption for data at rest and in transit, along with **multi-factor authentication** (**MFA**) and strict access controls based on the principle of least privilege.

- **Business associate agreements (BAAs)**: Ensured that all cloud service providers signed BAAs, securing a commitment to protect sensitive healthcare information.

Outcome: Achieved HIPAA compliance, ensuring the confidentiality, integrity, and availability of patient data, thereby reinforcing the provider's reputation and compliance status.

Case study: PCI DSS in hybrid cloud environment

Background: A financial services firm sought to expand its operations into the cloud while maintaining PCI DSS compliance for handling credit card transactions.

Objective: To implement robust security measures that comply with PCI DSS requirements while utilizing the scalability and flexibility of cloud computing.

Implementation:

- **Scope reduction**: Utilized tokenization and encryption to reduce the scope of PCI DSS by ensuring that actual cardholder data does not reside in the cloud.

- **Continuous monitoring**: Deployed advanced monitoring tools to continuously scan for vulnerabilities and ensure security controls remain effective over time.

- **Compliance training and policies**: Established strict security policies and conducted regular training sessions for employees on PCI DSS requirements and security best practices.

Outcome: Maintained strict PCI DSS compliance across both on-premises and cloud environments, enhancing security measures while enabling scalable and flexible payment processing solutions.

Conclusion

This chapter provided an in-depth exploration of the critical compliance and regulatory frameworks essential for operating securely in cloud environments. We delved into key standards, such as ISO/IEC 27001, HIPAA, GDPR, and PCI DSS, each of which addresses specific aspects of privacy, security, and data protection that are pivotal in cloud computing. The discussion highlights how these frameworks guide organizations in maintaining data integrity, ensuring privacy, and fulfilling legal obligations. Furthermore, the chapter outlines best practices for integrating compliance into cloud operations, including understanding the compliance landscape, choosing compliant cloud service providers, and implementing robust data governance and protection strategies. Through real-life case studies, the text demonstrates practical applications of these best practices in different sectors, illustrating how organizations can achieve compliance while leveraging the benefits of cloud technology. This comprehensive overview not only educates but also equips professionals with the knowledge to implement and sustain compliance, ensuring their cloud deployments are both secure and in line with global standards. proactive security measures. This approach not only secures the software development lifecycle but also enhances operational efficiency and compliance, illustrating the transformative potential of DevSecOps in today's digital landscape.

Key takeaways

- **Compliance is essential for trust and security**: Aligning with global standards like ISO/IEC 27001, HIPAA, GDPR, and PCI DSS helps organizations meet legal obligations, safeguard sensitive data, and build customer trust in cloud environments.

- **Different frameworks, different focus**: Each compliance standard addresses specific needs—HIPAA secures healthcare data, GDPR governs personal data in the EU, PCI DSS protects payment data, and FedRAMP ensures security for U.S. federal cloud use.

- **Best practices ensure ongoing compliance**: Success lies in practices such as data classification, encryption, continuous monitoring, selecting compliant cloud providers, and maintaining documentation for audits.

- **Compliance is a shared responsibility**: While cloud service providers offer baseline compliance, organizations must ensure proper configurations, access controls, and incident response to fulfill their end of the shared responsibility model.

- **Real-world applications reinforce concepts**: Case studies show how businesses across retail, healthcare, and finance implemented compliance strategies—demonstrating the importance of aligning cloud operations with sector-specific regulations.

- **Continuous monitoring and training are critical**: Proactive monitoring, regular audits, and compliance awareness training empower teams to maintain regulatory alignment even as cloud environments evolve.

Key terms

- **ISO/IEC 27001**: An international standard that specifies the requirements for establishing, implementing, maintaining, and continually improving an information ISMS within the context of the organization's overall business risks.

- **HIPAA**: U.S. legislation that provides data privacy and security provisions for safeguarding medical information.

- **GDPR**: A regulation in EU law on data protection and privacy in the EU and the European Economic Area, which also addresses the transfer of personal data outside the EU and EEA areas.

- **PCI DSS**: A set of security standards designed to ensure that all companies that accept, process, store, or transmit credit card information maintain a secure environment.

- **FedRAMP**: A U.S. government-wide program that provides a standardized approach to security assessment, authorization, and continuous monitoring for cloud products and services.

- **ISO/IEC 27017**: A code of practice for information security controls based on ISO/IEC 27002 for cloud services, providing guidelines for both cloud service providers and cloud service users.

- **ISO/IEC 27018:** A code of practice that focuses on protection of personal data in the cloud, addressing cloud-specific information security threats and risks.

- **SOX Act**: A U.S. law that sets requirements for all U.S. public company boards, management, and public accounting firms to enhance corporate responsibility, enhance financial disclosures, and combat corporate and accounting fraud.

- **Data classification**: The process of organizing data by relevant categories so that it may be used and protected more efficiently, often based on levels of sensitivity and/or the impact to the organization should that data be disclosed, altered, or destroyed.

- **Continuous monitoring**: The ongoing process of detecting, reporting, and responding to new information about the security state of network infrastructure and information systems in a timely manner to support risk management decisions.

Solved exercises

1. **What is ISO/IEC 27001 and why is it important for cloud service providers?**

   Answer: ISO/IEC 27001 is an international standard that outlines requirements for an ISMS. It is important for cloud service providers because it helps them establish, implement, maintain, and continuously improve their security management systems, thereby ensuring data security and building trust with customers.

2. **How does HIPAA impact cloud computing when dealing with healthcare data?**

   Answer: HIPAA requires that any entity dealing with PHI implement physical, network, and process security measures. In cloud computing, this means that cloud service providers must ensure appropriate safeguards are in place to protect PHI, potentially including encrypted storage and transmission, access controls, and audit logs.

3. **What are the key data protection principles outlined by the GDPR?**

   Answer: The GDPR emphasizes principles such as data minimization, accuracy, consent, transparency, and accountability. It requires that data be processed legally and fairly, kept secure from unauthorized access, and used only for explicitly stated purposes.

4. **Explain the significance of PCI DSS compliance for e-commerce platforms using cloud services.**

   Answer: PCI DSS compliance is crucial for e-commerce platforms to securely process credit card transactions and protect against data breaches. Compliance ensures that all cardholder data handled by the platform is protected with robust security measures, including encryption, access control, and vulnerability management, regardless of whether the data is stored in-house or in the cloud.

5. **Describe how the ISO/IEC 27017 standard supports cloud security.**

   Answer: ISO/IEC 27017 provides guidelines for information security controls applicable to the provision and use of cloud services. It extends the ISO/IEC 27001 and ISO/IEC 27002 standards by addressing cloud-specific information security threats and risks.

6. **What role does FedRAMP play in cloud adoption by U.S. government agencies?**

   Answer: FedRAMP standardizes the approach to security assessment, authorization, and continuous monitoring for cloud products and services used by U.S. federal agencies. It ensures that cloud services meet strict security and compliance requirements, facilitating safer cloud adoption across government entities.

7. **How should cloud services be evaluated to ensure compliance with the SOX?**

   Answer: Cloud services should be evaluated based on their ability to provide robust financial data integrity and security. This includes assessing data storage, processing capabilities, and audit trails to ensure they meet SOX requirements for financial reporting and record-keeping.

8. **Discuss the importance of implementing a data classification scheme in cloud environments.**

Answer: A data classification scheme is crucial in cloud environments to manage data according to its sensitivity and compliance requirements. It helps in applying appropriate security controls and complying with regulations like GDPR, HIPAA, or PCI DSS, which may have different requirements for different types of data.

9. **What are the best practices for managing data access in the cloud to comply with HIPAA?**

   Answer: Best practices include implementing strict access controls, using encryption for data at rest and in transit, ensuring proper authentication mechanisms are in place, and maintaining detailed access logs to monitor who accesses PHI.

10. **Why is continuous monitoring important in maintaining compliance in cloud environments?**

    Answer: Continuous monitoring is essential to detect and respond to threats in real-time, ensure that security measures are functioning as intended, and maintain compliance with dynamic regulatory environments. It helps identify potential compliance violations before they result in breaches or penalties.

Unsolved exercises

1. How do international compliance standards like ISO/IEC 27001 influence global data security practices in cloud computing?

2. What are the specific challenges faced by healthcare organizations in achieving HIPAA compliance when migrating patient data to the cloud?

3. Discuss how GDPR has impacted the design and operation of cloud services, particularly for providers operating both within and outside the EU.

4. What steps should an e-commerce company take to ensure PCI DSS compliance when storing and processing payment information in the cloud?

5. Explain the additional security measures that should be considered under ISO/IEC 27017 to protect cloud environments from unauthorized access.

6. Evaluate the effectiveness of FedRAMP in standardizing security assessments across cloud services used by U.S. government agencies.

7. What are the key considerations for ensuring SOX compliance for financial data stored and processed in the cloud?

8. How can organizations implement a robust data classification system in the cloud to meet varying compliance requirements across different jurisdictions?

9. Describe the role of continuous monitoring in maintaining compliance with multiple regulatory frameworks in a multi-cloud environment.

10. What are the best practices for cloud service providers to manage data sovereignty issues in light of varying international data protection laws?

Join our Discord space

Join our Discord workspace for latest updates, offers, tech happenings around the world, new releases, and sessions with the authors:

https://discord.bpbonline.com

Index